MYTH AND MYTHMAKING

Centre of South Asian Studies,
School of Oriental and African Studies,
University of London

COLLECTED PAPERS ON SOUTH ASIA

11. Local Agrarian Societies in Colonial India
P. Robb, K. Sugihara & H. Yanagisawa

12. Myth and Mythmaking
Julia Leslie

COLLECTED PAPERS ON SOUTH ASIA NO. 12

MYTH AND MYTHMAKING

Edited by

Julia Leslie

Routledge
Taylor & Francis Group
LONDON AND NEW YORK

First published 1996
by Curzon Press

2 Park Square, Milton Park, Abingdon, Oxon OX14 4RN
711 Third Avenue, New York, NY 10017, USA

Routledge is an imprint of the Taylor & Francis Group, an informa business

First issued in paperback 2016

British Library Cataloguing in Publication Data
A catalogue record for this book is available from the British Library

Library of Congress in Publication Data
A catalog record for this book has been requested

ISBN 0–7007–0303–9

ISBN 978-0-7007-0303-6 (hbk)
ISBN 978-1-138-99432-4 (pbk)

Contents

List of Tables and Figures

Acknowledgements

All but one of the papers in this volume began as a contribution to the weekly Hindu Studies Seminar which I have organized at the School of Oriental and African Studies since 1990. My thanks must therefore go first to Gez Hawting, then Head of the Centre of Religion and Philosophy, for suggesting a forum which would be greeted with such enthusiasm by its many and varied participants. Thanks are also due to Joyce Hutchinson who began the work of typing, and to Martin Daly of Research and Publications who cheerfully took over all administrative tasks while I was on sabbatical leave. I also thank the Publications Committee of the School for assistance in meeting the cost of preparing the work for publication. But it is, of course, the contributors who deserve my warmest thanks: for agreeing to pool their knowledge in a single volume on the elusive idea of 'mythmaking', and for their patience as the book all too slowly took shape.

Julia Leslie

12/1 Meghalaya
Vajarahalli
Kanakapura Road
Bangalore
April 1995

Note

Regarding conventions of spelling and transliteration, I have striven for consistency throughout the volume except in those cases where a rigid insistence on the rule would have struck a discordant note within the idiom of the period under discussion.

Contributors

N.J. Allen studied Classics at Rugby School, Medicine at the Universities of Oxford and London, and Social Anthropology at Oxford. After fieldwork in Nepal, he taught Anthropology at Durham. He was awarded a DPhil (Oxon) in 1976, and since then has been Lecturer in the Social Anthropology of South Asia at Oxford and Fellow of Wolfson College. Apart from more than fifty book reviews, he has published a grammar of a Himalayan language and some twenty-five articles, mainly on Himalayan ethnography and mythology, on kinship theory, and on Indo-European comparativism.

Indira Chowdhury-Sengupta took her first degree (BA with Honours in English) at Calcutta University in 1979. She completed her PhD on 'Colonialism, Cultural Identity and the Making of a Hindu Discourse: Bengal 1867-1905' at the School of Oriental and African Studies, the University of London, in 1993. She is currently Reader in the Department of English, Jadavpur University, Calcutta. Her research interests include: literary and cultural theory, contraception and reproductive rights in nineteenth-century India, and colonial and post-colonial literature and culture. Her publications include: *Femininity Redefined: The Politics of the Home and the World*, with J. Bagchi, R. Chatterjee and S. Bandyopadhyay (New Delhi: Kali for Women, forthcoming); and a revised version of her doctoral thesis (forthcoming).

Peter G. Friedlander lived in India from 1977 to 1982 where he studied Hindi in Benares. From 1983 to 1986, he was a student of Hindi and South Asian Studies in the School of Oriental and African Studies at the University of London (BA Hons). The title of his doctoral thesis was 'The Life and Works of Sant Raidās' which he completed, also at the School of Oriental and African Studies, in 1991. He is at present working on the cataloguing of Hindi and Panjabi manuscript collections in the library of the Wellcome Institute for the History of Medicine in London. He also teaches Hindi and the History of Buddhism in South Asia on the Antioch College Buddhist Studies Program. His publications include: *The Life and Works of Sant Raidās*, with W.M. Callewaert (Delhi: Manohar, 1992).

Julia Leslie studied Philosophy at the University of Sussex (BA Hons) and Classical Indian Religions at the University of Oxford (MPhil, DPhil). She has taught Indian Religions at Goldsmiths' College, University of London, Sanskrit at the University of Bristol, and Indian Religions and Philosophies at the Department of External Studies, University of Oxford. In 1987-8, she was Visiting Lecturer and Research Associate in the History of Religion in the Women's Studies in Religion Program at Harvard Divinity School. She is currently Senior Lecturer in Hindu Studies at the School of Oriental and African Studies, the University of London; and Senior Member of the Centre for Cross-Cultural Research on Women at Queen Elizabeth House, the University of Oxford. Her publications include: *The Perfect Wife: The Orthodox Hindu Woman according to the Strīdharmapaddhati of Tryambakayajvan* (Delhi: Oxford University Press, 1989; Penguin, 1995); *Rules and Remedies in Classical Indian Law*, editor (Leiden: Brill, 1991); *Roles and Rituals for Hindu Women*, editor (London: Pinter/Rutherford: Fairleigh Dickinson University Press, 1991; Delhi: Motilal Banarsidass, 1992); and a novel.

Laurie L. Patton studied History of Religions at the University of Chicago and completed her PhD on 'The Work of Language and the Vedic *Ṛṣi*: The *Bṛhaddevatā* as Canonical Commentary' in 1991. She is the author of numerous articles on Vedic commentary and mythology, as well as on interpretative issues in the study of religions. Her work has appeared in several edited volumes as well as in *Folklore, History of Religions*, and the *Journal of the American Academy of Religion*. She is the editor of two volumes of papers: *Authority, Anxiety, and Canon: Essays in Vedic Interpretation* (New York: SUNY Press, 1994); and *Out of Grandmother's House: Essays in Myth and Method* (Charlottesville: University Press of Virginia, in press). A revised version of her PhD thesis is in press in DeGruyter/Mouton's Religionsgeschichtliche Versuche und Vorarbeiten Series (general editors, Frits Graf, Hans Kippenberg and Larry Sullivan) under the title *Myth as Argument: The Bṛhaddevatā as Canonical Commentary*. She is currently Assistant Professor of Asian Religions at Bard College, Annandale-on-Hudson, New York; and Research Associate at the Southern Asian Institute at Columbia University, where she is Director of the Seminar on the Veda and its Interpretation, and of the Working Group on Gender and Vedic Authority.

Renate Söhnen-Thieme studied music in 1964-8 in Hanover; Musicology, German Literature and Philosophy in 1968-9, and Indology (Sanskrit, Pali, Hindi and Urdu) and Iranian Studies in 1971-8, at the University of Mainz. Her PhD thesis in Sanskrit literature was published in two volumes under the title, *Untersuchungen zur Komposition von Reden and Gesprächen im Rāmāyaṇa*' ('An Analysis of Dialogue Structures in the *Rāmāyaṇa*') (Studien zur Indologie und Iranistik 6, Reinbek, 1980). In 1974-9, she was Academic Assistant in the Department of Indology at the University of Mainz. In 1980, 1981, 1983 and 1987, she undertook fieldwork in Pakistan, especially in Baltistan, involving the collection and study of oral literacy and musical traditions. In 1982-6, she was a member of the Tübingen Purāṇa Research Project; publications in collaboration with Peter Schreiner include *Sanskrit Indices and Text of the Brahmapurāṇa*

(Wiesbaden, 1987) and *Brahmapurāṇa: Summary of Contents* (Wiesbaden, 1989). In 1986-8, she worked in Tübingen on a project on *Ṛgveda* lexicography together with Paul Thieme. She is currently Senior Lecturer in Sanskrit at the School of Oriental and African Studies at the University of London. Additional publications include: *A. S. Stenzler: Primer of the Sanskrit Language (Translation from the German with some Revision)* (London: SOAS, 1992); and articles on Sanskrit language and literature (Sanskrit-based studies in the Vedic, epic and Purāṇic traditions), and on the folklore of Baltistan.

Kathleen Taylor has a BA in Indian History and an MA in Religious Studies from the School of Oriental and African Studies, the University of London. She is currently completing her PhD thesis on Sir John Woodroffe's work and letters. She is also working on a biography of Woodroffe, and editing a small collection of the letters. She has lectured on Hinduism to adult education classes.

Lynn Thomas obtained a BA in Religious Studies from the University of Lancaster, and a DPhil from the University of Oxford (1987). Her doctoral thesis, entitled 'Theories of Cosmic Time in the *Mahābhārata*, explored the relationship between the *yugas* and the avatars. She is currently Lecturer in Hinduism at the Roehampton Institute, London, where she is working on Hindu mythology and mythology and women.

Introduction: Myths and Mythmaking

Julia Leslie

The Aim of the Book

This volume arose as a result of my increasing awareness that much of my own work and that of several of my colleagues working in Indian studies focus on the unravelling of mythical constructions. The constructions we analyse range from ancient narratives to traditional hagiographies to modern examples of (conscious or unconscious) fabrication. In this sense, the aim of the book was a modest one: to pull together between the covers of one volume a range of current studies of myths in the making from the earliest period of Indian studies to the present day.

This has proved to be a sortie into a promising and, it seems, ever fertile field. Indeed the field is vast. It includes an array of anthologies and dictionaries of myth[1] as well as an astonishing variety of studies on the nature and role of myth in the history of religions,[2] including comparative studies.[3] The objects of

[1] For examples of cross-cultural or 'world' collections of myth, see Campbell 1959-62, Cotterell 1986, Eliade 1967, Graves 1968, Larrington 1992, Willis 1993. For Indian collections, surveys or translations, see Dimmitt and van Buitenen 1978, Doniger O'Flaherty 1975 and 1982, Goldman 1984-, Hopkins 1915, Mani 1975, Roy and Ganguli 1884-96, Shastri 1957-9, Sörenson 1904-25, and van Buitenen 1973-8.

[2] Rooted in early Greek and Christian explanations of myth, and nourished by the rationalism of the Enlightenment and the vision of the Romantic movement, this mode of study reached a peak in the nineteenth century with its general theory of evolution. More modern studies include: Bolle 1984, Dundes 1984, de Vries 1977, Eliade 1961 and 1963, Maranda 1972, and Sebeok 1955. Studies of Indian mythical themes include: Biardeau 1968-76, Coburn 1984, Doniger O'Flaherty 1973, 1976 and 1980, Gombrich 1975, Hawley 1981 and 1983, Hawley and Wulff 1982, Kinsley 1987, Shulman 1976, and Zimmer 1946. Of course, none of these lists is exhaustive.

[3] Piatigorsky argues that 'any *thinking* on myth *is* comparative. (1993: Foreword). For an interesting recent study that is both comparative and interdisciplinary, see Doniger and Patton (in press).

study are correspondingly diverse and overwhelming in scale. According to Roy Willis, for example, the 'great themes of myth' include the origins and structure of the universe; the causes of life and death; supernatural beings such as gods and demons; cosmic disasters; heroes and tricksters as 'agents of change'; the body and the soul; marriage and the social order; and so on (1993:17-34). Wendy Doniger's survey of Indian mythic themes is more specific: animals; the tree and the mountain at the centre of the earth; cosmogony, theogony and anthropogony; eschatology and death; householder and renouncer, *dharma* and *mokṣa*; gods versus demons; illusion; and the pantheon. The components of each theme, each myth – the intricate details, startling twists of action, and layer upon layer of meaning – defy both enumeration and explanation. I am reminded of Robert Graves's remark that 'myths are seldom simple, and never irresponsible' (1968:viii).

A brief glance at this wealth of material clarifies at once what this book is not. It is not, and does not pretend to be, either an anthology or summary of Indian mythical traditions. Nor does it set out to provide a new theory or interpretation of myth. Nor does it try to identify and distinguish between the various categories of mythical construction or cultural belief: myth, legend, folklore, ideology, and so on. It does not even claim to touch on all the 'great', or specifically Indian, mythological themes.

What it does is present eight careful commentaries on, or reconstructions of, the making of a particular and precisely contextualized myth. In each case, the author's analysis of how and why that myth came to take its shape provides stimulating source material for the study of Indian culture.

Four Liaisons and a Wife (Allen)

In 'The Hero's Five Relationships: A Proto-Indo-European Story', Nicholas Allen draws on the work of Georges Dumézil to compare two versions – one Greek, one Indian – of a hero's journey. In the *Odyssey*, the hero's wanderings lead to four encounters with female figures in addition to his relationship with Penelope, his legal wife. In the *Mahābhārata*, the exiled Arjuna's pilgrimage to the holy bathing places of India leads to a parallel set of four encounters with females in addition to his relationship with Draupadī, his primary wife. After pointing out the major differences between the two narratives, Allen proceeds to tease out in precise detail the distribution of similarities.

These parallels are interesting enough, but Allen goes further. Returning to Dumézil's three classical 'functions' or 'clusters of ideas', he outlines his own proposition of a fourth function that can be either positively valued (hence 'transcendent') or negatively valued (hence the associations with death, destructions, demons and so on).

He then turns to the eight types of marriage listed in the *Manusmṛti*, with *svayaṃvara* as the ninth, reducing the nine to five 'modes of marriage'. As he demonstrates, these five reflect the classical three 'functions' together with both a positive and a negative value for the fourth. Finally, he compares these five 'modes of marriage' with the various relationships of the two epic heroes.

Allen concludes that the Proto-Indo-European corpus of oral narratives includes the voyage of a hero who temporarily leaves his wife and contracts four different types of liaison. He argues further that, of the Greek and Sanskrit versions derived from this, the Sanskrit is likely to be the more conservative, the one closer to their common Indo-European heritage. I would add that, for studies of Indian culture, this mythical gloss on the classical forms of marriage is an exciting addition to the study of the 'laws' of Manu.

Sex and Gender in Vedic Ritual (Patton)

In 'The Fate of the Female *Ṛṣi*: Portraits of Lopāmudrā', Laurie Patton focuses on the dialogue between Lopāmudrā and her husband, Agastya, to demonstrate the construction of gender roles in ancient India. The point at issue is the temptation of sex in the context of celibacy imposed by Vedic ritual. Patton's analysis of Lopāmudrā's role in the ensuing dialogue is based on a close examination of three textual versions: *Ṛgveda* 1.179, the later Vedic commentary provided by the fourth-century *Bṛhaddevatā*, and the epic rendering to be found in the *Mahābhārata*.

Drawing on the work of Hayden White and others, Patton begins by outlining her view of mythic narrative as 'a form of social argumentation' as opposed to 'a form of accurate, true-to-life representational discourse'. Taking White's notion of 'moralizing narrative', she asks how the 'complex set of social relations' implied by the term 'gender' moralizes the events described in the mythical dialogue. She also points out that many of the dialogue hymns in the *Ṛgveda* involve a negotiation or construction of gender roles in relation to sex, fertility and sacrificial ritual.

Patton describes how, in the *Ṛgveda*, Lopāmudrā represents the voracious demands of sexuality which Agastya first resists but by which he is subsequently overwhelmed. The end of the hymn celebrates Agastya as having attained immortality both through children and through ascetic practice, while Lopāmudrā remains marked by sexual desire.

Drawing on her own earlier work on the *Bṛhaddevatā*, Patton shows how the fourth-century version both cleans up the explicit sexuality of the dialogue and introduces a crucial new character, a celibate student who overhears the conversation and must atone for the intrusion. The result is a new hierarchical tension between senior and junior males. Patton concludes that 'Lopāmudrā is no longer simply the negotiator of sex and gender roles, but is surrounded by males for whom she is taboo'.

The more complex epic version subordinates gender roles to the demands of *dharma*. The independent Lopāmudrā of the *Ṛgveda* becomes literally the creation of Agastya, fashioned by him to provide him with children. The sexuality of the female *ṛṣi* is lost in the epic stereotype of the manipulative wife: Lopāmudrā now exploits her husband's need for children to force him to provide her with all manner of material things.

Patton concludes that gender roles are consistently reconstructed in line with changing brahminical norms. She further points out that the more 'participatory' role of women so often noted in the Vedic period is not always positive. Thus, in all three versions of the Lopāmudrā dialogue-story, the female protagonist acts in the service of her husband's ritual goals.

Seduction and Ascetic Rage (Söhnen-Thieme)

Renate Söhnen-Thieme's contribution, 'The Ahalyā Story through the Ages', tackles another well-known female character of Indian mythology. The standard epic version tells of Indra's seduction of the faithful Ahalyā by assuming the physical form of her husband, the ascetic brahmin Gautama. Like Allen, Söhnen-Thieme finds a parallel in Greek mythology: the seduction of the equally faithful Alkmene by Zeus in the guise of her royal husband, Amphitryon. Söhnen-Thieme's analysis of the Indian story involves an examination both of the popular renditions of the story (in the *Rāmāyaṇa*, in several *Purāṇas*, and in the *Kathāsaritsāgara*) and of the more fleeting allusions to it in other Sanskrit texts.

As in the Lopāmudrā story, the underlying tension is that between passion and ascetic practice. In the context of the standard epic version of the Ahalyā story, however, the passion of the seducer (that is, the sexual desire of Indra) is matched by the passion of the ascetic (that is, the rage of the cheated husband). Gautama's curse destroys both: Indra is castrated and Gautama loses his ascetic powers. Ahalyā is deemed guilty of adultery and she too is cursed. The details of the story – the narrative elements of the seduction, the innocence or otherwise of Ahalyā, whether her punishment follows from her guilt or her impurity, the particular manifestations of Gautama's curses and of their lifting – vary with each telling. Söhnen-Thieme combs through these variations in pursuit of the different layers of meaning and the probable sequence of the development of the story.

With reference to Ahalyā, Söhnen-Thieme concludes that the earliest reference describes her as Indra's lover but makes no mention of a husband. Later references depict her as married (either to Kauśika or to Gautama) but there is no suggestion that she deliberately betrays her husband or that she needs to be punished. It is not until the standard version in the *Rāmāyaṇa* that we find Ahalyā's guilt established and a punishment that is closely linked to her subsequent purification by the young Rāma. All later versions are programmed by this religious imperative. With reference to Indra, Söhnen-Thieme examines the intriguing epithets associated with him and links them to Gautama's curse. The notion of 'goldbeardedness' remains something of a mystery. The loss of Indra's penis, the destruction of his testicles, and their substitution with those of a ram may reflect the loss of power of the old gods. Indra's thousand eyes are explained in the first instance by the myth of Tilottamā and her eye-catching beauty, then by the curse of a thousand 'vulva marks' later mercifully transformed into eyes.

Söhnen-Thieme's careful unravelling of these and other strands of the Indra-Ahalyā story constitutes a graphic demonstration of the complex process of mythmaking in the Indian tradition, and the shifting variety of probable motivations.

An Exceptional Avatar (Thomas)

In 'Paraśurāma and Time', Lynn Thomas explores the unusual role of this avatar and in particular his intervention in the affairs of subsequent avatars. As Thomas explains, Paraśurāma is 'a strangely atemporal figure', the only avatar not confined to a particular place and time. Her study focuses on his interventions at two 'critical moments': at Rāma's marriage to Sītā, and during the great Bhārata war; the former at the juncture of the *tretā* and *dvāpara yuga*s, the latter at the juncture of the *dvāpara* and *kali yuga*s. Her primary sources are thus the *Rāmāyaṇa* for the first intervention and the *Mahābhārata* for the second.

Thomas pays particular attention to the battle between Paraśurāma and Bhīṣma during the Bhārata war, comparing this with his confrontation with Rāma in the *Rāmāyaṇa*. The parallels between the two accounts are striking: the sense of 'cosmic crisis'; the explicit links made with Paraśurāma's earlier annihilation of the *kṣatriya*s (described by Thomas as 'the essential deed of his avatar period'); and his humble acknowledgement of the superiority of his victor in the moment of defeat.

As Thomas explains, previous scholars have examined the various components of the myth separately, dismissing them as irrelevant interpolations, evidence perhaps of Bhārgava enthusiasm for the story but without any real significance. Her own assessment, based on an analysis of context and juxtaposition, contradicts such views. She argues that the Paraśurāma story is consistently found at key moments in the narrative, precisely when the reference to that earlier massacre will have greatest resonance. She further argues that Paraśurāma's unusually extended lifespan is equally deliberate, precisely to enable him to be present at the juncture of the *yuga*s.

She concludes that Paraśurāma's appearances are not haphazard. Emerging each time from the 'spatial and temporal sidelines' to which he has been deliberately assigned, he is associated in turn with three of the four *yugāntas* or junctures between the *yugas*. He is thus the mythical guardian of the end of the *yuga*, a mark of cosmic crisis.

Blood, Milk and Sex (Leslie)

'Menstruation Myths', my own contribution, explores notions of female sexuality and the inherent nature of women in the context of traditional discourses on menstruation. Two epic stories provide opposing views on female sexuality: Bhaṅgāśvana's positive preference for his/her sexual experience as a woman, and Aṣṭāvakra's negative discovery of the sexual depravity of even elderly women. I then relate the dominant myth about the origins of menstruation: the story of Indra's brahminicide with menstruation as the mark of innate impurity and guilt.

Finally, I examine the discourse on menstruation within three traditional frameworks. In the context of *āyurveda*, both menstrual blood and breast milk are perceived as sources of maternal nourishment. The ascetic discourse – and here I draw particularly on Padmanabh Jaini's work – betrays an alarming phobia about women's bodies: female breasts and genitals are viewed as prime sources of impurity, their existence alone being evidence of spiritual inadequacy. The normative discourse presented by *dharmaśāstra* is more ambivalent: menstrual blood is both impure and inauspicious ('proof of pregnancy lost'), but the onset of the woman's fertile 'season' on the fourth day is powerfully auspicious, rendering her 'incomparably pure'.

I conclude that it is the framing agenda that makes the substance of the discourse or myth. For *āyurveda*, the issue is health, that of the woman and her future child. For the male ascetic, the motive force is renunciation of the physical world, and hence contempt for both sex and women; to this, the Digambara Jain discourse adds the desire to denigrate their white-clad Śvetāmbara rivals by equating their spirituality with that of women. For *dharmaśāstra*, the overarching frame is that of the householder code and the need to control the sexuality and reproductive powers of women.

Spiritual Combat (Friedlander)

In 'The Struggle for Salvation in the Hagiographies of Ravidās', Peter Friedlander examines 'the textual exemplars of three oral traditions': the Hindu tradition referred to by the term *kathāvācak* ('teller of tales'), dating from the sixteenth to the eighteenth centuries; a Sikh tradition associated with the precursors of the Sikh gurus, with particular reference to a seventeenth-century account; and the tradition of the followers of the untouchable poet-saint for which the first textual source is located in the early twentieth century.

As Friedlander demonstrates, these hagiographies operate at several different levels. Some stories function primarily at the level of the general socio-religious context: they reveal the ongoing struggle between the heterodox traditions and brahmin orthodoxy, a struggle which admits of no ultimate resolution. Other stories demonstrate the conflicts between the different heterodox traditions, allowing for a variety of possible outcomes depending on the protagonists. For example, in stories about Ravidās and the goddess Gaṅgā, the assimilation of her hagiography into his own establishes his greater authority. In stories about Ravidās and Gorakhnāth, the latter is both defeated and excluded. In stories about Ravidās and Mīrābāī, she becomes his disciple and the hagiographies of the two are fused. A fourth example is provided by those stories in which Ravidās's greatness is included in, and subordinated to, a greater hagiography (in the *kathāvācak* tradition, for instance, or in the Sikh tales). The third level of interpretation is that of Ravidās's own personal struggle for salvation. As Friedlander points out, these stories may also be taken as metaphors for the inner struggles of his devotees as they strive for spiritual attainment.

Friedlander concludes that the hagiography of Ravidās – whether approached within a Vaiṣṇava, Sikh or Ravidāsī universe – depicts a life of constant conflict: persistent harassment by the brahmin élite, unending rivalry with other heterodox sects and, above all, the everlasting personal battle of the spiritual seeker.

The Sannyasi as Icon (Chowdhury-Sengupta)

Indira Chowdhury-Sengupta's chapter, 'Reconstructing Spiritual Heroism: The Evolution of the Swadeshi Sannyasi in Bengal', tackles the changing conceptualization of Hinduism in nineteenth-century Bengal. She argues that what is often called 'neo-Hinduism' is far more than a simple revivalism. It is a deliberate reconstruction of earlier religious ideas for the purpose of defining the emerging national culture. Central to this reconstruction is the remarkable 'icon of the sannyasi'.

She describes how nineteenth-century Hindu discourse appropriated elements of Orientalist and colonial debate: the dichotomy between the pure ancient past and debased modern practice, that between the gentle Hindu and the barbaric Muslim, and the British representation of the Indian (especially the Bengali) male as effeminate. These elements fed into the reformulation of Hindu masculinity in terms of the heroic ascetic, the sannyasi whose strength and sacrifice embraced both national politics and ancient religious ideals. Furthermore, as Chowdhury-Sengupta explains, the power of the celibate sannyasi lay in his ability 'to transmute sexual energy into inner spiritual strength'.

It is in this context that Chowdhury-Sengupta considers the role played by Swami Vivekananda. At the World Parliament of Religions in 1893, Vivekananda proclaimed himself a sannyasi 'of the most ancient order of monks in the world'. In his speeches, letters and writings, he sought to make this icon distinctly 'Indian' in appearance and demeanour. But his main project, referred to as his 'man-making mission', was to define a Hindu masculinity based on self-discipline (including celibacy) in opposition to the 'insensitive virility' exemplified by the colonizers. As Chowdhury-Sengupta argues, this formed the basis for the progressive construction of the Swadeshi sannyasi and helps to explain the significance of the icon for the early nationalist movement.

Orientalist and Pandit (Taylor)

The eighth and final contribution to the volume, Kathleen Taylor's 'Arthur Avalon: The Creation of a Legendary Orientalist', belongs to the twentieth century. She focuses first on the real-life figure of Sir John Woodroffe and the usual assumption that he is the man behind the pseudonym. She then looks at the persona implied by the pseudonym as it may be reconstructed from his works. There follows a useful contrast between the attitudes towards Tantra before the writing of 'Arthur Avalon' and the reception of those writings among the scholars of the day.

When Taylor pursues the implications of the pseudonym, the chapter begins to read like a detective story. Picking her way through twentieth-century revivals of occultism and esotericism, she finds Woodroffe's inspiration in a painting of the legend of King Arthur. She then sifts through his possible collaborators in the works of 'Arthur Avalon'. For, as Taylor points out, Woodroffe had once admitted that the 'Avalon' books were written 'with the direct cooperation of others and in particular with the assistance of one of my friends who will not permit me to mention his name'. Taylor at last identifies that man – Atal Behari Ghosh – in a photograph and in a collection of letters between the two friends. His identity established, Taylor is able to evaluate the different contributions of the two men, and the significance of their collaboration.

Taylor concludes that 'Arthur Avalon' was 'a far greater figure than either Sir John Woodroffe alone or Mr Ghosh of Calcutta could ever be'. This powerful creation combined the prestige of the European Orientalist and the scholarship of the Indian pandit, both of them disciples of a popular Tantric guru.

Conclusions

As this volume was nearing completion, I discovered a most welcome addition to the field, *Thamyris: Mythmaking from Past to Present*. This interdisciplinary journal, recently launched from Amsterdam under the joint editorship of Jan Best and Nanny de Vries, aims 'to engender an enjoyable debate among scholars and others interested in the processes of mythmaking and the unravelling of myths'. As the first editorial (1994:1/1,1) explains;

> ... the human need for myths seems inescapable, especially to legitimize dubious ideologies and cultural conventions or to explain away the exclusion of groups apparently contrasting with a dominant culture. Besides, many utopian movements or dystopian visions create their own compensatory myths in search of an alternative future or in order to recreate an empowering past. Obviously mythmaking... serves the needs of the moment by constructing a desired reality.

This volume speaks with the same purpose and much the same energy.

Our starting-point was that myths are made and remade – on a variety of topics and in wildly differing contexts – in a vast continuum stretching from the earliest periods of historical time to the present day. Each contributor has focused on one particular point in this continuum: 'a stretch of narrative' in the *Odyssey* and the *Mahābhārata* that suggests a common Proto-Indo-European heritage; three layers of the Lopāmudrā story, each betraying the socio-religious needs of its time; the tellings and retellings of Indra's seduction of Ahalyā in early Sanskrit texts; the development of the Paraśurāma figure and his strange relationship to mythical time; some traditional ideologies regarding menstruation and the way each fits the discourse that frames it; the dynamics behind the evolving hagiographies of the untouchable saint Ravidās; the ideal of the sannyasi in the progressive construction of an 'alternative masculinity'; and the deliberate merging of European Orientalist and traditional pandit in the pseudonym, 'Arthur Avalon'. These are just some of the ways in which myths have been made, and made to function, in the rich cultural history of India.

References

Biardeau, Madeleine. 1968-76. *Études de mythologie hindoue*. 4 vols. Paris.

Bolle, Kees W. 1984. 'Myths and Other Religious Texts.' In *Contemporary Approaches to the Study of Religions*, vol.1, ed. Frank Whaling. Berlin, 1984.

Campbell, Joseph. 1959-62. *The Masks of God*. 4 vols. Reprint: Harmondsworth, Penguin 1976.

Coburn, Thomas B. 1984. *Devī-Māhātmya: Crystallization of the Goddess Tradition.* Delhi: Motilal Banarsidass.

Cotterell, Arthur. 1986. *A Dictionary of World Mythology.* Revised edition. Oxford: University Press, 1990.

de Vries, Jan. 1977. *Perspectives in the History of Religions.* Berkeley: University of California Press.

de Vries, Nanny, and Jan Best. 1994. Editorial. *Thamyris: Mythmaking from Past to Present* 1/1 (Autumn 1994):1-8. Amsterdam.

Doniger, (O'Flaherty), Wendy. 1973. *Asceticism and Eroticism in the Mythology of Śiva.* London: Oxford University Press. Reprinted as: *Śiva: The Erotic Ascetic*, Oxford 1981.

—, tr. 1975. *Hindu Myths.* Harmondsworth: Penguin.

—. 1976. *The Origins of Evil in Hindu Mythology.* Berkeley: University of California Press.

—. 1980. *Women, Androgynes and Other Mythical Beasts.* Chicago: University Press.

—, tr. 1982. *The Rig Veda.* Harmondsworth: Penguin.

—. 1987. 'Indian Religions: Mythic Themes.' In *The Encyclopedia of Religion*, ed. Mircea Eliade, 7:182-90. New York: Macmillan.

—, and Laurie L. Patton, eds. In press. *Out of Grandmother's House: Essays in Myth and Method.* Charlottesville, VA: University of Virginia Press.

Dimmitt, Cornelia, and J.A.B. van Buitenen, trs. 1978. *Classical Hindu Mythology: A Reader in the Sanskrit Purāṇas.* Philadelphia: Temple University Press.

Dundes, Alan, ed. 1984. *Sacred Narrative.* Berkeley: University of California Press.

Eliade, Mircea. 1961. *Myths, Dreams and Mysteries.* New York.

—. 1963. *Myth and Reality.* New York.

—. 1967. *From Primitives to Zen.* New York.

Goldman, Robert, general editor. 1984-. *The Rāmāyaṇa of Vālmīki: An Epic of Ancient India.* Princeton: University Press.

Gombrich, Richard F. 1975. 'Ancient Indian Cosmologies.' In *Ancient Cosmologies*, ed. Carmen Blacker and Michael Loewe. London.

Graves, Robert, ed. 1968. *New Larousse Encyclopedia of Mythology.* Second edition. London: Hamlyn.

Hawley, John Stratton. 1981. *At Play with Krishna.* Princeton: University Press.

—. 1983. *Krishna, the Butter Thief.* Princeton: University Press.

—. and Donna M. Wulff, eds. 1982. *The Divine Consort: Rādhā and the Goddesses of India.* Berkeley: University of California Press.

Hopkins, E. W. 1915. *Epic Mythology.* Reprint: New York, 1969.

Kinsley, David. 1986. *Hindu Goddesses: Vision of the Divine Feminine in the Hindu Religious Tradition.* Berkeley: University of California Press.

Larrington, Carolyne, ed. 1992. *The Feminist Companion to Mythology.* London: Pandora.
Mani, Vettam. 1975. *Purāṇic Encyclopaedia.* Delhi: Motilal Banarsidass.
Maranda, Pierre, ed. 1972. *Mythology.* Baltimore.
O'Flaherty, see Doniger.
Piatigorsky, Alexander. 1993. *Mythological Deliberations: Lectures on the Phenomenology of Myth.* London: School of Oriental and African Studies, University of London.
Roy, Pratap Chandra, ed., and K.M. Ganguli, tr. 1884-96. *The Mahābhārata.* 12 vols. Second edition: Calcutta, 1970.
Sebeok, Thomas A., ed. 1955. *Myth: A Symposium.* Bloomington, Indiana.
Shastri, Hari Prasad, tr. 1957-9. *The Ramayana of Valmiki.* 3 vols. London: Shanti Sadan.
Shulman, David D. 1980. *Tamil Temple Myths: Sacrifice and Divine Marriage in the South Indian Śaiva Tradition.* Princeton: University Press.
Sörensen, Sören. 1904-25. *An Index to the Names in the Mahābhārata.* London.
van Buitenen, J.A.B., tr. 1973-8. *The Mahābhārata.* Chicago: University Press.
Willis, Roy, ed. 1993. *World Mythology: The Illustrated Guide.* London: BCA and Duncan Baird Publishers.
Zimmer, Heinrich. 1946. *Myths and Symbols of Indian Art and Civilization,* ed. Joseph Campbell. Reprint: Princeton University Press, 1972.

1

The Hero's Five Relationships: A Proto-Indo-European Story

N.J. Allen

Semigrand open crocodile music hath jaws
in James Joyce *Ulysses ('Sirens')*

Introduction

The main body of this chapter consists of straightforward comparison: I try and demonstrate that a certain stretch of the *Odyssey* and a certain stretch of the *Mahābhārata* tell two versions of the same story. Towards the end I argue that this story goes back to Proto-Indo-European times, and is related to Proto-Indo-European matrimonial law (or custom, if one prefers that word in a non-literate context). As for introduction, I take for granted some general knowledge of the Greek epic,[1] but say a little about the Indian. Similarly I take for granted the framework of Indo-European comparative linguistics, but comment briefly on the comparative study of other aspects of Indo-European culture.

Like the Greek (and this may or may not be coincidence), the Sanskrit tradition has preserved two epics, the *Rāmāyaṇa* and the *Mahābhārata*. The most obvious feature of the *Mahābhārata* (which includes a miniature version of the *Rāmāyaṇa*) is its length – eight times the *Iliad* and *Odyssey* put together. But it is not as intractable as this figure may suggest, and I shall be able to ignore the frame narrative (which tells how the story was first told), the

[1] See e.g. Camps 1980, or for the *Odyssey*, Griffin 1987.

embedded independent narratives, and the long didactic passages of Hindu philosophy (including the *Bhagavadgītā*). This leaves the main narrative, whose essential unity and coherence are nowadays widely recognized by scholars.[2] Apart from their well-structured narratives, the Sanskrit epics also have in common with the Greek that they enjoyed immense cultural and educational prestige. They too were carried overseas (notably to Indonesia), and provided the materials for a great deal of later creative work in poetry, drama and the plastic arts (not to mention television). Moreover both epic traditions were related to cultic activity.

In both cases the earlier history is uncertain and controversial. Homer seems to have been first committed to writing around 700 BCE, the *Mahābhārata* perhaps three to five centuries later, although the process in India may have continued into the first few centuries CE. However, both traditions were certainly oral before they were written (indeed to some extent oral transmission in Indian vernacular languages continues down to the present day), and it is the history during the oral phase that concerns me here.

I suppose most scholars envisage the Greek epic as taking shape from Mycenean times onwards (perhaps incorporating influences from the Middle East, as has been argued for instance by West 1988:169 ff.); and similarly, most Indologists probably envisage the Sanskrit epics as originating in India.[3] However, there is no a priori necessity to think in such local terms. Since the Greek and Sanskrit languages go back to Proto-Indo-European, the Greek and Sanskrit epics could go back to a Proto-Indo-European oral epic. For some decades the philologists have been reconstructing phrases belonging to a Proto-Indo-European poetic language (e.g. Schmitt 1968), and it is not inconceivable that comparative study of the epics should enable one similarly to reconstruct the narrative themes in the poets' repertoire.

A sceptic might argue that such a prospect is unrealistic. Morphology and lexicon change relatively slowly, and this is what makes it feasible for linguists to grasp the common language lying behind Greek and Sanskrit. Are not narratives a different matter altogether? For one thing, people make them up. For another, even if they are handed on over the generations, they would change at such a rate that even if a proto-epic did exist, we should have no hope of reconstructing it.

[2] Recent bibliographies can be found in Katz 1989 and Sharma 1991. The major specialists have been Biardeau (Biardeau 1985-6 provides a convenient summary and introduction to the epic), and Hiltebeitel (e.g. 1988, 1976). My own approach derives more from the systematic comparativism of Dumézil (1968).

[3] Thus van Buitenen writes: 'That the main story of *The Mahābhārata* was a conscious composition is, to me, undeniable, and one poet, or a small group of them, must have been responsible for it.... When was this old q lay first composed? Certainly after the very early Vedic period...' (1973:xxiv).

In the light of the work of Georges Dumézil, such a priori pessimism is unjustified. In his massive comparativist undertaking he has demonstrated that many aspects of culture, including some narratives, were in fact transmitted to different areas of Eurasia along with the Indo-European languages, and remain recognizable as having this history. I cannot hope to give in a few lines a satisfactory introduction to an *oeuvre* whose place in intellectual history will one day, I think, come to be seen as standing at least on a par with that of Lévi-Strauss.[4] I limit myself to four paragraphs.

First, one major reason for the relative neglect of Dumézil's work lies in the sociology of knowledge: the work does not conform to current disciplinary boundaries. For most anthropologists it lies on the other side of a boundary with philology. But Dumézil is not an Indo-European philologist in the ordinary sense since, although he knew and used the relevant languages, his main innovatory contribution lies not in linguistics but in cultural history. Yet if he is an ancient historian, it is not in the normal sense of a specialist in some well-recognized discipline such as Celtic, Germanic, Classical or Indo-Iranian Studies: he is essentially a comparativist, drawing on all of them. There are thus very few academics whose specific business it is to come to grips with his *oeuvre*, or teach it – and it is large.

Another reason for the widespread neglect, even hostility towards him, is no doubt that the ideology which he reconstructs for the Proto-Indo-European speakers, and of which he finds so many traces in the surviving materials, is of a type which, though anthropologically entirely plausible, is unfamiliar to the modern West. He describes it as based on three 'functions' – perhaps better thought of as three pigeon-holes. Each pigeon-hole is clearly characterized and, given any context or totality, the ideology will tend to organize or classify it into elements which are distributed neatly into the three holes. I shall return later to the functions (which I actually believe to have been four in number, one of them commonly subdivided). But I make one point here: since the general trend within the Indo-European world has been to move from pigeon-holing ideologies to non-pigeon-holing ones, cultural materials which manifest the functional pattern are likely to be more conservative than those which do not – other things being equal (cf. Allen 1987).

Dumézil in effect reconstructs not only the abstract ideological framework of the Proto-Indo-European-speakers but also aspects of certain domains in which the ideology manifested itself – social division of labour, law, ritual, theology and (what is most relevant here) narrative, both mythic and epic. When I say he 'reconstructs', I simplify. In practice, just as many comparative linguists are cheerfully agnostic about the phonetics of the starred forms they find it convenient to use, so Dumézil puts little emphasis on trying to imagine

[4] The best overview is Dumézil 1987. See also Allen 1993.

life in the original Proto-Indo-European homeland.[5] What he does is take for granted that a Proto-Indo-European culture once existed – somewhere, sometime – and use this uncontentious assumption to explore the similarities between surviving cultural products in different parts of the Indo-European-speaking world. The interest lies in the comparison, and the 'reconstruction' is left implicit. I shall mostly follow his example in this.

Finally, the greater part of Dumézil's Indo-Europeanist work relates the western and eastern extremities of the Indo-European world. Celtic, Italic and Germanic materials are confronted with Indo-Iranian ones, Rome and India providing the favourite comparisons. Greece in general, and Homer in particular, seemed to him to have diverged too far from the Proto-Indo-European cultural heritage to provide much material for the comparativist. However, as will become clear, this is not altogether the case.

So much for my main source of inspiration and guide to method. To summarize: I shall compare two stretches of narrative, emphasizing their similarity. I then argue that the similarity is due to a common Proto-Indo-European origin, and I try to strengthen the argument by exploring the relationship with the Indo-European functions.

The Wider Picture

Before beginning, I must contextualize the relevant section of the *Mahābhārata*. Of the work's eighteen books, the first five lead up to the great eighteen-day battle, which starts with the *Gītā* in book 6. From book 12 onwards is aftermath. The battle is between the Kauravas, who are on the whole the villains, and the Pāṇḍavas, a set of five brothers. The central one, third in birth order, is Arjuna, son of Indra king of the gods. Shortly before the great battle the five Pāṇḍavas undergo a twelve- or thirteen-year banishment (books 3-4), but this is not the first reference to the theme of exile. Two earlier exiles or quasi-exiles occur in book 1. At the end of the first, Arjuna wins the hand of Draupadī, and the five brothers collectively marry her. Soon afterwards, Arjuna infringes the rule they have established by interrupting his eldest brother while the latter is alone with Draupadī; and off he goes into exile again, this time without his brothers. I shall mention all three exiles, but it is Arjuna's that is my main Indian text. It is not very long – some ten pages in the translation by van Buitenen (1973:400 ff.).

[5] Thus he seldom draws on archaeology. For discussion from the standpoint of that discipline, see Renfrew 1987 (whose attack on Dumézil in chapter 10 is vitiated by serious misunderstandings, see Allen 1993: 127 f.) and Mallory 1989, who is broadly pro-Dumézil.

I can now start the comparison proper.[6] Arjuna's exile is presented as a pilgrimage around the holy bathing places of India: the four cardinal points are visited in order, moving clockwise. But the hero's ritual bathing is far less salient than his successive encounters with females, (in essence) one per quarter. Among Homeric heroes only Odysseus makes a journey bringing him in contact with a series of women, and my project is to relate the two journeys. More precisely, I shall try to demonstrate homologies between particular females as shown in Table 1. But before coming to the details, I look at the two narrative structures as wholes.

	Mahābhārata		*Odyssey*	
	Draupadī	(C: Indraprastha)	Penelope	(Ithaca)
I	Ulūpī	(N: Ganges Gate)	Circe	(Aeaea)
II	Citrāṅgadā	(E: Maṇipura)	Sirens etc.	('Straits')
II	Vargā etc.	(S: Southern Ocean)	Calypso	(Ogygia)
IV	Subhadrā	(W: Dvārakā)	Nausicaa	(Scheria)
	Draupadī	(C: Indraprastha)	Penelope	(Ithaca)

Table 1. Correspondences between females in the two narratives, the locations of the females being indicated in brackets. The hero leaves his main wife, encounters females I-IV during the four episodes of his journey, and returns to his main wife. Correspondences are shown horizontally, except as regards II and III: Citrāṅgadā corresponds to Calypso, Vargā plus friends to the Sirens plus Scylla and Charybdis.

Consider first some of the differences (incidentally, it is harder to be exhaustive, or even systematic, in the treatment of differences than in that of similarities). Arjuna, one of five brothers, is only just married, and has little warrior experience; Odysseus, brotherless, has a teenage son, and is a seasoned warrior. Arjuna, though not a king, incarnates a god; Odysseus is a king, but wholly human. Arjuna travels by land, although he visits sacred waters; Odysseus voyages, visiting land now and then. Arjuna goes where he wants; Odysseus is at the mercy of the supernaturals and the elements. For Arjuna the journey is ostensibly a fixed-term penalty for an offence, but it could well have been enjoyable (it is never explicitly the reverse); for Odysseus the journey involves much uncertainty and suffering. Arjuna's journey is schematic in that it conforms to the schema of centre and cardinal points; Odysseus' is not. Arjuna sets off from 'home'; at the point where Homer takes up the story, Odysseus has already been journeying from Troy for two years. Finally, as

[6] This paper derives from a book-length study which is still in progress. Hence the somewhat compressed style.

regards narrative technique, Arjuna's journey unrolls straightforwardly from start to finish; Homer tells the story by means of inserted retrospective narratives, so that the two episodes which actually happen first are only recounted in the course of episode IV.

On the other hand, there are some global similarities.

1. Both heroes are central to their respective epics, and neither journey could be excised without serious alteration to the overall plot (it is Subhadrā who ultimately ensures the continuity of the Pāṇḍava line).
2. Both heroes are married before their respective journeys, and return to this primary wife afterwards.
3. If the Greek sea monsters (Sirens, Scylla and Charybdis) are treated as a single narrative unit (a step in the argument which I shall justify later), and if Vargā is regarded as subsuming her four companions, then in the course of his journey each hero has four encounters or liaisons with females other than his primary wife.[7] The four encounters constitute the foci of the four episodes into which the journey can be divided.
4. Of these four encounters, in both cases three are with humans or with anthropomorphic supernaturals, while one is with water monsters (if the Sirens can be included under this heading). The former are either frankly sexual liaisons or (as in the case of Nausicaa) rich in hints of sexuality, while the encounters with water monsters are asexual relationships.
5. Both heroes start off in company; but their companions suffer attrition, and by episode 3 or 4 both heroes are alone.

Detailed Comparisons

I come now to details. But first I must emphasize one rule of method. Whenever attention is drawn to such and such a shared motif in episode x, then that motif occurs in no other episode of either journey. For each episode I shall summarize the *Mahābhārata*, but assume knowledge of Homer.[8]

[7] Encounters, liaisons, relationships – none of the terms applies perfectly to all and only the major hero-female interactions in both stories. 'Relationship' is the most abstract term and has the advantage of including the interaction of hero and first wife, which is more than an encounter. However the term is too inclusive to be ideal: for instance, Odysseus has a relationship with Arete, but this is not one of the five alluded to in the paper's title and is not included in Table 1.

[8] The main Homeric passages are as follows: for Circe 10.133-12.36; for Calypso 5.55-268, 7.244-66 and (cattle of the Sun) 12.127-41, 260-425; for the monsters 12.37-126, 153-259; 426 to end; for Nausicaa 5.441-end of 8, 11.333-76, 131.1-187.

Episode I is much shorter in India, and contains no equivalent for Odysseus' solo hunting expedition, for the companions turned to pigs, for the protective drug revealed by Hermes, for Elpenor with his broken neck, or for the dialogues with the dead in Hades. Nonetheless, there are enough similarities to make my case.

> **Ulūpī** (206).[9] Arjuna has set out with his brahmin friends and settled at the Gate of the Ganges. The priests light ritual fires and offer flowers on both banks of the river, so that the area becomes surpassingly beautiful. Arjuna bathes in the Ganges and makes an offering to his grandfathers. As he is about to emerge and perform a fire rite, Ulūpī, daughter of the King of the Snakes, pulls him under the water. Arjuna finds a fire in the underwater palace and performs the rite there. He then asks Ulūpī who she is and why she has brought him to this lovely land. She explains that, on seeing him enter the water, she has fallen hopelessly in love. She overcomes Arjuna's scruples by arguing that in giving himself to her he will save her from dying of love, and hence will be observing *dharma*, the highest law. Persuaded by this argument, he does as she wishes, but leaves the palace next morning with the rising sun.

6.[10] Both stories include a visit to the underworld. The Snake-king's palace is itself underneath the waters; Odysseus crosses the Ocean to Hades.

7. Both underworld visits involve a fiery ritual directed to the dead (Odysseus' two friends flay and burn sacrificial sheep).

8. Both females are ostensibly at risk of their lives, Ulūpī from amorous passion, Circe when Odysseus threatens her with his sword.

9. Both Ulūpī and Circe take the sexual initiative.

10. In neither case is the offer immediately welcomed. Both females must overcome the hero's scruples by means of words (respectively ethical argument and oath).

11. Both females possess magical powers over the human body. Circe can turn Odysseus' companions to swine and back again by the use of drugs; Ulūpī, as will be seen later, possesses a magic stone which she uses to resuscitate Arjuna when he has been (to all appearance) 'killed' by Babhruvāhana.

---

[9] For each of the four encounters I give the number(s) of the *adhyāya* (chapter) in the critical edition, which is the text translated by van Buitenen.

[10] I continue the numbering of similarities where I left off above.

12. Both females show a supernatural knowledge of the past. Circe knows the woes and wrongs suffered by the wanderers; Ulūpī already knows the reasons for Arjuna's exile.

These seven points will have to suffice, and I pass on to Sanskrit episode II, which corresponds to Greek episode III. A major difference concerns the girl's father: Calypso's father, Atlas, plays no role in the action.

> **Citrāṅgadā** (207). Arjuna travels onwards, visiting various mountains, fords and hermitages. In the course of this journey he makes donations of many thousands of cows, as well as giving dwellings to brahmins. At the gates of the kingdom of Kaliṅga the brahmins turn back, and the hero continues with only very few companions. Coming to Maṇipura or Maṇalūra, he happens to catch sight of the princess walking in the city, and desires her. The king agrees to the union on condition that the son born of it shall remain with him. Arjuna accepts, and stays for a longish period.

13. In both traditions this episode is sketchy relative to the others – events in Maṇipura are covered in fewer than ten *ślokas*.

14. Both episodes open with references to large numbers of cattle, which are disposed of in an act having religious significance. Arjuna makes his massive pious donation; Odysseus fails to prevent his companions impiously killing the cattle of the Sun.

15. Shortly afterwards, in both cases, the size of the party is abruptly reduced. The turning back of the brahmins corresponds to the death at sea of Odysseus' impious crew.

16. In both cases this liaison is much longer than the first one. Odysseus spends one year with Circe (plus twenty-four hours after the visit to Hades), seven years with Calypso. Arjuna spends one night with Ulūpī, three months or years (the point is debated) with Citrāṅgadā.

17. Now, for the first time, non-Homeric Greek epic becomes important. Homer says nothing of any offspring from Odysseus' liaisons with Circe or Calypso, let alone of course from his encounter with Nausicaa. However, according to later sources (see Frazer 1921:301-5), he had a son, Telegonus, by either Circe or Calypso. Much later on in the story, subsequent to the destruction of the suitors, Telegonus comes to Ithaca and kills his father with the spine of a sting-ray. Similarly, Arjuna has a son called Babhruvāhana by Citrāṅgadā. Much later on, subsequent to the great battle, Arjuna revisits the eastern quarter (critical edition 14.78-

80; tr. Roy 12:150-7), and Babhruvāhana kills his father with a snake-like poisonous arrow. Parricide is not a commonplace event, and the two sons must be cognate. In view of the other reasons for linking Calypso and Citrāṅgadā, the chances are that the obscure cyclic poet Eugammon of Cyrene was preserving the Proto-Indo-European tradition when he gave Calypso, rather than Circe, as the parricide's mother.

As for episode III, it has already been implied that a multiplicity of Greek monsters corresponds to a single type of Indian monster. The other main difference is that the Greek hero escapes from the monsters, while the Indian redeems them.

> **Vargā** (208-9). Arjuna approaches some bathing places in the South. Five of them were formerly favoured by religious ascetics, but are now occupied by large crocodiles which drag away visitors. Ignoring the warnings given by some ascetics, Arjuna visits one of the sacred *tīrthas*, and bathes in it. He is promptly seized by its crocodile, but he succeeds in pulling the reptile onto land, whereupon it turns into a beautiful woman. She is Vargā, a nymph who used to roam the forest with her four girl friends. Once, on a journey, the quintet had encountered a handsome brahmin practising his austerities. The girls sang and danced to seduce him, but after sternly resisting their temptations he cursed them to spend a century as crocodiles. In answer to their pleas for mercy he foretold their rescue. Another sage told them where to spend the period of their punishment, knowing that Arjuna would rescue them in due course. Indeed, having already rescued Vargā the hero now performs the same service for her four friends.

18. Both heroes receive warnings of the dangers awaiting them in certain waters, but are undeterred: Circe's warnings about the monsters correspond to those given by the ascetics.
19. In both cases the water monsters are somehow multiple. The six heads of Scylla correspond to the five-member group of crocodiles.
20. Both stories link the theme of female water monsters to that of seductive female singers, and in both cases the second theme in some sense precedes. In India the singers are the same beings as the crocodiles, but in an earlier phase of their lives. In Greece the Sirens are separate beings from the more obviously monstrous Scylla and Charybdis, but they are encountered just before them in the course of the journey. The unity of the quasi-Sirens and monsters in the Sanskrit is part of the justification for treating the Greek equivalents as a single narrative element (the

relationship with functions providing a further argument).

21. The duality of Scylla and Charybdis parallels the two phases in Arjuna's dealings with Vargā. First Vargā grabs the hero, as Scylla grabs Odysseus' six friends; then Arjuna pulls Vargā onto land, as Odysseus grabs the fig-tree over Charybdis.

22. To revert to post-Homeric sources (see e.g. Grimal 1982 s.vv.), in both cases the females have been metamorphosed into monsters by way of punishment. Moreover, both types of Siren figure undergo a second transformation as a result of the hero's visit. Vargā and friends change back into nymphs, the Greek Sirens die (Apollodorus, *Epitome* 7.19), perhaps by suicide.

Episode IV is particularly complex, in both traditions. The major difference is that Arjuna actually marries Subhadrā, while in Homer Odysseus does not even sleep with Nausicaa. In addition, Subhadrā's brother Kṛṣṇa plays a fundamental role in the whole *Mahābhārata*, and elsewhere, while the most obvious homologue in the Greek is a very minor character. I shall indicate later how at least the first of these discrepancies can be resolved.

> **Subhadrā** (210-13). Following a return visit to Maṇipura, Arjuna tours the bathing places in the west until Kṛṣṇa comes to meet him at Prabhāsa. They go together to Mount Raivataka where Kṛṣṇa has arranged entertainment – decorations and food, actors and dancers. After enjoying them, Arjuna goes to his bed, and while he is telling his friend about his journey, he falls asleep. The next day they go in a golden chariot to Dvārakā where Arjuna is welcomed by crowds. A few days later the local people hold a large festival on the same mountain. Again the mountain has been embellished, and there is music, dance and song. A number of those attending the festival are named, some of them being drunk.
>
> Kṛṣṇa and Arjuna are strolling through the confusion when the latter sees Subhadrā in the midst of her friends. He is smitten by the god of love. Recognizing this, Kṛṣṇa explains that the girl is his sister. Arjuna asks his advice. Of the two modes of marriage appropriate for a warrior, Kṛṣṇa points out the risks attached to 'marriage by concourse' (*svayaṃvara* – see below), and recommends marriage by capture.
>
> After they have returned to the city, Arjuna, well armed, sets off in a golden chariot yoked with Kṛṣṇa's two horses, pretending to be going hunting. Subhadrā has been attending the festival. After paying homage to the mountain and its deities,

she has finished her ritual circumambulation and is setting off for Dvārakā. Arjuna abducts her by force, and sets off for Indraprastha. Her armed escort raise the alarm. At the courthouse the magistrate sounds the war-drum, and the warriors assemble *en masse*. Drunk and angered at the abduction, they prepare to pursue Arjuna. Balarāma blames his half-brother for the guest's behaviour. Kṛṣṇa again discusses the modes of marriage, presents Arjuna's action as entirely right and proper, welcomes the union and proposes a diplomatic approach to the abductor. Arjuna is induced to return and hold a wedding at Dvārakā, before completing his exile and returning home.

23. In both cases the hero's hosts come from elsewhere. The Phaeacians migrated from Hypereia under Alcinous' father because they were being plundered by the Cyclops. The people of Dvārakā migrated from Mathurā during Kṛṣṇa's lifetime because they were being attacked by a more powerful king (2.13.35-50).

24. Both kingdoms eventually suffer what a modern might term a natural catastrophe. The sea-faring Phaeacians have their ports blocked with a mountain by Poseidon while, in book 16, Dvārakā sinks beneath the Ocean.

25. In both traditions this fourth episode unrolls in a multiplicity of locations, initially rural, later largely urban. The Scherian sea-shore corresponds to Prabhāsa and Mount Raivataka, the city of the Phaeacians to Dvārakā.

26. At a more detailed level of topography, in both cases the hero starts beside water (Prabhāsa is a *tīrtha* or sacred bathing place), and moves uphill. Odysseus climbs a *klitus* to his thicket, Arjuna ascends Raivataka.

27. Both heroes on their 'hills' are woken by a noise: Odysseus by the shout of the maidens when their ball falls into the river, Arjuna by songs, music and praises.

28. Both stories describe pleasures enjoyed in the countryside. Nausicaa sings and plays ball with her maidens; Arjuna enjoys watching singers and dancers on the decorated mountain.

29. Both heroes tell their stories just before falling asleep. Odysseus narrates the last part of his journey during his second night in Scheria before sleeping on the porch; Arjuna nods off while narrating to Kṛṣṇa.

30. Both stories involve wheeled vehicles. Nausicaa borrows her father's

mule cart; Arjuna rides in and later borrows Kṛṣṇa's splendid horse-drawn chariot.

31. When encountering their females both heroes are assimilated to hunters. Odysseus emerging from a thicket is compared, in a typical Homeric simile, to a lion going hunting among cattle, sheep or deer. When setting off to abduct, Arjuna pretends to be going hunting.
32. Both heroes are, or claim to be, amazed by the sight of the female. (The point may seem banal, but I recall my rule of method: not one of the other encounters inspires similar amazement in the hero.)
33. Both traditions here describe at least two crowd scenes, large gatherings of the citizens or of particular categories of citizens.
34. At one of these gatherings, both epics include lists of names of males who, as individuals, play a minimal or even totally unspecified role in events. Although I cannot find any etymological links between the eleven 'empty' names of the noble youths at the Phaeacian games and the thirteen 'empty' names of warriors who attend the Raivataka festival, it is the presence of the lists that is striking.
35. Both heroes encounter from the local youths an initial hostility which is later resolved. The details are particularly complicated, and I merely note that the insult of Euryalus, for which Alcinous makes him apologize, corresponds to the vilification of Arjuna by Balarāma, who is pacified by Kṛṣṇa.
36. In both cases the female's brother is on particularly friendly terms with the hero. Nausicaa's brother Laodamas, an exquisite dancer, corresponds to Subhadrā's brother Kṛṣṇa, also a notable dancer (in later Hindu tradition). As I have said, since Laodamas is such a minor figure, while Kṛṣṇa's role in Hinduism is comparable to Christ's within Christianity, the homology is intriguing.
37. At the end of episode 4 both heroes receive magnificent gifts, Odysseus simply on the initiative of Alcinous, Arjuna as dowry accompanying Subhadrā.
38. On their return home, both heroes encounter from their original wives an initial distrust or reserve.

A Complication

These thirty-eight points of similarity are a selection from about twice as many, some of which relate to quite small details in the language of the two texts. But I hope that enough has been said to show that the similarities between the two traditions cannot be ascribed to accident, or to vague resemblances between societies 'at a similar stage of development'. The strongest argument against that idea is the distribution of the similarities. These are not isolated clichés of the epic genre scattered at random across the story, but narrative particulars located precisely in one or other of the four episodes which make up the structure specified by Table 1 and by the global resemblances 1-5.

However, the analysis cannot stop at this point. The relationship between the two epics is more complex than the comparison between the two journeys indicates. It is true that the end of Odysseus' wanderings corresponds to the second of the three exiles in the *Mahābhārata*, but it seems that the start of the voyage corresponds to some extent to the first exile, and that the end has superimposed on it certain features from the third exile (book 3). I concentrate on the end, doing little more than hint at comparisons which need to be explored in much greater depth.

> **Urvaśī** (38-40, 163-4).[11] During the great twelve-year exile, Arjuna goes off by himself to the north. He undertakes increasingly severe religious austerities, ultimately subsisting for a month on wind alone. He is taken to Heaven, where he sees a nymph called Urvaśī. He studies dancing and singing with the *gandharva* Citrasena, who becomes his friend. [Now comes a passage rejected from the main text of the critical edition.] Urvaśī receives from Indra a divine messenger who tells her to prepare for love-making with Arjuna. She goes to visit him at night. But Arjuna's attitude is one of embarrassed reverence, not love, since the nymph is a distant forebear of his. She departs angrily.

The comparisons are with Odysseus' involuntary austerities resulting from storm and sea; the blissful, quasi-heavenly land of Scheria; Nausicaa being told by Athene to prepare for her wedding; Odysseus' sense of *sebas* (reverence) when he accosts her. Citrasena parallels Nausicaa's friendly brother, Laodamas the dancer.

One major discrepancy between the Greek and Sanskrit episode IV was the lack of sexual relations between the Greek hero and heroine, but this is precisely paralleled by Arjuna's unconsummated encounter with Urvaśī. One can reasonably say that Nausicaa, the nubile female of the fourth encounter, corresponds structurally to Subhadrā, but corresponds in much of her content to Urvaśī. The other major discrepancy was the relative insignificance of Laodamas as compared to Kṛṣṇa. This too finds a parallel in the relative insignificance of Citrasena.

---

11 The Urvaśī episode in the narrower sense is in appendix 1.6 of the critical edition (vol.4: 1047-53), tr. Roy 2:102-6.

Four-Functional Interpretation

What is to be made of the historical relationship between the Greek and Indian narratives? If Homer was written down half a millennium earlier, was the story perhaps carried to India, maybe by Alexander's troops, or later, or even earlier? One objection to this, out of many, is the order of events in the narrative. By the fourth century at any rate the Homeric texts were no doubt well on their way to being standardized, and it would be surprising, to say the least, if the Indian bards had managed to rework the narrative so as to eliminate all traces of Homer's sophisticated embedded narrative technique. But I have an additional and more interesting line of argument.

The time has come to return to Dumézil and his functions, bearing in mind that the presence of a functional pattern in narratives is probably an index of conservatism. I assume that Dumézil is essentially right in recognizing within the Indo-European ideological inheritance three clusters of ideas: F1 pertaining to religion and the sacred, F2 to physical force and war, F3 to fecundity, wealth and associated ideas. I have argued in other papers that Dumézil's view of the ideology needs to be expanded (Allen 1991, in press). The three classical functions are as it were 'framed' by a fourth function pertaining to what is other, outside or beyond. Frequently one finds two contrasting representatives of the fourth function. One of them is positively valued and often in some sense transcendent, while the other is negatively valued and may be associated with death, destruction, demons and the like. I refer to such elements as $F4^+$ and $F4^-$ respectively. So, are the five relationships shown in Table 1 a manifestation of this pattern?

A good deal of the work needed to answer this question has already been carried out by Dumézil in a study (1979) which starts off with a comparison between Sanskritic and Roman matrimonial law. The best-known Indian text to discuss the topic is the *Manusmṛti* or Code of Manu (again dating from around the turn of the eras). Manu (3.20-34) actually presents a list of eight types of marriage, but, as Dumézil notes, the first four are very similar, and the list can readily be reduced to five major types, three of which are clearly related to his functions. Using a single label for the first (conflated) type (cf. Trautmann 1981:288 ff.), I introduce English labels and order the list in the simplest way. These then are the types on which Dumézil focuses attention:

gift of a bride (*kanyādāna*)	F1
marriage by capture (*rākṣasa*)	F2
purchase of a bride (*āsura*)	F3

Very briefly, the gift of a bride is assimilated to an offering to the gods, and is specially recommended for priests; marriage by capture involves the use of physical force and is recommended for warriors; bride purchase connotes haggling with the bride's father over the price (*śulka*), and in comparison to the others is somewhat dishonourable and most appropriate for merchants. These modes relate respectively to the realms of religion, force and wealth; and each has a related form in Rome, which adds further weight to the argument that the classification is Proto-Indo-European (cf. also Sergent 1984).

Manu lists two other major modes, marriage by mutual choice (*gāndharva*) and the *paiśāca* mode. The latter occurs when a man unites in secret with a woman who is asleep, drunk or mad – that is (my gloss), not in her normal state. But marriage by mutual choice is closely related to a ninth type, *svayaṃvara*, or marriage by concourse, which is not mentioned by Manu but is common in the epics. This type occurs when a princess chooses from a group of princes who have assembled for the purpose, and who may participate in a contest. In a somewhat confused listing, the *Mahābhārata* (1.96.7 ff.) rates it the best of the types. Conversely, the law codes generally agree that the *paiśāca* mode is the worst; indeed they often treat it last, and sometimes (Āpastamba, Vasiṣṭha) omit it altogether. So these two modes are both to some extent excluded and heterogeneous, and thereby qualify as F4; and one is valued, the other the converse. Dumézil's analysis can therefore be supplemented as follows:

marriage by concourse (*svayaṃvara*)	$F4^{+}$ [12]
paiśāca union	$F4^{-}$

The question can now be rephrased (I conflate two issues which are theoretically distinct and start with the *Mahābhārata*): do Arjuna's five relationships conform either to the five modes of marriage or to the functions?

The marriage with Draupadī is by concourse ($F4^{+}$). Being polyandrous, it is in any case heterogeneous and wholly outside the norm. But although it is a scandal, it is one for which the text offers religious justifications of several sorts, and it is certainly presented as correct for the Pāṇḍavas.

The encounter with Vargā and friends is not even sexual, let alone a marriage; and the females are not asleep, drunk or mad. But, *qua* monsters, they are certainly heterogeneous relative to the others and – more important – they are not in their normal state. It is also worth noting the symmetry. The

[12] Dumézil regards marriage by concourse as having developed in the context of chivalry as a public and orderly variant of the more intimate mutual choice mode, and he construes both as F2. As I hope to argue elsewhere, the relationship should be reversed. The mutual choice mode is probably a privatized and democratized variant of the $F4^{+}$ concourse mode. The point need not be argued here since none of Arjuna's unions is by mutual choice (*pace* Katz (1990:62) who interprets the Ulūpī encounter in this way).

$F4^+$ relationship with Draupadī involves five males and one female, the $F4^-$ encounter involves five females and one male; all the other liaisons are one-to-one. Thus, in spite of the absence of sexual union, the encounter can reasonably be aligned with the $F4^-$ *paiśāca* union – perhaps sexuality was present in earlier versions of the story (maybe even pre-Proto-Indo-European ones).

The Subhadrā union is explicitly a marriage by capture (F2).

The remaining two liaisons are not explicitly labelled in the Sanskrit. However, that with Citrāṅgadā involves Arjuna taking the initiative, submitting to the bride's father's demands, and conceding to him a 'price'. The term *śulka*, used nowhere else in the story, is precisely the term used in Nārada's definition of the F3 marriage by purchase.

The union with Ulūpī resembles marriage by gift in that the initiative comes from the bride's side, and the text specifically refers to gifts, using the root *dā* - (*pradānam*).[13] Moreover the whole episode is pervaded by references to religion and ritual.

The results of the analysis can be summarized as in Figure 1.

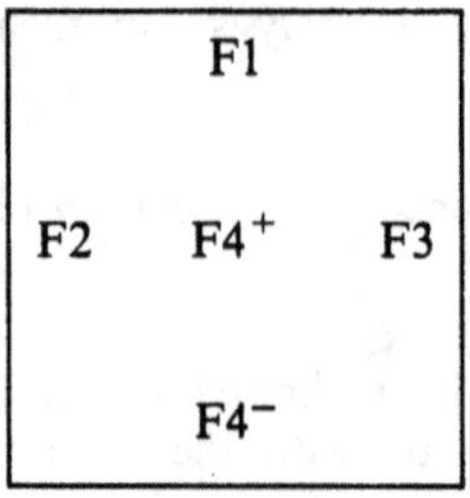

Figure 1. Relationship between cardinal points and modes of marriage in the Sanskrit.

The argument has been that the Greek relationships correspond one-for-one with the Sanskrit, but they do not relate directly to the cardinal points. The next question is whether they relate directly either to the functions or to the modes of marriage.

In some post-Homeric sources the marriage of Odysseus and Penelope somewhat resembles a marriage by concourse (Pausanias 3.12.1), and it is closely associated with the gathering of the princes of Greece to woo Helen (e.g. Apollodorus, *Bibliotheke* 3.10.8). To a certain extent it therefore conforms to the type which in India would be $F4^+$ (no doubt too, Odysseus stringing the bow amidst the suitors is participating in an event of a similar type). The

[13] Since the text presents Arjuna, not the bride's side, as making the gifts, the union does not in fact exemplify the F1 mode, but it does relate to the F1 complex of ideas.

various monsters might be thought sufficiently heterogeneous relative to the other females to point in the direction of $F4^{-}$, although the gap between the Sirens and Circe is perhaps not really very great. As for the other episodes, none of them as they stand relate unambiguously either to functions or to modes. At most there are odd hints: in Circe's case, as in Ulūpī's, the sexual initiative comes from the bride's side.

Let me sum up the implications of what has been said about functions. The Proto-Indo-European-speakers tended to organize all sorts of domains and contexts into clear-cut structures such that the elements involved were distributed into a number of ideological pigeon-holes, technically called functions. Dumézil says that there were three functions, the first of which was sometimes split (into Mitra and Varuṇa aspects, roughly speaking into close and distant). I say that there were four functions, and that the fourth was very often split into positively valued and negatively valued. We both draw on a great deal more evidence than is even alluded to here.

In the particular case of matrimonial law, the trifunctionalist attributes to Proto-Indo-European culture the recognition of three modes of marriage, each related to a function; the implication is that in increasing the number of types the Indians innovated. The quadrifunctionalist looks at the matter the other way round. The Proto-Indo-European-speakers would have recognized five modes, and in retaining these the Indians were conservative; if they innovated, it was only in increasing the number from five to eight. In either case Proto-Indo-European culture related some marriage types to functions. The present paper shows that the Proto-Indo-European corpus of narratives included one (myth, epic, legend – it hardly matters here) in which a hero contracted five types of union or relationship. If the proto-narrative resembled the *Odyssey*, the relationships were not clearly related to functions, and India innovated in making the link. But I have already accepted Dumézil's argument that in 'legal' contexts at any rate the Proto-Indo-European-speakers did relate marriage types to functions, and if so, it is much more likely that the proto-narrative also made the connection – unlike the *Odyssey*, but like the *Mahābhārata*. In other words, in this respect too the Indian epic is far more likely to be the conservative one. This helps to confirm the earlier conclusion that the narrative similarities are not due to influences from Greece on India. Incidentally, it also shows that Dumézil was right in thinking that Homer had moved a long way from his Indo-European heritage; if there was a mistake, it was in underestimating the amount of heritage that remains recognizable.[14]

[14] During the 1980s Dumézil did in fact propose a number of Homeric analyses, notably a convincing trifunctional analysis of the modes of action used by and against Circe (1982:166 ff.).

Final Remarks

In conclusion, I note a few areas that invite further work.

- At the most general anthropological level, the paper relates to the conceptualization of marriage outside as well as inside the Indo-European world, a topic which is sometimes approached simplistically in terms of bride-price versus dowry.
- The paper presents another manifestation of the four-functional ideology, together with an example of how easily manifestations of F4 can be overlooked (cf. Allen 1987:35).[15] There are certainly many more.
- The association between functions and cardinal points might repay further attention (cf. Allen 1991:148-50).
- As regards India, it ought to be possible to relate what has been said above about Kṛṣṇa to the rise of Vaiṣṇavism. Would it be possible to argue that Kṛṣṇa not only corresponds to Laodamas and Citrasena but has also, so to speak, expanded his role so as to take on much of the narrative and conceptual material which in the *Odyssey* is distributed among other characters? In a general sense, Kṛṣṇa is to Arjuna as Athene is to Odysseus.
- Coming to narrower problems, the comparison casts a little light on the composition of the epics, that is, on what used to be called 'the Homeric question', and on its Indian equivalent. Significant parts of both narratives go back to Proto-Indo-European times, and it is certain that some material contained in 'post-Homeric' sources, as well as some material condemned in the Pune critical edition, belongs in this archaic category (comparisons 17 and 22; Urvaśī episode). At least in one case (comparison 31), a 'Homeric' simile seems to be equally old.
- Finally, and obviously, how extensive is the relationship between Greek and Indian epic outside the passages we have been considering? It cannot be coincidence that fairly soon after the Urvaśī episode Arjuna finds himself in disguise at the court of King Virāṭa, while fairly soon after the Nausicaa episode Odysseus finds himself in disguise in his own palace.

---

[15] Dumézil rightly ascribes the inclusion of the *paiśāca* mode in the Indian codes to the pandits' desire for completeness in their enumerations (1979:33), although he does not wholly appreciate the force of his own remark. Here is a further example of the understandable tendency to overlook the heterogeneous F4 and its representatives. The *Mahābhārata* is widely available in India in the form of comic strips, and 'Arjuna's Twelve-Year Exile' is covered in Pai 1989. The 'text' covers all four encounters (quite accurately), but the accompanying map (p.11) omits the visit to the Southern Ocean (presumably because of the vagueness of the localization).

References

Allen, N.J. 1987. 'The Ideology of the Indo-Europeans: Dumézil's Theory and the Idea of a Fourth Function.' *International Journal of Moral and Social Studies* 2: 23-39.

—.1991. 'Some Gods of Pre-Islamic Nuristan.' *Revue de l'histoire des religions* 208(2):141-68.

—. 1993. 'Debating Dumézil's Recent Studies in Comparative Mythology.' *JASO* 24/2:119-31.

—. Forthcoming. 'Romulus and the Fourth Function.' In *Indo-European Religion After G. Dumézil* (JIES Monographs 13), ed. E. Polomé. Washington: The Institute for the Study of Man.

Apollodorus. *The Library* [*Bibliotheke*] and *The Epitome*. See Frazer 1921.

Biardeau, M., and J.-M. Péterfalvi. 1985-6. *Le Mahābhārata*. 2 vols. Paris: Flammarion.

Camps, W.A. 1980. *An Introduction to Homer*. Oxford: Clarendon.

Dumézil, G. 1968. *Mythe et épopée*, vol.1. Paris: Gallimard.

—. 1979. *Mariages indo-européens*. Paris: Payot.

—. 1982. *Apollon sonore et autres essais*. Paris: Gallimard.

—. 1987. *Entretiens avec Didier Eribon*. Paris: Gallimard.

Frazer, Sir James G. 1921. *Apollodorus: The Library* (2 vols., Loeb). London: Heinemann.

Griffin, J. 1987. *Homer: The Odyssey*. Cambridge: University Press.

Grimal, P. 1982. *Dictionnaire de la mythologie grecque et romaine*. Paris: Presses Universitaires de France. Tr., Oxford: Blackwell, 1985.

Hiltebeitel, A. 1976. *The Ritual of Battle*. 2nd edition 1990. Ithaca: Cornell University Press.

—. 1988. *The Cult of Draupadī, Vol.1. Mythologies: From Gingee to Kurukṣetra*. Chicago: Princeton University Press.

Katz, Ruth. 1990. *Arjuna in the Mahābhārata*. Delhi: Motilal Banarsidass.

Mahābhārata. 1933-60. Critical edition (19 vols.) by V.S. Sukthankar *et al.* Pune: Bhandarkar Oriental Institute.

—. 1883-96. Tr. K.M. Ganguli, ed. P.C. Roy. Calcutta: See also van Buitenen 1973.

Mallory, J. 1989. *In Search of the Indo-Europeans: Language, Archaeology and Myth*. London: Thames & Hudson.

Manu. 1983. *Manusmṛti*, ed. J.L. Shastri. Delhi: Motilal Banarsidass.

—. 1991. *The Laws of Manu*, tr. W. Doniger and B.K. Smith. London: Penguin.

Pai, Anant, ed. 1989. *Mahābhārata -14 ('Arjuna's Twelve-year Exile')*. Part 2 of Amar Chitra Katha bumper issue no. 55. Bombay: India Book House.

Pausanias. 1926, *Description of Greece*, vol.2, tr. W.H.S. Jones and H.A.

Ormerod (Loeb). London: Heineman.

Renfrew, C. 1987. *Archaeology and Language: The Puzzle of Indo-European Origins*. London: Cape.

Schmitt, R., ed. 1968. *Indogermanische Dichtersprache*. Darmstadt: Wissenschaftliche Buchgesellschaft.

Sergent, B. 1984. 'Three Notes on the Trifunctional Indo-European Marriage.' *Journal of Indo-European Studies* 12:179-91.

Sharma, A., ed. 1991. *Essays on the Mahābhārata*. Leiden: Brill.

Trautmann, T.R. 1981. *Dravidian Kinship*. Cambridge: University Press.

van Buitenen, J.A.B. 1973. *The Mahābhārata. Vol.1: The Book of the Beginning*. Chicago: University Press.

West, M. 1988. 'The Rise of the Greek Epic.' *Journal of Hellenic Studies* 108:15-172.

2

The Fate of the Female *Ṛṣi*: Portraits of Lopāmudrā

Laurie L. Patton

Introduction

The *Virāṭaparvan* of the *Mahābhārata* opens with the sorrow of Draupadī, who must bear the unwelcome advances of the boorish marshal Kīcaka while the Pāṇḍava brothers are living in the kingdom of the Matsyas. When Bhīma attempts to console her, he invokes a Vedic model of the patient virtuous wife: 'Just as Lopāmudrā gave up all of her human comforts and followed Agastya… so too you shall prevail with all of your virtues.'[1] A glance at the Vedic hymn in which Lopāmudrā appears, however, reveals that in her role as poetess she is anything but a model of patience. In *Ṛgveda* 1.179, Lopāmudrā attempts to persuade her husband, Agastya, away from his illustrious ascetic practices and back to the joys of sexual union.

How can we make sense of these diverse mythological portrayals of this Vedic *ṛṣi* and poetess, and the gender roles they illustrate? While much has been done at a general level to outline the position of women in early Indian

This chapter was originally given as a talk in November 1992 at Ālocana, a Documentation and Resource Center for Women in Pune, India, and in April 1993 at Columbia University's Southern Asian Institute, at the conference on Gender and Vedic Authority. I would especially like to thank Michèle Dominy, Peggy Kraft, Nancy Leonard, Paul Griffiths, and the staff at Ālocana, Medha Kotwal Lele and Simrita Singh, for their input. In addition, members of the Working Group on Gender and Vedic Authority – Stephanie Jamison, Ellison Findly, Mary McGee, Vasudha Narayanan, and Julia Leslie – have made many helpful suggestions in the preparation of this article.

[1] *Mahābhārata* 4.20.10-12.

mythology and ritual,[2] more specific studies are just now beginning to emerge.[3] In this chapter I will add to these studies by providing a close reading of the myths about Lopāmudrā. In doing so, I want to provide a more nuanced understanding of the narrative representation of gender roles in the Vedic period.

The Problem with 'Women'

When previous authors have written on women in the *Ṛgveda* they usually include human, semi-divine, and divine figures in a single category. Bhagwat Saran Upadhyaya's book, *Women in Ṛg Veda* (1974), is a case in point: a potpourri of female *ṛṣis, apsaras*es, and goddesses, such as Vāc, Uṣas, and others, are all placed together in a single category, with only a superficial typological treatment of differences between these figures. This is also the case in Shyam Kishore Lal's more recent *Female Divinities in Hindu Myth and Ritual* (1980). This tendency to create a separate category of 'female', which distinguishes only sketchily between various kinds of 'female', is inherently problematic. The move is similar to the tendency of colonialist writers to create a unified Hinduism where, as Fryckenberg and many others have recently pointed out, no such Hinduism existed.[4] The assumption made is that because women, human, semi-divine, or divine, are all essentially different from men, they must all share the same characteristics.

Despite the difficulties inherent in such a task, scholarship on women in early India might fruitfully avoid the dangers of ghettoizing women in a single intellectual category by recognizing gender identity as a necessary point of departure, but always as a construction in and of itself. Following the lead of several feminist writers on colonial India,[5] we might move beyond the large, unwieldy, and confusing category of 'the female' in ancient India as well. The study of myths about women in early Indian religions is no different from any other arena of South Asian Studies: we must avoid creating an 'essence' where none exists, but focus instead on a complex set of social relations, referring to a changing set of historically variable processes.[6] Such a view necessitates smaller

---

[2] See Upadhyaya 1974, Lal 1980, Haddad and Findly 1985, Sharma 1987 and Bhattacharji 1994.

[3] See especially Smith 1991, and Menski 1991. While Bhattacharji's recent *Women and Society in Ancient India* (1994) is a more general overview, it is quite detailed in its use of textual materials.

[4] See Fryckenberg 1991, Guha and Spivak 1988, Bayly 1988, and Prakash 1992.

[5] See Chatterji 1989 and Mohanty (1984:337-8) for a comparison of the ways in which Western feminism imitates colonial discourse in its depiction of 'Third World Women' under a homogeneous category.

[6] See Jane Flax's section, 'Thinking in Relations' (1987:628-30) for a fuller theoretical elaboration of this idea for feminist theory.

studies of individual myths about individual Vedic figures, and how they might change over time. Moreover, the treatment of such myths might concentrate not only on the representation of 'women', but also on the dynamic of gender relationships that are sanctioned by the prevailing ideologies of the period in question.[7]

With this view in mind, I will examine three periods of Vedic and post-Vedic texts to show the development and change in gender role of the particular character of Lopāmudrā – wife of the famous *ṛṣi* Agastya and poetess of several verses of RV 1.179. More specifically, I will examine how she is represented in the *Ṛgveda* (c.1200 BCE), and how that representation changes in texts of later Vedic commentary (400-100 BCE) and in the *Mahābhārata* epic (200 BCE-200 CE).

Myth as Argument

Before turning to Lopāmudrā, however, some preliminary thoughts about the role of myth are in order. I have come to view the role of mythic narrative as a form of social argumentation.[8] In this I follow historians and philosophers such as Hayden White, Gyan Prakash Pandey, and others, who disagree with the idea that narrative is a form of accurate, true-to-life representational discourse. Narratives, they argue, are a form of speaking about events, whether real or imaginary. Distinguishing between discourse and narrative, Hayden White writes,

> The 'subjectivity' of the discourse is given by the presence, explicit or implicit, of an 'ego' who can be defined 'only as the person who maintains the discourse'.

In other words, we know who is speaking, what their background is, and why they are speaking in the manner that they are. White goes on to say:

> By contrast, the 'objectivity of narrative is defined by the absence of all reference to the narrator.' In the narrativizing discourse, then, we can say, with Buenveniste, that 'truly there is no longer a "narrator". The events are chronologically recorded as they

[7] As Flax (1987:629) puts it, 'From the perspective of social relations, men and women are both prisoners of gender, although in highly differentiated but interrelated ways. To the extent that feminist discourse defines its problematic with the category of 'woman', it too privileges 'man' as unproblematic or exempted from determination by gender relations.

[8] See Patton 1993 and forthcoming.

> appear on the horizon of the story. No-one speaks. The events seem to tell themselves.' (1987:3).

According to White, the assumed pattern of narrative can contribute to the sense of objectivity any story presents. Such narratives are concerned with presenting a principle, which is shown to be self-evident through the unfolding events of the story. Hayden White illuminates this aspect of narrativity in the following way (p.14):

> If every fully realized story, however we define that familiar but conceptually elusive entity...endows events, whether real or imaginary, with a significance that they do not possess as a mere sequence, then it seems possible to conclude that every historical narrative has as its latent or manifest purpose the desire to moralize the events of which it treats.

White's idea of 'moralizing narrative' can be productively broadened to include the strategies of mythological narrative; both kinds of narrative impose a certain ordered, higher significance onto a sequence of events. Such narratives reveal to us a world that is putatively 'finished', done with, over, and yet not dissolved, not falling apart (p.21).

Despite its rather abstract nature, I think this view of narrative has important implications for gender studies' perspectives on the female *ṛṣi*. These theoretical perspectives generate a fruitful set of questions. How does the factor of gender, and by implication, practices of sexuality, moralize the events told in the stories of the female *ṛṣi*s? What is the higher order imposed upon these events and the characters who bring them about? If gender is in fact a complex set of social relations, referring to a changing set of historically variable processes, how do they become represented as a so-called objective reality, to use Hayden White's term again, as if they had always been there, never to be questioned?

The Construction of Gender Through Dialogue

While White's understanding of the construction of mythic objectivity dovetails well with recent feminist understandings of the construction of gender, it also seems to fit with the particular literary genre in which many of these early Vedic hymns about women are cast – the dialogue. By virtue of the design of many of these hymns, we can witness the construction of gender ideology taking place in the progress of the conversation between two or more mythological characters. These hymns are called *saṃvāda*, or dialogue hymns, and are part of a genre that is found through the *Ṛgveda*. Generally speaking, they involve rather touching, human situations that are also, both directly and indirectly, related to the performance of the Vedic sacrifice.

A brief description of some of the *saṃvāda* hymns that do not involve women might be helpful here. RV 10.135 is sung during the funeral rite, and consists of a conversation between a dead father who has gone to the realm of Yama, and his son, who longs to be in his company and fantasizes about building a magical chariot so that he may follow him. RV 10.51 involves the gods trying to persuade Agni, or fire, out of the waters, where he has fled because he fears that he will perish, as have his brothers, earlier sacrificial fires. RV 10.108 depicts Saramā, the dog of Indra, roving through the galaxies and crossing the mythical river Rasa in order to rescue the valuable cows that have been stolen by the demons who live on the other side, and having a conversation with the demons upon her arrival. To take a final example, RV 10.28 depicts a scolding conversation between Indra and his son, who has become pretentious enough to pretend he is Indra himself.

Such familial themes aside, many of the dialogue hymns are particularly associated with hymns that relate to fertility, and are explicitly sexual in nature. Sketching out the context for Lopāmudrā, Vedic hymns that involve dialogues with women *ṛṣi*s all represent situations in which one member of the pair attempts to persuade the other to engage in some sort of sexual activity. In RV 10.10, the conversation between the twins Yama and Yamī, Yama, the first son of the solar god and king of the dead, rejects the solicitations of his twin sister Yamī. Yamī invokes the gods of procreation and argues that the human race must be preserved; Yama counters by invoking moral gods and their laws.

Ṛgveda 10.95 is the basis of the well-known story of Purūravas and Urvaśī, which is retold in a rather different fashion in a number of different texts from the more devotional tradition of the Purāṇas. The hymn is a dialogue between two lovers who have been separated for reasons that are not entirely clear. However, what is clear is that Urvaṣī is not as happy with her husband as he has been with her, and this is in part the source of the friction.

In the much analysed hymn of Apālā and Indra (RV 8.91), the young woman Apālā is described as *pati-dvíṣ-* a woman who hates her husband.[9] The first and last verses narrate the story of Apālā, and the rest of the hymn consists of verses spoken by her. Apālā finds *soma*, presses it in her mouth and offers it to Indra in order to be cured. Indra makes love to her, which she first resists and then consents to. She then asks him to cure her and to restore fertility to her father and to his fields. This hymn, along with that of the female *ṛṣi* Ghoṣā, are thus

---

[9] Stephanie Jamison (1992:170) and Hanns-Peter Schmidt (1987:16) have both remarked upon the relevant compound, *pati-dviṣaḥ*, and conclusively resolved the ambiguity as to whether it should be interpreted as 'husband-hating' or 'hated by her husband'. The alternative *pâti-dviṣṭā-* would normally have been used by the poet if he had meant 'hated by her husband', with little metrical change in the verse. The fact that the poet did not choose this expression seems to indicate that he meant 'husband-hating'.

quite specific illustrations of the ways in which fertility and female *ṛṣi*s are linked in Vedic ideology.[10]

Other hymns are even more explicitly sexual in nature and yet, at the same time, seem to be linked with the very public progress of the sacrifice. The hymn to Vṛṣākapi is one such hymn, which has been called by many one of the strangest hymns in the *Ṛgveda*. It involves a dialogue between Indra and Indrāṇī, Indra's wife, and Vṛṣākapi, the monkey, and the monkey's wife. While the details of the hymn would be too much a digression here, suffice it to say that various possible sexual liaisons are alluded to, such as those between the monkey Vṛṣākapi and Indra's wife, and various sexual powers are extolled, such as that of Indra and Vṛṣākapi. Yet in addition, there is a great deal of sacrificial imagery: in the course of the hymn, offerings of *soma* and other mixtures are frequently mentioned.

I mention all of these hymns here not only for background, but also for a theoretical reason: their dialogical natures underscore the recent move in feminist theory to concentrate on the social construction, and not the given nature, of gender roles within culture. Ideas about gender are enacted, or practised, as well as portrayed, and they thus have an ongoing, mutually dependent relationship with the large ideologies that they represent. We might productively view gender as constituting social relations which are practised as well as learned – models for as well as models of, to revitalize an old Geertzian framework. As Jane Flax also remarks in this regard: 'Both men's and women's understanding of anatomy, biology, embodiedness, sexuality is partially rooted in, reflects and must justify pre-existing gender relations. In turn, the existence of gender relations helps us to order and understand the facts of human existing' (1987:637).

With this view in mind, then, one can argue that these dialogical hymns lend themselves particularly easily to this view of gender. They are literally constructing ideologies about gender; all of them involve some kind of negotiation about male and female roles, and those roles' relationship to sexuality, fertility, and the sacrifice. What is more, all of them possess some kind of resolution in which gender relations are finally fixed and 'given', to use Hayden White's term, in a particular way, despite their radical instability in the progress of the *saṃvāda* hymn. And that resolution is literally constructed, negotiated, through dialogue.

---

[10] Ghoṣā is a similar female *ṛṣi*, author of another hymn (RV 10.40) in which she asks the Aśvins to cure her of a skin disease. She is described in the hymn as a widow, and in Vedic usage this often means the wife of an impotent husband. Ghoṣā reminds the Aśvins of how many people they have helped in the past, particularly to regain their virility. The hymn invokes images of a happy marriage, at which the bride's parents weep and reminisce, and the people wear wedding clothes rather than funeral clothes (v. 9-10). Ghoṣā also asks them to bless her future husband (v.11-13).

Lopāmudrā and Agastya

Ṛgveda 1.179[11] follows quite easily along such constructed lines. The hymn opens within the context of asceticism (the fourteenth-century commentator Sāyaṇa implies that *both* Lopāmudrā and her husband are engaging in ascetic practice). Lopāmudrā says to her husband in verse 1: 'For many autumns [and for] age-producing dawns I have worked – day and night. Age distorts the glory of bodies; [thus] virile men should go to their wives.'[12] Lopāmudrā is claiming an ideology that is quite clear; she describes herself as *śaśramāṇā,* 'toiling' – a word which could mean either her own work of asceticism, or her common labour. In either case, such work delays the basic fulfilment of their gender roles; Agastya is *vṛṣṇa,* or fertile, bursting with seed, and should go to his wife.

In verse 2, Lopāmudrā goes on to say: 'Even those men of the past, who acted according to the sacred order, and discussed the sacred order with the gods, stopped [their asceticism] when they did not find the end. Wives should unite with virile men.'[13] Lopāmudrā wishes to persuade her husband out of his asceticism, since even the archetypal men, the *ṛṣi*s of old, stopped when they failed to become successful in their practices.

Agastya then replies in verse three: 'Not in vain is all of this work (*śrāntáṃ*) of asceticism, which the gods themselves encourage. Let us two take on all enemies; and through this we will win the contest of a hundred ways when we two, as a united pair, drive against (the enemies).'[14] Agastya thus argues with her that there is more than one way to achieve happiness, and implies that their union will be that much happier if they remain in their separate, ascetic state now. Notice here that Agastya accepts her understanding of the respective duties of their gender. Ironically to twentieth-century ears, however, it is the virile but celibate male who, using the imagery of war, suggests that one must combat the temptation to sex in as many ways as possible.

---

[11] My translation of the hymn is in part inspired by Wendy Doniger O'Flaherty's (1981). However, it departs from hers in several respects.

[12] *pūrvī́r ahámṃ śarádaḥ śaśṛamāṇā́ doṣā́ vástor uṣáso jaráyantīḥ/minā́ti śriyaṃ jarimā́ tanū́nām ápy ū nú pátnīr vṛ́ṣaṇo jagamyuḥ//*

[13] *yé cid dhī́ pū́rva ṛtasā́pa ā́sant sākáṃ devébhir ávadann ṛtā́ni/ té cid ávāsur nahy ántam āpúḥ sám ū nú pátnīr vṛṣabhir jagamyuḥ//*

[14] *ná mṛ́ṣā śrāntáṃ yád ávanti devā́ḥ visvā́ ít spṛ́dho abhy àśnavāva/ jáyāvéd átra śatánīthaṃ ājíṃ yát saṃyáñcā mithunā́v abhy ájāva//* The verse implies that the contest could require one hundred strategems of the contestants, or possess one hundred strategems of its own. The translation, 'contest of a hundred ways', attempts to leave this ambiguity in. Certainly, if, as Thieme argues, the hymn is about the temptations of sex, and a portrayal of combatting the temptations of sex, then the battle would have one hundred strategems of its own to overwhelm the hapless ascetics. I part from him in his taking *saṃyañcā mithunau* as the object, however, since, as Stephanie Jamison has argued (correspondence, April 1994), the three dual verbs in *pāda*s bcd suggest that she is his partner, and their joint endeavour should be directed to fighting external battles.

It is important to note here that it is ambiguous whether the contest requires one hundred strategems by the people who are contesting, or whether the contest has one hundred strategems of its own. Paul Thieme, in a persuasive interpretation of the hymn, chooses the latter reading. In a psychologically realistic portrayal of the struggle of the pair, he has suggested that the hymn compares the battle against temptation that celibacy involves to a chess game (or even a real battle) with changing situations, surprise attacks and defences.[15]

The next verse has been attributed to Lopāmudrā, to Agastya, and to the poet: 'Desire of my swelling reed has overwhelmed me – desire from this side, that side, all sides; Lopāmudrā makes the virile one flow; the unwise woman sucks the panting, wise man.'[16] Interpretations of this physically graphic verse, like those of the previous verse, vary. Several Indian commentaries, one of which I shall discuss below, suggest that Agastya is the speaker.[17] Thus one should read *nadásya mā rudhatáḥ* as '[desire] of my swelling reed'. The verse would then be Agastya's acquiescence to his wife's voraciousness. However, other interpreters[18] believe that Lopāmudrā speaks the verse. In the mouth of Lopāmudrā, this verse would read, 'Desire has overwhelmed me for the bull who roars', with a pun on the phrase, *nadásya rudhatáḥ*. Translated in this way, the phrase would show Lopāmudrā's ultimate triumph over Agastya's will.

Siding with the Indian tradition, Paul Thieme (1971:209) again provides several persuasive arguments that the verse is Agastya's. First, if this verse is given to Agastya, the hymn is a more symmetrical dialogue where each speaker utters two verses. Second, it would be unlikely that Agastya would end with verse 3, an explicit rejection of Lopāmudrā's advances, when it is clear from the rest of the hymn that he gives in to her advances. More important, since Lopāmudrā has already articulated her desire in verses 1 and 2, it makes no

---

[15] '*Man könnte geradezu auf den Gedanken kommen, daß der Dichter bei seinem Bild vom, "Streit der hundert Strategeme" an ein Brettspiel wie das Schach denkt, bei dem es sich um ein lang ausgedehntes Ringen mit wechselnden Situationen, mit überraschenden Angriffen und Verteidigungen handelt* (1971:208).

[16] *nadásya mā rudhatáḥ kā́ma ā́gann itá ā́jāto amútaḥ kútaś cit/ lópāmudrā vṛ́ṣaṇam ní riṇāti dhī́rám ádhīrā dhayati śvasántam//* *Rudhatāḥ* can also mean 'growing, rising', and refers to the growing or rising of the reed, or penis. As Jamison (correspondence 1994) also points out, *ni riṇāti* has the connotation of 'sucking', usually in the form of breast-feeding. It may well refer to the physical movements of Lopāmudrā in sexual intercourse. Semen is frequently seen as the 'milk' that the wife milks out, such as RV 1.105.2: *tuñjā́te vṛ́ṣnyaṃ páyaḥ, parìdā́ya rásaṃ duhe* ('The two express the bullish milk; having yielded, she milks the sap.'). Jamison further conjectures that the words *dhīra* and *adhīra* may also be a low-level pun on *dhayati*, 'suck' with its attendant connotations of sucking in the context of breast-feeding.

[19] See *Sarvānukramaṇī* and *Sāyaṇa* on RV. 1.179; also *Bṛhaddevatā* 4.57-60, discussed below.

[18] See *Nirukta* 5.2; Sieg 1902:120 ff.; Geldner 1923: 232; Hillebrandt 1913:136 ff.; and Oldenberg 1885:65 ff.

sense for her to claim that desire has suddenly overtaken her, from an indeterminate place. It is only Agastya who struggles against desire, and who would thus be overtaken so suddenly by it – victim of a 'sudden attack' in the contest of a hundred ways.

Read in this way, the gender implications of the hymn are quite clear. After his initial protests in verse 3, Agastya remains the valiant, heroic struggler who is abandoned by his partner to the call of desire. Instead of initiating sex, he first rejects, then submits to the will of Lopāmudrā. Lopāmudrā acts as the less valiant warrior, the persuasive agent of desire who, in keeping with her character, feels herself ageing and questions the value of celibacy.

A similar interpretative dilemma faces the reader of the fifth verse, which reads as follows: 'By this *soma* which I have drunk in my innermost heart I say, "Let him forgive whatever wrong we have committed, for a mortal is full of many desires." '[19] Some interpreters have proposed that Agastya speaks this verse, and others, to be discussed at greater length below,[20] have argued that a *brahmacārin* (celibate) student of Agastya is the speaker. If the verse is Agastya's, it is a kind of acquiescence to the husbandly role that he should play – a role that is in direct conflict with his asceticism. In this context, he must drink *soma* in order to replace the semen that he has lost. In contrast, as we shall see below, the celibate student is presented by many commentators as the embarrassed eavesdropper on the conversation between Agastya and Lopāmudrā.

However, Thieme (1971:210-11) again proposes the most reasonable solution to the problem. The last two verses are thus spoken as a kind of response to the *mise-en-scène* that has been created in the first four verses. They are verses of atonement which are spoken by the *brahmacārin* poet. Building on the wording of one commentary,[21] Thieme argues that the *brahmacārin* does not need to be the student of Agastya living in the same house as his teacher, but simply a *brahmacārin* who, after learning the first four verses, saw the last two as a kind of revelatory incantation which would counteract the breaking of celibate vows.

This view is supported by the fact that the consumption of *soma* accompanied by a *sāman*, or chant, is used elsewhere in the *Ṛgveda* as a method of atonement, as *Sāmavidhānabrāhmaṇa* 1.7.9. suggests. Moreover, there is further evidence for the introduction of a new speaker in the fact that the metre changes from *triṣṭubh* in verses 1 to 4, to *bṛhatī* in verse 5. As Thieme also notes of RV 3.33.13 and 10.108.11, the change of metre implies that a new speaker has entered the scene. Thus the first four verses act as an artistic portrait of a kind of human truth: celibate people break their vows, and must

---

[19] *imám nú sómaṃ ántito hṛtsú pītám úpa bruve| yát sīm ā́gaś cakṛmā́ tát sú mṛḷatu pulukā́mo hí mártyaḥ||*

[20] Sāyaṇa on RV 1.179.5; *Sarvānukramaṇī* 1.12; *Bṛhaddevatā* 4.58-60.

[21] *Sarvānukramaṇī* 1.12.

atone for the rupture. The fifth verse acts as an incantation that counteracts the effects of such a wrong, and could be used by later *brahmacārins* as a kind of ritual of self-absolution after a sexual transgression.[22]

Finally, it is agreed by all that in the sixth verse the poet ends the narration: 'Agastya, digging with spades, wishing for children, progeny, and strength, was nourished both ways, for he was a powerful sage. He found fulfilment of his real hopes among the gods.'[23] Thus Agastya has achieved immortality through children and through asceticism.

Despite the flexibility shown by Agastya in verse 4, remarked upon above, an ideology of gender is explicitly constructed in this hymn. Lopāmudrā's is the desire which must be resisted and which ultimately overwhelms; she has a unidimensional role as the voracious one. Agastya, on the other hand, plays the role of the male who, although giving in to temptation, nonetheless achieves a kind of holistic unity involving both *tapas* and offspring, spirit and body. In line with what Kristeva (1981), Flax (1987), and many other gender theorists have remarked, in this hymn gender roles are negotiated so that the female stands for the partial (the *adhirā*, or unwise desire) and the male stands for the whole (the *dhira*, or wise, unity which enacts and encompasses opposites). Certainly, we can see foreshadowings of the Purāṇic myths of Śiva and Pārvatī, where Pārvatī, despite her demonstrated skill at asceticism, is portrayed as the soul of desire, longing, and household life. Śiva, on the other hand, moves between his ascetic mountain-top and his desire-filled household with the greatest of ease.

The Representation of Gender in Later Commentary

While *Ṛgveda* 1.179 may well have been biased towards the *brahmacārin* from the very beginning, one can also see a progression from negotiated gender identity to regulated gender identity in the treatment of the hymn by later commentators. Through a deft use of exegetical techniques, the later Vedic scholars, writing at a time when the maintenance of brahminical norms was paramount, 'clean up' the offensively free sexual dialogues in an effort to make them acceptable. These techniques are demonstrated in a text called the *Bṛhaddevatā*, a fourth-century BCE commentary on the *Ṛgveda* which contains a series of stories about how the *Ṛgvedic* hymns were composed. In other words, the *Bṛhaddevatā* gives a fourth-

[22] As Jamison (correspondence, 1994) suggests, this ritual use formulated by Thieme is also supported by the fact that verse 5 begins with a strong deictic *imám*. Such a linguistic construction suggests a 'here-and-now' kind of situation which would be used in ritual performance.

[23] *agastyaḥ khánamānaḥ khanítraiḥ prajā́m ápatyaṃ bálam icchámānaḥ| ubháu várṇāv ṛ́ṣir ugráḥ pupoṣa satyā́ devéṣv āśiṣo jagāma||*

century BCE brahmin's version of what the female *ṛṣi*s in the *Ṛgveda* are supposed to say, in addition to what the *Ṛgveda* actually says. Moreover, the manipulation of the character of the *brahmacārin*, discussed above, is evident. As can be seen from *Ṛgveda* 1.179, there is nothing in any of the verses about a student, or about a conversation being overheard.

The hymn is interpreted as follows:

> The *ṛṣi*, through desire for a secret intercourse, began to chat up (*upa jalp*) [his] wife, the illustrious Lopāmudrā, when she had bathed after menstruation. With two verses – **'For many autumns [and for] age-producing dawns I have worked; day and night. Age distorts the glory of bodies; [thus] virile men should go to their wives. Even those men of the past, who acted acted according to the sacred order, and discussed the sacred order with the gods, stopped [their asceticism] when they did not find the end. Wives should unite with virile men.'** (RV 1.179, 1-2) – she declared her intention. Then Agastya, lusting, pleased her with the two following verses: **'Not in vain is all of this work (*śrāntaṃ*) of asceticism, which the gods themselves encourage. Let us two take on all battles; and through this we will win the contest of a hundred ways when we two, as a pair, drive against [the enemies]. Desire of my swelling reed overwhelms me, desire engulfing me from this side, that side, all sides.'** (3-4) The student, having known by *tapas* of the existence of the two lusting [after each other], [thinking] 'I have committed a sin [by] having listened' sang the last two verses: **'By this *soma* which I have drunk in my innermost heart I say, "Let him forgive whatever wrong we have committed, for a mortal is full of many desires. Agastya, digging with spades, wishing for children, progeny, and strength, nourished both ways, for he was a powerful sage. He found fulfilment of his real hopes among the gods."'** (5-6). The teacher and his wife praising and embracing him, kissed him on the head; smiling they both said to him, 'You are without fault, son.' (BD 4.57-60).[24]

A close reading of this passage reveals the addition of distinct elements, such as the embarrassed *brahmacārin* to be discussed below. Notice too that neither

---

[24] *ṛtau snātām ṛṣir bhāryāṃ lopāmudrām yaśasvinīm/ upajalpitum ārebhe rahaḥsaṃyogakāmyayā//* (4.57) *dvābhyāṃ sā tv abravīd ṛgbhyāṃ pūrvīr iti cikīrṣitam/ riraṃsus tām athāgastya uttarābhyām atoṣayat//* (58) *viditvā tapasā sarvaṃ tayor bhāvaṃ riraṃsatoḥ/ śrutvainaḥ kṛtavān asmi brahmacāry uttame jagau//*(59) *praśasya taṃ pariṣvajya gurū mūrdhny avajaghratuḥ/ smitvainam āhatuś cobhāv anāgā asi putraka//*(60)

the element of the couples' embrace of the embarrassed *brahmacārin* nor the words of 'forgiveness' from the two love-makers ('You are without fault, son') are derived from the *Ṛgvedic* hymn at all; both are supplied by the *Bṛhaddevatā*.

Yet if we are to avoid the 'dumb scribe' theory and assume, as Hayden White does, that all narratives have a purpose, there is a reason for this change other than stupidity. In the original Ṛgvedic hymn, as Thieme has suggested, the *mantras* restore a balance from sexual excess. They take away the effect of the efficacious and lustful words in the previous lines, and may possibly have had ritual efficacy for those who broke the rules of celibacy. The potential ritual use of the hymn is underscored by the fact that one other Vedic text comments that the main deity of the hymn is Rati, or Desire, as does the later commentator Sāyaṇa. In contrast, in the *Bṛhaddevatā* the imbalance is not a result of the desire, or excess, or the *ṛṣi* himself – but of that of his student. The *mantra* takes away the 'wrong' caused by the outside character of the *brahmacārin*.

To be even more specific here, by telling the story the way it does, the text omits several possibilities. Let us take the first possible option. If the hymn is taken as a dialogue, then verse 5, which the *Bṛhaddevatā* argues is uttered by the *brahmacārin*, could in fact also be uttered by Agastya, as Geldner suggests. Yet if that were the case, then Agastya would be explictly asking for pardon in this verse. Because the *ṛṣi* has committed the sin of excess of lust in the hymn, he would then be asking pardon or, to be more accurate, would be replenishing his own virility via *soma*.

This is not, however, the appropriate conduct for a *ṛṣi* according to first-century BCE brahminical norms. The *Bṛhaddevatā*, being a product of these norms, thus does not entertain the possibility of Agastya's apology. If one were to consider the idea that the *ṛṣi* was apologizing or, as the Sanskrit says, that he is *anaga*, 'needing to be forgiven', then the *ṛṣi* would be less perfect; he would have a fault. One effect of the *Bṛhaddevatā* story, then, is to augment the power of the *ṛṣi* and the gods, at the expense of the woman. To put the verses of apology in the mouth of a *brahmacārin* is an ingenious way of allowing the *ṛṣi* to remain virile, as *ṛṣi*s should be, as well as without fault.

Moving to the second option, the *Bṛhaddevatā* could be simply following Indian tradition in claiming that the verse was uttered by the *brahmacārin*. As mentioned above, the commentary of the *Sarvānukramaṇī*, a text probably earlier than the *Bṛhaddevatā*, introduces a *brahmacārin* as the author of verse 5 of the hymn. However, as Thieme argues, the earlier text does not necessarily imply that the *brahmacārin* was Agastya's student, nor that he was living in the house with the couple at the time of the lustful conversation.

The *Bṛhaddevatā* constructs this story to good effect, however. By placing the *brahmacārin* in the house with Agastya, he sets up an explicit hierarchical contrast between the senior *ṛṣi* and the junior one, again augmenting the power of Agastya. The first four verses of the hymn cease to be even an illustration, or portrayal, of a 'human truth' where people break their vows of celibacy, as

Thieme suggests in his interpretation. The 'wrong' is entirely different from that: it is the wrong of intrusion upon the private life of a powerful *ṛṣi*, not the wrong that the *ṛṣi* and his wife themselves committed.

In the story of the *Bṛhaddevatā*, then, gender roles become even more circumscribed. By placing the verse of atonement in the mouth of the *brahmacārin*, the scribe achieves a certain effect: he keeps Agastya's reputation intact, and thus he implicitly maintains Agastya's hierarchical relationship with Lopāmudrā and the student. Lopāmudrā is caught in the middle, however. She is the lustful woman in contrast with Agastya, who attempts to resist her; she is also contrasted with the Agastya-to-be, the *brahmacārin*, for whom her sheer presence is forbidden, let alone her sexually explicit words. Lopāmudrā is no longer simply the negotiator of sex and gender roles, but is surrounded by males for whom she is taboo.

It is worth adding a footnote here that the embarrassment at the couple's love-making is not only that of the *Bṛhaddevatā*'s *brahmacārin*. One nineteenth-century French Indologist, Abel Bergaigne, (1878-83:2.394) give the hymn a 'mystical interpretation', similar to that given by Biblical exegetes to the Song of Solomon. For Bergiane, Agastya is the god Soma, and Lopāmudrā, in a 'prayer' draws him down from his dwelling place! His approach is perhaps a subtle reminder that modern as well as ancient interpretations of uncomfortable material can be just as manipulative, if not more so, than Indian ones.

Fashioning the Female: The *Mahābhārata*

In the *Mahābhārata* 3(33)94-97, the tale of Agastya and Lopāmudrā is significantly more elaborate. While I do not have space here to narrate the entire tale, which covers several pages of the *Āraṇyakaparvan*, I will summarize the important elements here. Agastya discovers a number of his ancestors hanging upside down in a cave; when he askes them why they have been given this fate instead of progressing to heaven, the ancestors say that they are waiting for future progeny to be born to perform the appropriate rites to release them from a curse. It is thus the sage Agastya's responsibility to produce the appropriate progeny in order to overcome the plight of his ancestors (3.94.11-15).

He fashions for himself a woman whose limbs are matchless, and gives her to the king of Vidarbha in order to keep her safe for himself (3.94.16-28). After Lopāmudrā has grown up as a princess, King Vidarbha gives the full-grown Lopāmudrā to Agastya for fear of his terrible ascetic's curse. Lopāmudrā marries Agastya only to be ordered to throw away her finery and retire with him to the forest to practise austerities. Once she has proved, in a fashion similar to Pārvatī, that she is his equal in her powers of asceticism, or *tapas*, Agastya approaches her for intercourse (3.95.1-14).

Instead of giving in to his demands, Lopāmudrā manipulates Agastya into giving her a significant amount of wealth. Just as he is about to approach her, she demands that before they make love she must be given all the wealth that she has been accustomed to as a princess. In the stereotype of the manipulative wife, she demands such things as a bed like the one she was accustomed to in her father's house, and jewels to her taste. Agastya must go and find these before she will give in to him (3.95.15-25).

Agastya searches the realms of Kings Śrutārvan, Vadhryaśva, and Trasadasyu, and judges that the taking of income from these realms would mean hardship for the subjects (3.96.1-20). After searching in these three kingdoms, Agastya goes to the kingdom of the Asura Ilvala and, as a test, is presented with the brother of Ilvala, Vātāpi, cooked on a plate. The great sage Agastya eats him, digests him successfully, and is given the wealth he needs. As a result of this demonstration of his power in both the secular and the sacred realms, Agastya is allowed into Lopāmudrā's bedroom and, as a result of their union, Dṛḍhasyu is born – a seer of tremendous power, who has learned the Vedas in the womb and comes into the world reciting them (3.97.1-25).

In terms of the construction of gender, the role of Lopāmudrā takes on several new aspects in this version of the myth. First, she is entirely derivative of her male *ṛṣi*'s counterpart: she is his creation, made for the service of freeing his ancestors because of their lack of progeny. Moreover, the couple's lustful love-making is not presented on its own, but instead becomes the occasion for Lopāmudrā to demand of Agastya that he provide for her as she was provided for in her father's house. Thus, although Lopāmudrā acts as a negotiator here, this is not an expression of her own sexual desire. In her demands, she sets up the contrast not between *ṛṣi* and *brahmacārin*, as the *Bṛhaddevatā* does, but between king and sage, testing Agastya to see if he can match the wealth of a *kṣatriya.*

Thus, through this 'cardboard cut-out' Lopāmudrā, a third element is added to Agastya's personality: he not only creates progeny and is a truly powerful ascetic, but he can also garner wealth like the best of kings. He does this not through the polluted processes that kings use, but through his vision and guile, as a brahmin would. The desire for progeny is also no longer Lopāmudrā's, but Agastya's – no longer an expression of Lopāmudrā's version of gender ideology but Agastya's altruistic, salvific act for his ancestors. Gender roles have thus been quite differently configured; Lopāmudrā has no desires save that of being pampered in the manner to which she has been accustomed, and Agastya's fame is augmented in a material as well as a spiritual way. Needless to say, gender roles have become subordinate to the idea of *dharma* – Agastya in saving his ancestors and Lopāmudrā is dutifully following her husband to the forest, and giving birth to a powerful son and sage.

Conclusions

From this study of Lopāmudrā we can make an argument that gender roles were explicitly constructed through dialogical hymns, most of which were connected, either implicitly or explictly, to the public, fertility-oriented sexuality of the sacrifice. While Lopāmudrā's role within the *śrauta* tradition remains obscure, she probably does play a role as a figure in the ritual of absolution that Thieme has argued constitutes the background of RV 1.179. Moreover, she is openly participatory in sexual negotiation, and holder of a sexual power which infused much of the ritual rules of the sacrifice itself.[26]

Once such sacrificial concerns changed, so too gender roles and attendant attitudes toward sexuality changed. First, as the little red-faced *brahmacārin* of the *Bṛhaddevatā* indicates, the hierarchy of man over woman is more rigidly presented, with woman remaining as the advocate of sexuality, standing between two generations of men for whom sex is taboo. Finally, in the *Mahābhārata*, sexuality becomes the means of fulfilling rights and obligations of the dharmically oriented brahmin, such as the honour of the ancestors. The woman ceases to become the negotiator of *rati*, or desire, but simply the means by which the ancestors are freed. Even her role as an implicit advocate for progeny is taken away from her in the epic.[27]

These changing roles of Lopāmudrā raise important questions about the representation of gender in Vedic times. Although many have remarked upon the more 'participatory' role of women in the Vedic period, their assumption remains that participation *per se* is an intrinsic good. Yet, if one asks, 'participation in service of whose goals, in the construction of what kind of gender roles?', the answer is not always positive. In the case of Lopāmudrā, both the retention of seed in asceticism and the making of progeny are goals of the *ṛṣi* Agastya, and, in all three versions of her story, Lopāmudrā acts in service of these goals. Moreover, as her tale is retold, she is portrayed more and more derivatively, almost anaemically, as she helps her husband/creator to promote the abstract ideal of *dharma*. Thus, despite Lopāmudrā's strength of voice, her myths remain arguments for specific ideologies of gender, and her participation is proscribed in intriguing ways from the very beginning.

---

[26] See Stephanie Jamison's forthcoming book, *Sacrificed Wife/Sacrificer's Wife*, for a detailed study of the role of women within the *śrauta* tradition.

[27] There is an oral version of the tale, mentioned to me by Vasudha Narayanan of the University of Florida, which does not circumscribe Lopāmudrā's character so stringently. In this version, similar to that in the *Mahābhārata*, Lopāmudrā is all the time aware of her husband's need for progeny, and of the intentions and machinations of the demon king Ilvala, and so forth. She is thus able to manipulate events so that her husband will be victorious.

References

Sanskrit Sources

Bṛhaddevatā. Ed., tr., A.A. Macdonell. 2 vols. Harvard Oriental Series. Cambridge: Harvard University Press, 1904.

— : *Or an Index to the Gods of the Rig Veda by Śaunaka, to which have been added Ārṣānukramaṇī Chandonukramaṇī and Anuvākānukramaṇī* in the form of Appendices. Bibliotheca Indica Sanskrit Series 722, 760, 794, and 819 (new series). Calcutta: Baptist Mission Press, 1893.

The Mahābhārata. Critical edition (19 vols.) by V.S. Sukthankar *et al.* Pune: Bhandarkar Oriental Research Institute, 1933-60.

—. 3 vols. Ed., tr., J.A.B. Van Buitenen. Chicago: University of Chicago Press, 1973-8.

Nirukta. The Nighantu and the Nirukta, The Oldest Indian Treatise on Etymology, Philology, and Semantics, Critically Edited From Original Manuscripts and Translated by Lakshman Sarup. London/New York: Oxford University Press, 1920-7.

—. *Indices and Appendices to the Nirukta with an Introduction*. Lahore: University of the Panjab, 1929.

—. *Yāska's Nirukta with Durga's Commentary*. 2 vols. Ed. H.M. Bhadkamkar. Bombay Sanskrit and Prakrit Series 73 and 85. Bombay: Government Central Press, 1918.

Ṛg Veda Saṃhitā, together with the Commentary of Sāyaṇa Āchārya. 4 vols. Ed. F. Max Müller. Varanasi: Chowkhamba Sanskrit Series, 1966.

Secondary Sources

Bayly, C.A. 1998. 'Rallying Around the Subaltern.' *Journal of Peasant Studies* 16.1:110-20.

Bhattacharji, Sukumari. 1994. *Women and Society in Ancient India*. Calcutta: Basumati Corporation Limited.

Bergaigne, Abel. 1878-83. *La Religion Védique*. 3 vols. Paris: F. Vieweg.

Chatterjee, Partha. 1989. 'Colonialism, Nationalism and Colonized Women: The Contest in India.' *American Ethnologist* 16.4:634-60.

Flax, Jane. 1987. 'Postmodernism and Gender Relations in Feminist Theory.' *Signs* 12/4:621-43.

Fryckenberg, Robert. 1991. 'The Emergence of Modern "Hinduism" as a Concept and as an Institution: A Reappraisal with Special Reference to South India.' See Sontheimer and Kulke 1991:29-50.

Geldner, Karl F. *Der Rigveda*. Göttingen: Vandenhoeck and Ruprecht.

Guha, Ranajit and Spivak, Gayatri. 1988. *Selected Subaltern Studies*. New

York: Oxford University Press.
Haddad, Yvonne Yazbeck, and Findly, Ellison Banks, eds. 1985. *Women, Religion, and Social Change.* Albany: State University of New York Press.
Hillebrandt, Alfred. 1913. *Lieder Des Rgveda.* Göttingen: Vandenhoeck and Ruprecht; Leipzig: J.C. Hinrichs.
Jamison, Stephanie. 1992. *Ravenous Hyenas and the Wounded Sun.* Ithaca: Cornell University Press.
—. Forthcoming. *Sacrificed Wife/Sacrificer's Wife.*
Kristeva, Julia. 1981. 'Women's Time.' Reprinted in *The Feminist Reader: Essays in Gender and the Politics of Literary Criticism*, ed. Catherine Belsey and Jane Moore. New York: Blackwell, 1989.
Lal, Shyam Kishore. 1980. *Female Divinities in Hindu Mythology and Ritual.* Pune: University of Pune.
Leslie, Julia, ed. 1991. *Roles and Rituals for Hindu Women.* Rutherford: Fairleigh Dickinson University Press.
Menski, Werner. 1991. 'Marital Expectations as Dramatized in Hindu Marriage Rituals.' See Leslie 1991:47–67.
Mohanty, Chandra. 1984. 'Under Western Eyes: Feminist Scholarship and Colonial Discourses.' *Boundary 2*: XII/3, XIII/1.
O'Flaherty, Wendy Doniger. 1980. *Women, Androgynes, and Other Mythical Beasts.* Chicago: University of Chicago Press.
—. tr. 1981. *The Rig Veda.* Harmondsworth: Penguin Books.
Oldenberg, Hermann. 1883. 'Das altindische *Ākhyāna, mit besonderer Rücksicht auf das Suparṇākhyāna.' Zeitschrift der Deutschen Morgenländischen Gesellschaft* 37:54-86.
—. 1885. *Ākhyāna-Hymnen im Rigveda.' Zeitschrift der Morgenländischen Gesellschaft* 39:52-83.
—. 1916 (second edn.). *The Religion of the Veda.* Tr. Shridhar B. Shrotri. Delhi: Motilal Banarsidass, 1988.
Patton, Laurie L. 1993. 'Beyond the Myths of Origin: Narrative Philosophizing in Vedic Commentary.' In *Myths and Fictions: Their Place in Philosophy and Religion*, ed. S. Biderman and B. Scharfstein, 225-54. Leiden: E. J. Brill.
—. Forthcoming. *Myth as Argument: The Bṛhaddevatā as Canonical Commentary.* In the Religionsgeschichtliche Versuche und Vorarbeiten Series, ed. Lawrence Sullivan, Fritz Graf, and Hans. G. Kippenberg. Berlin: DeGruyter/Mouton.
Prakash, Gyan. 1992. 'Can the "Subaltern" Ride? A Reply to O'Hanlon and Washbrook.' *Comparative Studies in Society and History* 34.1:168-84.
Schmidt, Hanns-Peter. 1987. *Some Women's Rites and Rights in the Veda.* Pune: Bhandarkar Oriental Research Institute.
Sharma, Arvind, ed. 1987. *Women in World Religions.* Albany: State University of New York Press.
Sieg, Emil. 1902. *Die Sagenstoffe des Ṛg Veda und die indische Itihāsa-tradition.*

Stuttgart: W. Kohlhammer.

Smith, Frederick M. 1991. 'Indra's Curse, Varuṇa's Noose, and the Suppression of the Woman in the Vedic *Śrauta* Ritual.' See Leslie 1991:17-45.

Sontheimer, Günther, and Kulke, Hermann, eds. 1991. *Hinduism Reconsidered.* New Delhi: Manohar.

Thieme, Paul. 1971. 'Agastya und Lopāmudrā.' In *Kleine Schriften*, 1. Wiesbaden: Franz Steinder Verlag GMBH.

Upadhyaya, Bhagwat Saran. 1974. *Women in Ṛg Veda.* (Foreword by S. Radhakrishnan.) New Delhi: S. Chand.

White, Hayden. 1987. *The Content of the Form: Narrative Discourse and Historical Representation.* Baltimore: Johns Hopkins.

3

The Ahalyā Story through the Ages

Renate Söhnen-Thieme

Introduction

If Indra is imagined as a 'womanizer' in Indian Literature, one may well ask who were the women who became his prey. An Indian, asked this question, answered without hesitation, 'Oh, so many!' Asked to name some of them, he replied, 'Well, Ahalyā, for instance.' Asked for other names, he was in some difficulty. Evidently there is only this one instance, and it may be worth while looking at it more closely.

About the beginnings of the relationship between Indra and Ahalyā we do not know much. It does not belong to the old stock of Vedic lore, such as the story of Śunaḥśepa (the young brahmin who was sold by his father as a sacrificial animal but was able to release himself from the sacrificial post by 'beholding' Ṛgvedic hymns), or the story of Purūravas and Urvaśī, which is the topic of a particular dialogue hymn in the tenth Maṇḍala of the *Ṛgveda*. The name Ahalyā is not mentioned at all in the *Ṛgveda*; the name Indra of course occurs very frequently, but never in connection with an adultery story.

The First Version: *Rāmāyaṇa* Book 1

The first explicit narrative of Indra and Ahalyā (see Table 2, Column B: 1) is attested comparatively late, in the first book of the *Rāmāyaṇa*, which is generally considered to be a later complement of the *Rāmāyaṇa*, adding the story of the hero's birth and early exploits to the epic. It is in the context of Rāma's journey from Viśvāmitra's hermitage to the court of King Janaka that the Ahalyā story is narrated.

The core of the narrative may be summarized as follows: Indra, the king of the gods, has fallen in love with Ahalyā, the wife of an ascetic brahmin

	A. Allusions				B. Full story: epics	
Text stratum	Brāh-maṇas	Mahā-bhārata	VDhP 1.128	PadmaP 2.57	Rāmāyaṇa 1	Rāmāyaṇa 7
Prehistory: creation of Ahalyā			30		(+)	+
education of Ahalyā						+
marriage with Gautama		5.12.6	31			+
Place					Mithilā-upavana	
Indra in love with Ahalyā	+					
" in the shape of Gautama	(+?)				+	(+SR)[1]
" in his own shape						
Indra's cohabitation with Ahalyā	+	+	+	+	+	+
(a) she takes him for her husband						(+SR)
(b) she recognizes him and...				(agrees?)	agrees	
Indra is caught by Gautama						
" flees in the shape of a cat					+	+
Indra's punishment:						
(a) castration		(+?)	+	+	+	
(b) loss of his rank				(+?)		+
(c) 1000 vulvas					(D1!)[2]	
(d) 'goldbeardedness'		+				
Ahalyā's punishment:						
(a) bodiless					+	
(b) loss of her rank					(D1!)	+
(c) rock, stone				+		
(d) dry river						
Ahalyā defends herself						(+SR)
" tells the truth						
Ahalyās release from the curse:						
(a) by Rāma					+	(+SR)
(b) by the river Gautamī						
Indra obtains: (a) a ram's testicles		(+?)			+	(+NR)[3]
(b) his former rank						+
(c) 1000 eyes		12	28			
by means of...		seeing Tilottamā				Vaiṣṇava sacrifice

1 Southern Recension.
2 One Devanāgari manuscript.
3 Northern Recension.

Table 2: The narrative elements of the Ahalyā story.

C. Full story: Purāṇas					D. Classical Skt. poetry	
BrahmaP ch.87	BrahmavaivartaP 4.47	4.61	PadmaP ASS 5.51 (=1.54)	SkandaP 5.3.136	Raghuvaṃśa 11.33-4	KSS 17.137-48
+			+			
+			+			
+			+			
bank of the Godāvarī	Puṣkara Svarṇadī	Mandākinī	Puṣkara	bank of the Narmadā		
+	+	(2nd time)	+	+	+	
		(1st time)				+
+	+	+	+	+	+	+
+		(2nd time)	+		(+?)	
		refuses		(agrees?)		agrees
+	+	+	+			
biḍāla			*mārjāra*			*mārjāra*
			+			
			+			
+	+	+	+	+		+
			nirdehā			
	+	+	*asthimayā*	+	+	
+			(*śuṣkā?*)			
+		+	+			
						'maj-jāra'
	+	+	+	+	+	+
+						
			+			
+	+	+	+	(+?)		
			+	+		+
river Gautamī	worship of Sūrya		praise of Devī	intervention of the gods		Tilottamā

named Gautama. In order to seduce her, Indra takes on the shape of her husband. When caught in the act, he is cursed by the ascetic to lose his testicles (and thereby, naturally, his male powers), a punishment which no doubt reflects an archaic sense of justice and is actually prescribed in the *Āpastambadharmasūtra*:

> If sexual intercourse is performed, cutting off the penis and testicles.[1]

An ascetic brahmin will not execute the castration directly, with his own hands; a word of his, which is imbued with ascetic power, suffices to effect the punishment.

The beginning of this narrative looks quite similar to a well-known story found in Greek mythology: that of Alkmene and Amphitryon (the first explicit narrative is also attested rather late). In this myth, the great Zeus sees no other way of making love to Alkmene, the faithful wife of King Amphitryon, than by appearing in the shape of her husband. Zeus achieves his goal: Alkmene does not become aware of the deceit until the false Amphitryon is confronted with the real one.

So far the two stories seem to be fairly similar; the second part of the stories, however, shows characteristic differences which reflect the background of religious development in the two societies. In the Greek version, the main emphasis rests on the result of this divine intermingling with human beings: the birth of the semi-divine hero Hercules; even very early allusions to the story in Hesiod and Homer attest this feature. The betrayed husband turns his wrath against his wife whom he believes to be guilty of adultery, and who can only be cleared of suspicion by either Zeus himself or the blind seer Tiresias. (An early vase painting in the British Museum depicts Alkmene about to be burnt at Amphitryon's command: the pyre is already alight when Zeus complies with Alkmene's prayers and has water poured down in order to extinguish the fire.) The idea that Amphitryon might take revenge on the king of the gods is absolutely out of question.

The betrayed husband in the Indian story reacts quite differently. To him, Indra, the king of the gods, no longer means what he meant to the Indo-Aryans at the time of the composition of the Ṛgvedic hymns. Many centuries of development of religious history lie in between, during which a new world-view evolved, one which might be called 'mechanistic': the once powerful gods no longer have any influence on human affairs, but they are more and more dependent on those human beings who know about the secret correspondences between the world of gods and demons on the one hand, and the world of gods

[1] *saṃnipāte vṛtte śiśnaś chedanaṃ savṛṣaṇasya* (2.10.26.20).

and human beings on the other, about the correspondences of microcosm and macrocosm, and who can put this knowledge into effect when performing the traditional sacrifices: these are the brahmins, who in their own way have become more powerful than even the gods. (This development can only be attested with respect to the educated class of those who composed and transmitted the Sanskrit texts which are our sources; as for the ideas or beliefs of other layers of the population, information can be derived only indirectly, for instance in the older parts of the epics or in the Buddhist *Jātaka* tales.)

It was probably this development of new concepts in the *Brāhmaṇa* texts which made it seem at all possible that a human might curse a god, be he even the highest god of the Ṛgvedic pantheon: Gautama is both a brahmin and an ascetic, who has accumulated immense powers that can be used for putting an effective curse upon whomsoever he chooses. This is quite a common motif in Indian literature: an ascetic, offended by some insignificant slight, invokes a vengeful curse which then becomes the starting-point of dramatic complications (as is the case in Kālidāsa's drama *Śakuntalā*).

Such a curse uttered in rage, however, uses up all the powers accumulated by ascetic practice, and this means that the ascetic has to start afresh, just as he would have to if he had seen a beautiful woman and desired her – another favourite motif in Indian literature (the gods, in order to deprive an ascetic of those powers that seem to be so dangerous for them, send a beautiful *apsaras* who, in most cases, is successful in her task). Passion, be it that of wrath or desire, destroys ascetic powers. Thus, in our story, all the ascetic powers accumulated by Gautama have been exhausted in the curse called down on Indra; indeed Indra can now boast of a deed salutary to the gods and ask a recompense from them; and this is indeed described in our story as it is told in the first book of the *Rāmāyaṇa* (1.47.15-48.10). The gods ask the deceased ancestors to make over to them, on behalf of Indra, the testicles of a ram (*meṣavṛṣaṇau*) offered at an ancestral rite, which in turn explains why henceforward, as the story states, the ancestors are worshipped with an offering of a castrated ram.

There is another feature in our story from the first book of the *Rāmāyaṇa* which reflects a new development in the history of religion. Ahalyā, guilty of adultery, is also cursed by her husband, but with the rider that she will be released by Rāma when he passes this place on his way to King Janaka's court. This element of the narrative is clearly connected with the context in which the story is told: the sage Viśvāmitra had sought Rāma from his father as protection against some *rākṣasas* who were disturbing his sacrifices; he is now guiding Rāma and his brother to Mithilā, where they are to attend King Janaka's sacrifice. On their way, Viśvāmitra, as a true traveller's guide, tells stories about the places they visit and about their former inhabitants. Shortly before they reach Mithilā, they come across the deserted hermitage of the ascetic Gautama. Viśvāmitra tells Rāma about the adultery that was once committed by Indra and Ahalyā and led to them being cursed. In this version of the story, Ahalyā (unlike Alkmene in the Greek myth) has some inkling as to who her lover is, but she agrees to his wish 'out of curiosity for the king of the gods' (*devarājakutūhalāt*). Thus not only Indra but also Ahalyā deserves punishment, and Gautama's curse is that she should abide in the ashes, observe a strict fast, and be invisible to everybody, until Rāma, son of Daśaratha, enters this hermitage; by this she would be purified, and by showing hospitality to Rāma she would be allowed to return to her husband. Viśvāmitra completes his story by reporting how Indra regained his sexual powers by means of a ram's testicles (see above), and then invites Rāma to enter the hermitage. Inside Rāma beholds Ahalyā who is invisible to everyone else but appears to him in her beauty and splendour (although obscured by smoke) 'like some divine illusion fashioned by the creator'; Rāma and Lakṣmaṇa touch her feet, and she offers them hospitality. Thereupon showers of blossoms fall down from heaven, celestial drums are sounded, and gods, *gandharvas* and *apsarases* appear and cry, '*Sādhu, sādhu*!' ('Well done!'), while Gautama accepts Ahalyā again as his wife.

Now these phenomena, which are also known from the Buddha legend, appear only at outstanding events: in the *Rāmāyaṇa* they occur, for example, after Rāma's final victory over Rāvaṇa; in the *Mahābhārata*, frequently in connection with Arjuna and Kṛṣṇa (Arjuna's birth, and his stringing of the bow at Draupadī's *svayaṃvara*; during Kṛṣṇa's diplomatic mission in the fifth book, where he reveals himself as Viṣṇu). In the context of our story, the emphasis appears to be on the beneficial effect of even the young Rāma, which in turn points to the concept of Rāma as an *avatāra* of Viṣṇu, as which Rāma appears in the *Bālakāṇḍa*.

On the other hand, it may seem strange that so much honour should be paid to the rehabilitation of an adulteress. Would it not be more sensible to assume that, as in the Alkmene story, it is rather the rehabilitation of an unjustly suspected person? Why else would Indra take the shape of the husband of the woman to whom he wants to make love? It is unlikely that he hopes to deceive the husband who knows only too well that the other man cannot be he; his disguise can only be meant to deceive the wife, who would not have agreed to make love to anyone but her husband, not even the king of the gods. Narrative logic would suggest that in a – hypothetical – original form of the story, Ahalyā was actually innocent, that is, she believed that it was her husband to whom she yielded.

Further Attestations in the Epics

There are, however, other versions of the story. The *Rāmāyaṇa* itself provides another story about Indra and Ahalyā (see Table 2, column B), in the last book (7.30.15-41), which is presumably even later than the first book, but may of course contain older material. This version agrees with that of book 1 only in the fact that Indra had intercourse with Ahalyā (without specifying in which shape, or whether or not she was willing), and that both were cursed by Gautama. The curses, however, are quite different from the ones discussed above and they are not softened – at least if one follows the Baroda edition and rejects the seven and a half verses transmitted only in the southern recension, in which Ahalyā claims to be innocent and induces Gautama to soften his curse in the same way as in the first book (i.e. that she would be purified by the sight of Rāma and then be accepted again by her husband). Most probably this interpolation is influenced by the version of the first book (although she certainly did not claim to be innocent there); for in the version of the last book, the story centres not on Ahalyā, but on Indra. At the end of a long battle between gods and demons (in this context, the *rākṣasas*), Indra has been taken prisoner by Rāvaṇa's son, Indrajit; after being released from prison, he asks Prajāpati why this shame had come upon him. He is then told (or reminded) how he once violated Ahalyā and was consequently cursed by Gautama to fall into the hands of his enemy. This motif must be seen in connection with the idea that Indra's rank, his rule over the gods, has become unstable, so that neither he nor anyone else who might replace him would be able to enjoy this position for long.

This idea points to the other ancient Indian epic, the *Mahābhārata*, and in particular to a passage in which Indra's transgression with respect to Ahalyā is used as an argument: the Nahuṣa episode (see Table 2, column A: *Mahābhārata*). Being persecuted by Brahminicide personified (because he has killed the brahmin demon Vṛtra), Indra hides in the water. His office, which is thus vacated, is assigned to Nahuṣa, a grandson of Purūravas. In his new high rank, Nahuṣa soon loses all sense of proportion and claims Śacī, Indra's wife, too. Śacī takes refuge with Bṛhaspati, but Nahuṣa sticks to his claim, adducing in his favour the fact that Indra himself was not restrained from having intercourse with Ahalyā:

> Formerly Indra violated Ahalyā, the renowned sage's wife, although her husband was alive; why did you not prevent *him*?[2]

Like the version in *Rāmāyaṇa* book 7, this brief allusion does not state whether Indra appeared in the disguise of the ascetic husband. As for Ahalyā, it seems here that she must have been innocent: this is suggested by the parallel story of Śacī, who refuses to belong to anyone other than Indra, and by the word *dharṣitā* ('violated'), which conveys the idea of a forceful act against the will of

---

[2] *ahalyā dharṣitā pūrvam ṛṣipatnī yaśasvinī jīvato bhartur indreṇa sa vaḥ kiṃ na nivāritaḥ//* *Mahābhārata* 5.12.6.

the person concerned; moreover, the positive epithet *yaśasvinī* ('renowned') would probably not have been applied to an adulteress.

There are two other allusions to the seduction of Ahalyā in the *Mahābhārata* (one in book 12 and one in book 13), which are mainly concerned with Indra's punishment. The latter (13.153.6) states only that Gautama cursed Indra when the god was making love to Ahalyā, but for the sake of *dharma* (*dharmārtham*) did not harm him. The other, more interesting one (12.329.14,1-2; see Table 2, column A: *Mahābhārata*) belongs to a prose passage and presents a list of incidents at which gods and others were disfigured by curses. In this list, the first two examples are as follows:

> Indra obtained from Gautama('s curse) the condition of being gold-bearded, on acount of his violating Ahalyā.
> And on account of Kauśika, Indra lost his testicles and obtained the condition of having a ram's testicles.[3]

These two statements are intrigung since they seem to separate two narrative elements (found also in the version of the first book of the *Rāmāyaṇa*), namely Indra's transgression and his punishment, and to combine them with other quite unexpected elements. Why should 'gold-beardedness' (*hariśmaśrutām*) be deemed a punishment? Why should it be an appropriate punishment for the violation of Ahalyā? And in the second statement, what does the name Kauśika (a family name associated with Viśvāmitra) signify?

The *Subrahmaṇya* Formula and its Explanation in the *Brāhmaṇas*

An answer to at least the last of these questions may be provided by an investigation of the oldest mention of the relationship between Indra and Ahalyā (see Table 2, column A: *Brāhmaṇas*). This is found in the so-called *subrahmaṇya* formula, used at the beginning of the sacrifice to invite the main participants, Indra, the gods, and the brahmins. This formula occurs in much the same form in the *Jaiminīyabrāhmaṇa* (2.79), the *Ṣaḍviṃśabrāhmaṇa* in the *Sāmaveda* tradition (1.1.20-1), the *Śatapathabrāhmaṇa* (3.3.4.18-19), the *Taittirīyāraṇyaka* in the *Yajurveda* tradition (1.12.4), and in two Śrautasūtras (*Lāṭyāyanaśrautasūtra* 1.3.1, *Drāhyāyaṇaśrautasūtra* 1.3.3). It runs as follows:

---

[3] *ahalyādharṣaṇanimittaṃ hi gautamād dhariśmaśrutām indraḥ prāptaḥ/ kauśika-nimittaṃ cendro muṣkaviyogaṃ meṣavṛṣaṇatvam avāpa//*

Come here, O Indra, come here with your golden steeds!
(You who are/took the shape of) Medhātithi's ram,
(You who are/took the shape of) Vṛṣaṇaśva's co-wife;
(You who) as a wild ox leapt down,
O lover of Ahalyā (lit. 'the unploughable one'?);
O Brahmin belonging to the Kuśika family,
(You who are) called (or called yourself) Gautama![4]

The *Brāhmaṇa* sources also provide some explanation, in particular those belonging to the *Sāmaveda* tradition. Interestingly, the latter differ from each other, but the explanations of the *Jaiminīyabrāhmaṇa* tend to agree with those of the *Śatapathabrāhmaṇa* of the White Yajurveda. Only the last three invocations are relevant for the discussion of the *Mahābhārata* quotation above. The first of these names Indra as 'Ahalyā's lover'. The *Jaiminīya-brāhmaṇa* and the *Ṣaḍviṃśabrāhmaṇa* are in this case unanimous in declaring that, 'He was the lover of Ahalyā Maitreyī' (*ahalyāyai ha maitreyyai jāra āsa*). In his commentary on the *Ṣaḍviṃśabrāhmaṇa*, Sāyaṇa explains that 'Maitreyī' is the 'daughter of Mitrā (f.)' No husband is mentioned in any explanation given in the *Brāhmaṇas*.

As for the *Śatapathabrāhmaṇa*, after this invocation, there is simply a statement summarizing the preceding invocations (and thus separating them from the following ones):

> With these, which are his special adventures, he (=the priest) wishes to please him at this (occasion of the sacrifice).[5]

Of the remaining two invocations, the first (*kauśika brāhmaṇa*) is explained in the *Jaiminīyabrāhmaṇa* with the following story: 'At the battle with the Asuras he destroyed the Vedas; he learned them from Viśvāmitra, that is why he called himself Kauśika.' The *Ṣaḍvimśabrāhmaṇa* suggests another explanation: 'As a brahmin of the Kuśika family he used to go to her' (*kauśiko ha smaināṃ brāhmaṇa upanyeti*).

This might be exactly what is needed to explain the allusion in the *Mahābhārata* (book 12), in which Indra is cursed to lose his testicles not by Gautama but by Kauśika. Such a curse is, however, not mentioned at all in any of the *Brāhmaṇa* explanations, since there was obviously no husband to curse him.

---

[4] *índrā́gacha hā́riva ā́gacha/ médhātither meṣa vṛṣaṇaśvasya mene//gaúrāvaskandin áhalyāyai jāra/ kaúśika brāhmaṇa gaútama bruvāṇa//*

[5] *íti tád yā́ny évāsya cáraṇāni/ tair évainam etát prámumodayiṣati//*

The last invocation (*gautama bruvāṇa*), which would fit our story best, seems to be an optional addition invented, according to the *Śatapathabrāhmaṇa*, by the celebrated Āruṇi. The *Jaiminīyabrāhmaṇa*, however, rejects the wording and corrects it to *kauśika bruvāṇa*, which it does not explain separately. The *Ṣaḍviṃśabrāhmaṇa* tells a different story, in order to explain *gautama bruvāṇa*:

> In the battle between gods and *asuras*, Indra asked Gotama, who was practising austerities between the two battle lines, to be a spy for the gods. When the ascetic refused, Indra obtained permission to assume the shape of the ascetic in order to be a spy himself. That is why he called himself Gautama.

Thus it is fairly obvious that in the *Brāhmaṇas* the explanations are by no means unanimous and that there is not yet any connection made between Ahalyā and Gautama. In the *Mahābhārata*, there seems to be a kind of bifurcation: although Gautama is named as Ahalyā's husband, it is Kauśika's curse that leads to Indra's characteristic punishment.

I shall now sum up the elements which eventually led to the development of the Ahalyā narrative. In the *subrahmaṇya* formula, Ahalyā appears as Indra's beloved, but without any husband; in the explanation provided by the *Ṣaḍviṃśabrāhmaṇa*, Indra assumes the shape of the brahmin Kauśika when he visits Ahalyā (it is not said that Kauśika was her husband, but this may be suspected); and in the *Mahābhārata*, she appears as Gautama's wife. But there is no mention of her being guilty of betraying her husband, nor of any punishment she has to suffer, before the detailed versions of the *Rāmāyaṇa*, where, in the version found in book 1, her punishment is closely connected with the motif of purification through Rāma. This motif with its religious implications can then be traced in all later versions or adaptations of the Rāma story: for example, in Kālidāsa's *Raghuvaṃśa* (11.33-4), in the relevant sections of the *Purāṇas*, in the *Adhyātmarāmāyaṇa* (1.5), and of course in the *Rāmcaritmānas* of *Tulsīdās (1.242-3)*.

Indra's Epithets and the Prehistory of Ahalyā

I shall now turn to the question of Indra's punishment. I have already described three procedures in the epics: the curse to lose his testicles, a misfortune then alleviated by providing him with a ram's testicles; another curse making him inferior to his enemy Indrajit and thereby destabilizing his rank as king of the gods; and the curse of 'gold-beardedness'. The loss of testicles appears to represent a primitive form of justice, whereas the substitution of a ram's testicles may be traced back to the invocations of the *subrahmaṇya* formula: *médhātither meṣa vṛṣaṇaśvasya mene* may have suggested the epithet *meṣavṛśaṇa*, 'having a ram's testicles'. The roots of Indra's inferiority to his enemy can be found in the general attitude of the *Brāhmaṇas* towards the old Ṛgvedic gods, according to which even Indra as king of the gods wielded little real power. In attempting to explain the 'gold-beardedness', a look at an older stratum of text sources, namely Indra's epithet's in the *Ṛgveda*, may be helpful: they seem to have been partly misunderstood, partly reinterpreted in later strata. One of these epithets is *hariśmaśru* (*hariśmaśāru* in the RV) 'having a golden or yellowish beard'; why it should be a punishment to have a golden beard, is not immediately understandable. Perhaps the ideal of beauty had somehow changed after the immigration of the ancient Aryans, who were presumably fair-haired, and in later periods blond hair and beard were regarded as abnormal.

Far more important for the further development of the Ahalyā story is another well-known epithet of Indra in the epics: 'having a thousand eyes' (*sahasrākṣa* or synonymous formations). This epithet is used in the *Ṛgveda* mainly for other gods (Varuṇa, Soma, the moon, Indra and Vāyu in the dual, etc.). It probably refers to the thousand spies through whom a mighty king may come to know everything that is going on in his realm. This interpretation certainly fits for Varuṇa and Soma, who are often called kings in the *Ṛgveda*. Someone who 'has a thousand eyes' (that is, has his eyes everywhere) comes to know if anything is wrong and can take measures against crime and injustice. This was certainly valid also for Indra, the mighty king of the gods and ideal ruler of the world, as he appeared to his believers. As a common epithet of Indra, *sahasrākṣa* is used frequently in the epics (thus it also occurs in the first version of the *Rāmāyaṇa* before Indra is cursed by Gautama).

Later tradition, however, tended to take this epithet literally and tried to explain how these thousand eyes that are so characteristic of Indra came into existence. Such an explanation can already be found in the *Mahābhārata* (1.203) where the following myth is told. In order to cause disunion between two dangerous demons, Sunda and Upasunda, Brahmā causes an extremely beautiful *apsaras* (named Tilottamā) to be made by Viśvakarman, the divine sculptor. When she respectfully circumambulates the gods, they feel such desire to look at her that Śiva grows three other faces, one in each direction, so that he may watch her continuously, whereas Indra develops eyes everywhere on his body, a thousand in total.

A similar myth about beautiful Tilottamā can be found in the *Viṣṇudharmottarapurāṇa*, in a passage about the origin of celebrated *apsarases*, among whom, surprisingly, Ahalyā is listed as well. The origin of Tilottamā is described thus:

> In order to destroy (the demons) Sunda and Upasunda, Viśvakarman collected sesamum seed after sesamum seed (*tilam*) and created Tilottamā ('best of all sesamum seeds')

> adorned with all jewels, at whose circumambulation the holder of the trident (= Śiva) became four-faced, and illustrious Śakra with the thunderbolt, the slayer of (the demon) Pāka became thousand-eyed (*sahasrākṣa*).[6]

The origin of Ahalyā is described as follows (see Table 2, column A: VDhP):

> The Grandsire (= Brahmā), wishing to see all loveliness of shape assembled in one place, created a singular beauty in the three worlds, named Ahalyā. And Brahmā with his auspicious four faces gave her to Gautama: it was for her sake that Śakra was bereft of his testicles by Gautama.[7]

This prehistory of Ahalyā, her outstanding beauty and her marriage to Gautama, is also related in the version of the Ahalyā story found in book 7 of the *Rāmāyaṇa* (7.30.16-42). It starts with the following report: 'Among all living beings created by Brahmā, who were originally similar in shape, it was first Ahalyā who was different from all the rest because of her special beauty; for this purpose Brahmā had created her.' This feature of the narrative may be traced back to the fanciful comparison in the first version of the *Rāmāyaṇa*, where Ahalyā appeared to Rāma 'like some divine illustion fashioned by the creator' (see above), which seems to have been taken literally. (In the southern recension, it is also connected with an etymology of the world *ahalyā*, which is said to mean something like 'without any disfigurement or flaw' but might also be understood from the context as 'incomparable'.) Such a beautiful woman is naturally desired by the other gods too; Brahmā, however, decides to entrust her to the celebrated sage Gautama for education, and finally to marry her to him, at which point Indra in particular, becomes enraged. In this context, Indra's motive for intruding into Ahalyā's married life is obviously jealousy or envy of Gautama. Ahalyā's punishment for having intercourse with Indra is, in this version, the loss of the uniqueness of her beauty, which from now on she has to share with other beings, so that jealousy would never again arise on account of there being only one beautiful woman. In addition to this, she is repudiated by her husband (a parallel to Sītā's fate in the same book of the *Rāmāyaṇa*), a punishment which is softened in the southern recension, as mentioned earlier. As for Indra, to whose mind Brahmā had recalled this story

---

[6] *sundopasundanāśāya nirmitā viśvakarmaṇā| tilaṃtilaṃ samādāya sarvaratnais tilottamā|| yasyāḥ pradakṣiṇāj jātaś caturvaktraḥ pinākadhṛk| sahasranayanaḥ śrīmān vajrī śakraś ca pākahā||* 1.128.27-8.

[7] *ekasthaṃ rūpasaundaryaṃ draṣṭum icchan pitāmahaḥ| ahalyāṃ nāma kṛtavāṃs trailokyasyaikasundarīm|| gautamāya ca tāṃ prādād brahmā śubhacaturmukhaḥ| yasyāḥ kṛte gautamena śakro vivṛṣaṇaḥ kṛtaḥ* // 1.128.30-1.

as the explanation for his shameful defeat, he is given the advice to purify himself by means of a Vaiṣṇava sacrifice; acting accordingly, he regains his rank of the king of the gods.

The allusion in the *Viṣṇudharmottarapurāṇa* seems to be closely connected with this second version in the *Rāmāyaṇa*, as far as the prehistory is concerned (but which is dependent on which I would not venture to say). Indra's punishment to be *vivṛṣaṇa* ('without testicles') goes back to the common epic tradition, whereas the image of Indra's thousand eyes is obviously borrowed from the *Mahābhārata* passage about Tilottamā, which had nothing to do with the Ahalyā story.

A Full Account in the *Brahmapurāṇa*

This short version of the *Viṣṇudharmottarapurāṇa* may well have been the starting point for the version of the Ahalyā story in the *Brahmapurāṇa* (87.44), or, more precisely, in the section entitled 'the magnification of (the river) Gautamī' (*gautamīmāhātmya*), Gautamī being a name for the Godāvarī. One of the salutary places on its banks is the confluence with the river Ahalyā, the origin of which is told by Brahmā to Nārada, in a new version of our Ahalyā story, a version which is adapted to the context in a characteristic way (see Table 2, Column C). As an introduction, the prehistory of Ahalyā is told in full detail: Brahmā reports that he once created many beautiful young girls, the most praiseworthy being Ahalyā. After reflecting for a long time on who might deserve to bring her up, he decided on Gautama, a knowledgeable and in every respect excellent brahmin, and entrusted her to him. When she reached marriageable age, Gautama returned the girl well adorned and well educated. As soon as they see her, all the gods want her and ask Brahmā for her hand. Brahmā secretly wishes to give her to Gautama, but officially he states that whoever, after circumambulating the earth, returns first shall marry her. All the gods immediately start on their journey. Gautama, staying behind, beholds the pregnant wishing-cow Surabhi and circumambulates her, knowing that she is *urvī* ('broad', a term meaning 'pregnant' as well as 'the earth'). He also circumambulates a Śiva *liṅga* and then returns, being the first of all to arrive. Brahmā accepts him as the winner and marries Ahalyā to him. The gods, when they arrive one after the other, are made to understand that they are too late, so they return to heaven, while Ahalyā and Gautama settle in a hermitage on the Brahmagiri and live happily together. Thus runs the prehistory which, in this version, is especially colourful.

The main story presents further new and interesting details. Indra in his heaven learns about the happy married life of the couple. Assuming the guise of a brahmin, he sets out for the place in order to see for himself. When he sees Ahalyā, he loses his senses: without considering the consequences, he stays near the hermitage, waiting for his chance. One day, when Gautama has set off with his pupils to perform a morning ritual on the bank of the Gautamī (which must have been at some distance from the hermitage), Indra makes use of his absence. Assuming Gautama's shape, he approaches Ahalyā, tells her that he has been overcome by desire for her beauty, takes her by the hand and leads her into the hut where she yields to him, believing him to be her husband:

> Ahalyā, however, did not recognize him; she took her lover (*jāram*) for Gautama, enjoying love with him according to her pleasure...[8]

The choice of the word *jāra* ('lover') undoubtedly recalls the *subrahmaṇya* formula (*ahalyāyai jāra*).

Meanwhile Gautama returns with his disciples. He wonders why Ahalyā does not rush out joyfully to greet him in her usual way. Instead the servants approach full of surprise that he should be in the hut as well as outside it, and praise the ascetic powers which enable him to multiply himself. Full of foreboding, Gautama enters the hut and calls for Ahalyā who, on hearing his voice, immediately rises from the bed and accuses her lover of deceiving her. Being afraid of Gautama, Indra turns himself into a cat (*biḍāla*). Gautama, however, threatens to turn him to ashes unless he makes himself known. Thereupon Indra confesses who he is and asks for forgiveness for his deed, the responsibility for which he lays upon Kāmadeva's arrow. Gautama nevertheless curses him to become *sahasrabhagavat*: since his sin consisted of enjoying the vulva (*bhaga*), his body would be marked by a thousand (*sahasra*) of them.

In order to understand the background of this curse, one may again turn to the juridical literature. A relevant *śloka* occurs in the *Bṛhaspatismṛti* (24.14, quoted in Kane, vol. III, p.532):

> If anyone performs the sexual act in disguise, his punishment is the confiscation of all his wealth; he should be branded with the 'vulva mark' (*bhagāṅka*), and then be expelled from the town.[9]

This description of the transgression fits perfectly with Indra's deed: by pretending to be Ahalyā's husband he has managed to seduce her; in consequence, his punishment is to be branded by the *bhaga* mark, which the curse multiplies by a thousand – a new motif which has become very popular in

---

[8] *na bubodha tv ahalyā taṃ, jāraṃ mene tu gautamam/ ramamāṇā yathāsaukhyam...* (BrP 87.44).

[9] *chadmanā kāmayed yas tu tasya sarvaharo damaḥ/ aṅkayitvā bhagāṅkena purān nivāsayet tataḥ//*

the Purāṇic versions of the story.

Ahalyā in this version is cursed by her husband to become a dried-up river – a motif which only appears in this specific narrative context. When she claims to be innocent and even produces the servants as witnesses, her husband softens his curse by announcing that she will retain her former shape as soon as she (as a river) joins the river Gautamī with its purifying power.

Indra also asks Gautama for mercy, and Gautama announces that his punishment too will be softened by the power of the Gautamī: after bathing in its water, he will be purified from sin and the shameful marks will turn into eyes. With this, a new and obviously convincing explanation is provided for the epithet *sahasrākṣa* ('having a thousand eyes'), which in the *Viṣṇudharmottara-purāṇa* was explained by the face- or eye-creating effect of Tilottamā's beauty, an explanation which appeared, however, already in the direct vicinity of the Ahalyā story, so that the replacement of the old curse (deprivation of testicles) by the new one (being branded with *bhaga* marks, which resemble eyes) may have suggested itself.

The characteristic features of the Ahalyā story in the *Brahmapurāṇa* may be summed up as follows:

1. The prehistory is provided with particular imaginative features (such as the competition for Ahalyā's hand).
2. The Alkmene motif, as I would call it, is prominent: Ahalyā is innocent, since Indra appears effectively as her husband; even the servants believe that Gautama has duplicated himself and can attest to Ahalyā's innocence.
3. Afraid of being discovered, Indra takes the shape of a cat.
4. Indra is cursed to be branded with a thousand 'vulva marks', which are later mercifully turned into eyes; his old epithet 'thousand-eyed' (*sahasrākṣa*) is thereby explained in a naturalistic way.
5. The softening of the curses is effected by the purifying contact with the river Gautamī; thus two new auspicious places of pilgrimage are established, one called 'Indratīrtha', the other 'Ahalyāsaṃgama' ('confluence of the Ahalyā'). This narrative context seems also to be responsible for the specific curse called down upon Ahalyā: that she should become a dried-up driver.

A Mixture of Motifs in the *Padmapurāṇa*

There are three other *Purāṇas* in which the Ahalyā story is retold in full detail: the *Padmapurāṇa*, the *Brahmavaivartapurāṇa* (two versions which stresss quite different aspects and are thus complementary to each other), and the *Skandapurāṇa* (see Table 2, column C). I cannot deal with these in the same detail, but a few distinctive characteristics should be highlighted.

I shall start with the *Padmapurāṇa* version, which is in several respects similar to that of the *Brahmapurāṇa*. There is a shorter version of the prehistory of Ahalyā's marriage; then the main story starts with Indra waiting for Gautama to absent himself. At some point, Gautama leaves the hut in order to take a ritual bath. Ahalyā is occupied with performing a *pūjā* to the divinities when Indra appears in Gautama's shape and demands a kiss. Ahalyā first rejects him, pointing out that it would be inappropriate to neglect her duties towards the gods for the sake of love. Her fake husband, however, instructs her regarding the duties which she, as a faithful wife, owes to him, especially concerning the very point he has in mind, and insists on having his will despite her reluctance. Meanwhile, by means of his supernatural gifts of knowledge, Gautama realizes what is going on and returns to the hermitage. Indra immediately turns himself into an *ākhu* (a rat or a mole?), but leaves the footprints of a cat (*vṛṣadaṃṣṭra*). Thereupon Gautama asks him: 'Who are you, assuming the shape of a cat (*mārjāra*)?' (5.51.27). Thus the motif of Indra turning himself into a cat appears again, but here the two terms used for the animal (*vṛṣadaṃṣṭra, mārjāra*) are different from that used in the *Brahmapurāṇa* (*biḍāla*).

Indra's punishment in this version is a strange mixture of motifs: he is cursed, first, to be marked by a thousand vulvas (*sahasrabhaga*), then to lose his male organ (*liṅgaṃ*), and finally his shame should be visible to all the inhabitants of heaven (which presumably means that he cannot retain his rank as king of the gods).

Having cursed Indra, Gautama now interrogates Ahalyā, who declares herself innocent. However, since she has become impure by intercourse with Indra, she is cursed to become a mere skeleton of skin and bones. She asks for a limitation on this curse. Gautama prophesies that at some point in the future Rāma will come here together with Vasiṣṭha (not Viśvāmitra, strangely enough, as in the *Rāmāyaṇa*) and will laugh about her (5.51.36):

> (Gautama speaks:) Seeing you (= Ahalyā), afflicted, dried out, without body, standing (or lying) on the path, Rāma will laugh and say to Vasiṣṭha, 'Who is this unlucky figure, dried up and consisting only of bones?'[10]

Here the attribute *nirdeha* ('bodiless') calls to mind the first version of the

[10] *ḍṛṣtvā tvāṃ duḥkhitāṃ śuṣkāṃ nirdehāṃ pathi saṃsthitām/ gadiṣyati ca vai rāmo vasiṣṭhasyāgrato hasan/ kim iyaṃ śuṣkarūpā ca pratimāsthimayāśivā//*

Rāmāyaṇa, while *śuṣkā* or *śuṣkarūpā* ('dried out, dried up') recalls the dry river (*śuṣkanadī*) in the *Brahmapurāṇa* version. The phrase 'standing (or lying) on the path' (*pathi saṃsthitā*) may also be said of a stone or a rock, although in this context it appears to describe a skeleton, which may also be called *śuṣkarūpā*. But *nirdeha* ('bodiless') and *asthimayā pratimā* ('bony image') seem to contradict each other, which in turn suggests that different ideas have been intermingled again.

As for Indra, he hides in the water, full of shame, and praises the deity for whom the vulva (*yoni*, here termed *indrākṣi*, 'Indra's eye') is characteristic. Pleased by his praise, Devī grants him a boon. He asks for his former shape, in order to regain his rank as ruler of the gods, but this is more than can be done for him by her or anyone else. However, she can create a thousand eyes in the middle of the 'vulva marks'; as Sahasrākṣa ('characterized by a thousand eyes') he will again be able to rule over the gods. Finally she restores his male organ (*śiṣna*) and provides it with a ram's testicles (*meṣāṇḍa*) – again we find a combinaton of various well-known motifs, none of which could evidently be given up once it had entered the tradition.

The special characteristics of this version can now be summarized:

1. Ahalyā and Indra in the form of Gautama have a dispute before they make love.
2. Indra appears to Gautama as a cat.
3. Many different (and partly contradictory) elements are combined in the curses and their softening.
4. Unlike in the other versions, but in accordance with the prescription in the *Āpastambadharmasūtra*, Indra loses his penis (that is, not only his testicles).
5. Ahalyā is released by Rāma, Indra by the Goddess. The latter may seem remarkable in a Vaiṣṇava context, but is probably explained by the fact that she is the deity of the *yoni* (here euphemistically called 'Indra's eye').

Other versions in the *Brahmavaivartapurāṇa* and *Skandapurāṇa*

The *Brahmavaivartapurāṇa* presents us with two versions, one is told by Kṛṣṇa Nārāyaṇa to Rādhā (4.47), the other is told to Nārada, the messenger of the gods (4.61). The latter is discussed by G. Bonazzoli in an article about seduction stories in the *Brahmavaivartapurāṇa* (*Purāṇa* XIX/2: 321 ff.). According to him, these stories have an underlying common structure which shows how they are influenced by the Caitanya movement, a structure which is manifest in the presentation of the development of a love story in five steps:

(1) falling in love (on the part of the man), (2) description of the female beauty, (3) dialogue in which the woman rejects her lover, (4) obstacle to, or interruption of, the love affair, (5) performance of the act of love. In this structure Bonazzoli sees the reflection of the 'Caitanya doctrine about the importance of the body and *līlā*' (p. 339), love being successful in overcoming every obstacle, even moral scruples.

This may indeed by valid for the second version (4.61); as for the first version (not analysed in Bonazzoli's article) which deals explicitly with 'the breaking of the pride of the king of the gods' (*surapater darpabhaṅgaṃ*), it appears to me to convey quite a different message. It begins by showing Indra in his power, which he has secured for himself by a hundred sacrifices (according to his epithet *śatakratu*, which originally meant 'having a hundred powers of will', but was later interpreted as 'characterized by a hundred sacrifices'). Unfortunately, Indra forgets to pay due respect to some venerable persons and is consequently cursed (not unlike Śakuntalā, incidentally). His mother Tārakā tries to comfort him by assuring him that, even if he has to bear the effect of his actions now, after bad days good days are to come. In order to have a bath, Śakra goes to the (or a) heavenly river (*svarṇadī*) one day, where he sees Ahalyā washing herself and is totally confused by the beauty of her limbs. Regaining his senses, he approaches her in the form of her husband, embraces her, and makes love with her until they sink down, happily exhausted. At this moment, the enraged Gautama interrupts them. Indra throws himself at the brahmin's feet. Gautama curses him to be marked by a thousand vulvas (*yoni*), but since Indra has approached him for protection, he is compelled to soften his curse so that these vulva marks will be changed into eyes if Indra worships the sun-god. Gautama further explains the whole incident as being connected with the curses in the introductory passage of the story. Ahalyā's fate in this version is to be a stone for sixty thousand years, since she, though innocent, has become impure and can no longer perform her duties as a housewife. She submits to her husband's verdict. After the sixty thousand years have been completed, Rāma happens to stumble over this stone, whereupon Ahalyā is purified and allowed to return to her husband.

It seems to me that in this version, which certainly describes the act of love in some detail, much greater emphasis is placed on the inevitability of fate, and especially on the idea that curses must be fulfilled. As for the structure of the development of a love affair in five steps, only the first and the last one, falling in love and fulfilment of love, can be identified; they are, however, integrated into a quite different thematic structure centring on non-intended transgression and its unavoidable consequences, Indra's transgression being explained as a result of curses that he inadvertently provoked due to the whim of fate.

As for the second version, it centres rather on the question of how the flawless, virtuous, chaste wife of Gautama could possibly be seduced. Kṛṣṇa Nārāyaṇa's answer to Nārada's question gives a more detailed narrative, which involves a new peculiar feature. Indra first sees Ahalyā in Puṣkara on a pilgrimage and falls in love with her. The next day, he finds an opportunity to watch her secretly while she takes a bath in the Mandākinī river. Out of his senses, he immediately approaches her and praises her beauty in every detail, a beauty to which he, as an expert in love, can certainly do better justice than the ascetic Gautama, who knows nothing about *kāmaśāstra* (the science of love). He promises to place her even above his wife Śacī and wonders how Brahmā could be so foolish as to give her to an ascetic disinclined towards love (obviously all this presupposes versions like that of the *Brahmapurāṇa*). Ahalyā, however, is not impressed. Instead she rebukes him, tells him how despicable his intentions are, and informs him that, although beautiful women are created for the purpose of bewitching the minds of men (if only for the sake of procreation), a wise man should resist this bewitchment; in any case, intercourse with another's wife leads directly to hell. Then she returns home and tells the whole story to her husband, providing much amusement to them both.

Indra, however, does not give up. When Gautama happens to be absent one day, Indra takes advantage of this opportunity and makes love with Ahalyā in the guise of her husband. Gautama realizes what is going on and curses them both, Indra to have his body covered with vulvas (*bhagāṅga*), and Ahalyā to become a stone in the forest. In spite of her entreaties, Gautama refuses to change his mind on the grounds that she has become impure, whether or not she intended to do so, or even knew about it; however, her curse is limited in the same way as in the other version (that is, until Rāma kicks the stone with his foot).

In this version, Indra's first encounter with Ahalyā, especially the description of her beauty and Indra's attempt to seduce her, is indeed presented in more erotic detail – there is no doubt that people enjoyed telling and listening to a story like this – but, in my view, the main concern is with moral concepts. On the one hand, Ahalyā's blamelessness is contrasted with Indra's immorality; on the other, the consequences of even unconscious transgression are strictly observed (in Ahalyā's case, for instance, punishment is the result of her impurity rather than her guilt). But the most striking feature of this version is the duplication of Indra's meeting with Ahalyā, first in his own shape and without success, then in Gautama's shape as usual. This feature I have found in only one other version, that of the *Skandapurāṇa* (5.3.136). Here too Indra first appears in his own form and tries to persuade Ahalyā in a way similar to that in the second *Brahmavaivartapurāṇa* version (the arguments are, by the way, much the same as Rāvaṇa's arguments before he abducts Sītā in the *Rāmāyaṇa*.) Ahalyā does not respond; she seems to be unresolved. Indra interprets this in his favour and approaches her again, this time in Gautama's shape. The rest of the story does not differ much from the versions of the *Brahmavaivartapurāṇa*.

The narrative elements of the versions told in the *Purāṇas* (see Table 2, column C) may now be summarized as follows:

1. The most elaborate version of the prehistory (that is, the creation and education of Ahalyā and her marriage to Gautama) is presented in the *Brahmapurāna*. This fits the allusion in the *Viṣṇudharmottarapurāṇa* (see Table 2, column A: VDhP 1.128), from which its core may have been borrowed, and is probably the basis for the shorter version in the *Padmapurāṇa*.
2. In all the versions, Indra approaches Ahalyā in her husband's form in order to make love to her without being recognized by her. A special development can be observed in the second version of the *Brahmavaivartapurāṇa*, as well as in the *Skandapurāṇa*, where Indra appears twice – once in his own form, without success, then in the form of Gautama – so that no one might suspect Ahalyā of being curious to experience the love of the king of the gods.
3. Caught in the act, Indra assumes the form of a cat in the *Brahmapurāṇa* and in the *Padmapurāṇa*, whereas in the *Brahmavaivartapurāṇa* and *Skandapurāṇa* he immediately asks Gautama for mercy.
4. The 'vulva marks' have become the most popular form of punishment for Indra; only in the *Padmapurāṇa* version has the old curse that he should lose his testicles been integrated with it.
5. Ahalyā's punishment is less consistent: in the *Brahmapurāṇa* she is cursed to become a dry river, in the *Padmapurāṇa* a skeleton, but the adjectives 'bodiless' and 'dried up' also recall the *Rāmāyaṇa* and *Brahmapurāṇa* versions. The two versions of the *Brahmavaivartapurāṇa* as well as that of the *Skandapurāṇa* agree in that she is cursed to become a stone or a rock – a motif which then gains more and more popularity and which also appears in allusions to the story (e.g. in the *Raghuvaṃśa*).
6. Ahalyā is released from the curse by Rāma's visit to the hermitage; the only exception to this is found in the *Brahmapurāṇa* where, as befits the context, she is released by the river Gautamī.
7. The softening of Indra's curse so that he becomes *sahasrākṣa* ('thousand-eyed') is common to all versions. They differ only in the way in which this is achieved: in the *Brahmapurāṇa* by bathing in the Gautamī, in the *Padmapurāṇa* by praising the Goddess (the tutelary deity of the *yoni*), in the *Brahmavaivartapurāṇa* by worshipping the sun-god, and in the *Skandapurāṇa* by Gautama himself after the intervention of the gods.

An Anecdote in the *Kathāsaritsāgara*

In conclusion, I should like to glance at one other popular version of the story, that of the *Kathāsaritsāgara*. Here we find a nice detail, a pun by means of which Ahalyā can avoid the sin of telling a lie. In this version, she has recognized Indra in his disguise but has nevertheless accepted him as her lover (as in the first *Rāmāyaṇa* version). As in the *Padmapurāṇa* and *Brahmavaivartapurāṇa*, Gautama becomes aware of what is happening by his superhuman knowledge, and interferes. In a panic, Indra assumes the shape of a male cat (*mārjāra*), as in the *Padma-* and *Brahmapurāṇa* versions. Instead of asking Indra who he is, Gautama asks his wife. She replies '*majjāra*', which can be interpreted either as the Prakrit form of *mārjāra* 'cat' or of the compound *majjāra*, 'my lover'. Gautama laughs and softens his curse that she should become a rock by adding that, since she has at least spoken the truth, she will be released by Rāma. Indra is cursed to have what he has so desired a thousandfold on his own body; but when he sees the *apsaras* Tilottamā, they will turn into eyes (which recalls the *Viṣṇudharmottarapurāṇa* and *Mahābhārata* stories about Tilottamā).

The date of the composition of the *Kathāsaritsāgara* is comparatively late (eleventh century AD), but its Prakrit source, Guṇabhadra's *Bṛhatkathā* must have been much older, presumably of the first or second century AD. The Ahalyā narrative may well go back to a Prakrit original, but it also appears to presuppose the first version of the *Rāmāyaṇa* as well as the Tilottamā story of the *Viṣṇudharmottarapurāṇa,* as the softening of the curses shows. The narrative problem of the first *Rāmāyaṇa* version (that is, why Indra should assume the form of Gautama, when he is recognized by Ahalyā) is, however, eliminated here: Indra does not bother to take the form of Gautama. The motif that, in order to escape, Indra takes the form of a cat (shared with the *Brahma-* and *Padmapurāṇa* versions) may have been invented for this version where it is needed for the pun (which consequently also serves to justify the softening of Ahalyā's curse). If so, it will then have been borrowed by the *Brahmapurāṇa* version, even though it was not needed there. Alternatively, it may be that the motif of feline stealth was invented independently and did already exist in a version which was made use of either by the *Bṛhatkathā* or by the *Kathāsaritsāgara* (for we cannot rule out the possibility that the latter introduced the pun when recomposing the Prakrit version in Sanskrit). The word *mārjāra* does not appear in the *Brahmapurāṇa* which uses the term *biḍāla,* a vernacular term well attested in the epics and in Pali (but which does not occur in the *Kathāsaritsāgara* at all). Thus we are not compelled to assume that the *Brahmapurāṇa* presupposes the *Kathāsaritsāgara*; and in any case the idea of taking the form of a cat in order to escape easily is not particularly far-fetched.

Whether this version, interspersed as it is with the moralizing comments usually found in fables, is the most skilfully told (as Rau (1966) has opined) is a matter of taste. To some extent, the narrative culminates here in a kind of joke based on the pun, which is certainly entertaining. On the other hand, it lacks the tragic dimension of the Alkmene motif that is fully developed in the

Purāṇic versions, as well as the connection with the mythical and sacrificial background from which the legend started to grow (the *subrahmaṇya* formula, the explanations of how Indra came to lose his former rank, and so on.)

Turning back to the initial question of who were the many women who became the prey of Indra the womanizer, the answer may now be given, 'Yes, there are indeed many incidents, but it is always the same Ahalyā, who is multiplied by the various versions in which her story exists'.

Abbreviations

BrahmaP	*Brahmapurāṇa*
BrahmavaivartaP	*Brahmavaivartapurāṇa*
KSS	*Kathāsaritsāgara*
PadmaP ASS	*Padmapurāṇa, Ānandāśrama Sanskrit Series*
RV	*Ṛgveda*
Skanda	*Skandapurāṇa*
VDhP	*Viṣṇudharmottarapurāṇa*

References

Texts and Translations

Adhyātmarāmāyaṇa. Critical edition. by N. Siddhantaratna. Calcutta Sanskrit Series XI. Calcutta, 1935.

Āpastambadharmasūtra

—. *Āpastambīyadharmasūtram: Āpastambha's Aphorisms on the Sacred Law of the Hindus*, ed. G. Bühler. Bombay Sanskrit Series XLIV, L. 3rd edn.: Bombay, 1932.

—. Bühler, G. (tr.). *The Sacred Law of the Aryas, as taught in the schools of Apastambha, Gautama, Vasishṭha and Baudhāyana*, part I. Sacred Books of the East 2. Oxford: Clarendon Press, 1879. Delhi: Motilal Banarsidass, 1986.

Brahmapurāṇa

—. *Brahmapurāṇa*. Ānandāśrama Sanskrit Series 28. Pune, 1895.

—. P. Schreiner and R. Söhnen*: Sanskrit Indices and Text of the Brahmapurāṇa*. Purāṇa Research Publications 1. Wiesbaden: Harrassowitz, 1987.

Bṛhaspatismṛti, ed. by K.V.R. Aiyangar. Gaekward Oriental Series 85. Baroda, 1941.

Brahmavaivartapurāṇa, ed. V.G. Apte. Ānandāśrama Sanskrit Series 102. Pune, 1935.

Jaiminīyabrāhmaṇa. Critical edition by Raghu Vira and Lokesh Chandra. 2nd

rev. edn. Delhi, 1986.
Kathāsaritsāgara. 2nd edn. Delhi: Motilal Banarsidass, 1977.
Mahābhārata. Critical edition by V.S. Sukthankar, S.K. Belvalkar, P.L. Vaidya, and others. Pune: Bhandarkar Oriental Research Institute, 1927-66.
Padmapurāṇa
—. *Padmapurāṇa,* ed. Viśvanātha Nārāyaṇa Maṇḍalīka. Ānandāśrama Sanskrit Series Extra No. 1. Pune, 1893-4.
—. *Padmapurāṇa*. 4 vols. Bombay 1927. Delhi: Nag Publishers, 1984-5.
—. *Padmapurāṇa*, tr. N.A. Deshpande. Parts 1-3. Ancient Indian Tradition and Mythology 39-41. Delhi, 1988-90.
Raghuvaṃśa of Kalidāsa. Ed. by G.R. Nandargikar. 4th edn. Delhi, 1971.
Rāmāyaṇa
—. *Rāmāyaṇa*. Critical edition by G.H.Bhatt and others. Baroda: Oriental Institute, 1960-73.
—. Goldman, R.P. (transl.): *The Rāmāyaṇa of Vālmīki: An Epic of Ancient India*. Vol. 1. Princeton: University Press, 1984.
Rāmcaritmānas
—. Tulsidās: *Rāmcaritmānas*. Allahabad: The Indian Press, 1940.
—. Growse, F.S. (tr.): *The Rāmāyaṇa of Tulasī Dāsa*, ed. R.C. Prasad. Delhi, 1978.
Ṣaḍviṃśabrāhmaṇa, ed. H.F. Eelsingh. Thesis. Utrecht, 1908.
Śatapathabrāhmaṇa
—. *Śatapathabrāhmaṇa*, ed. A. Weber. 2nd ed. Chowkhamba Sanskrit Series no. 96. Varanasi, 1964.
—. Eggeling, J. (tr.): The *Śatapatha-Brāhmaṇa according to the Mādhyandina School*. Part II, Books III and IV. Sacred Books of the East 26. Oxford: Clarendon Press, 1885. Delhi, 1972.
Skandapurāṇa. Gurumaṇḍala Series 20. Calcutta: Manasukharāya Mora, 1960-.
Śrautasūtras
—. Parpola, A. *Śrautasūtras of Lāṭyāyana and Drāhyāyaṇa and their Commentaries*. 2 vols. Helsinki, 1968.
Taittirīyāraṇyaka, ed. with Sāyaṇa's commentary by Rājendralāla Mitra. Calcutta, 1871.
Viṣṇudharmottarapurāṇa. Bombay: Veṅkaṭeśvara Press, 1912.

Secondary Sources

Doniger O'Flaherty, W. 1975. *Hindu Myths*. Penguin Classics.
Kane, P.V. 1946. *History of Dharmaśāstra: Ancient and Mediaeval Religious and Civil Law*, vol. III. Pune: Bhandarkar Oriental Research Institute.
Lindberger, Ö. 1956. *The Transformations of Amphitryon*. Stockholm: Almqvist & Wiksell.
Bonazzoli, G. 1977. 'Seduction Stories in the Brahmavaivarta-Purāṇa: A Study

in Purāṇic Structure'. *Purāṇa* XIX/2:321-41.
Oertel, H. 'Contributions from the Jaiminīya-Brāhmaṇa to the History of the Brāhmaṇa Literature.' JAOS 1897: 15-48.
Rau, W. 1966. 'Fünfzehn Indra-Geschichten.' *Asiatische Studien* 20: 72-100.
Rocher, L. 1986. *The Purāṇas*. A History of Indian Literature vol. II, fasc. 3. Wiesbaden: Harrassowitz.
Söhnen. R., and P. Schreiner. 1989. *Brahmapurāṇa: Summary of Contents*. Purāṇa Research Publications 2. Wiesbaden: Harrassowitz.
Söhnen, R. 1991. 'Indra and Women'. *BSOAS* LIV: 68-74.
Varma, Dh. 1937. 'Evolution of the Myth of Ahalyā Maitreyī.' *Jha Commemoration Volume*, Allahabad: 427-33.

4

Paraśurāma and Time

Lynn Thomas

Introduction

Paraśurāma, the complex Bhārgava figure who comes to be viewed as the sixth avatar (*avatāra*) of Viṣṇu, is associated with a large body of myths and has been the subject of a number of different studies (e.g. Gail 1977). Most of these studies have concentrated on the central myths which go to make up his story in the classical texts, or on later deeds assigned to him in the regional traditions of South and West India. One area of Paraśurāma's career which has remained relatively unexplored, however, is his intervention in the affairs of the avatars who follow him, Rāma Dāśarathi and Kṛṣṇa, as told in the narratives of the two epics. This involvement in stories subsequent to his own avatar period, and the strange relationship to mythical time which it confers on Paraśurāma, is the subject which I should like to explore.[1]

I should like to thank Nick Allen, John Brockington and Freda Matchett for their comments on this chapter, and also Jim Benson for comments on a previous version.

[1] It should be pointed out that although the story of Paraśurāma first appears in the *Mahābhārata* and the main features are carried over into most subsequent tellings, he is not in fact consistently recognized as an avatar until the Purāṇic accounts, and only one of the epic references gives him that status: 12.326.77. This and all other references to the *Mahābhārata* are to the critical edition edited by V.S. Sukthankar *et al.* Although this change between epic and Purāṇic accounts is important for our understanding of the development of the myth, most of the important details of the deeds themselves remain the same in both. This means that the elements which make it suitable to be counted as an avatar story are already present, even where that status is not yet conferred. Consequently, I shall bring this awareness into my discussion of the epic accounts where relevant. A similar, though less important, problem is encountered with the name of this figure, for Paraśurāma is not used in the epics, where he is more commonly called Rāma Jāmadagnya, Rāma Bhārgava or simply Rāma. Again, however, for simplicity, I shall keep to the name Paraśurāma throughout. For further discussion of Rāma Jāmadagnya's association with this name, see Goldman 1972.

The story of the events proper to Paraśurāma's own myth is first told in detail in the *Mahābhārata* and it will be useful to begin by briefly reviewing it. The fullest account is given at 3.115-17 and consists of three parts: Paraśurāma's conception through an accidental mixture of the powers and features of the top two castes which leaves him as a brahmin with the characteristics of a warrior; his slaughter of his mother Reṇukā at his father's behest; and his extermination of the *kṣatriyas* twenty-one times.[2] This last is the act for which he is best known in the *Mahābhārata*, and comes to be considered the essential deed of his avatar period, where it is seen as a necessary purging of a caste which had become corrupt and overbearing (12.326.77). The immediate cause of the massacre arises from Paraśurāma's feud with Arjuna Kārtavīrya and the consequent death of his father Jamadagni at the hands of Kārtavīrya's sons.[3] Paraśurāma vows to avenge his father's death, and does so by killing Jamadagni's murderers, along with the entire *kṣatriya* caste. The slaughter is repeated over several generations of *kṣatriyas* and Paraśurāma creates five lakes with their blood, in which he offers oblations to his ancestors (*pitṛ*). Finally dissuaded from further slaughter by the ancestors themselves, he undertakes a great sacrifice and gives the whole earth as the sacrificial fee to his priest, Kaśyapa.

Unlike the other avatars, however, when the purpose of his incarnation is completed Paraśurāma does not die or reunite with Viṣṇu. Instead he goes, or in some versions is banished, to Mount Mahendra and there he lives on, seemingly unageing, to intervene in the affairs of the world at two other critical moments: Rāma Dāśarathi's marriage to Sītā at the juncture between the second and third ages of the world, the *tretā* and *dvāpara yugas*; and then during the events surrounding the Bhārata war thousands of years later, at the juncture between the third and fourth ages, the *dvāpara* and *kali yugas*. Thus of all the avatars, Paraśurāma is the only one who is not confined historically to a particular place and time, but presents instead a strangely atemporal figure who

[2] The constituent parts of the myth are told in more detail elsewhere in the epic. The telling at 12.49 elaborates on the slaughter of *kṣatriyas*, while 13.4 concentrates on the *brahman/kṣatra* conception, being more concerned with the other product of the same mix, the sage Viśvāmitra. Although it is likely that the three parts of Paraṣurāma's myth were originally distinct, Madeleine Biardeau argues convincingly for their structural relationship in the myth as we have it (1976:190).

[3] The role and status of Arjuna Kārtavīrya is rather interesting. Although he is presented as a villain in the account at 3.115-17, in the longer version of the conflict at 12.49, an attempt is made to absolve him partially from blame: he is described as 'highly virtuous' (*paramadharmavid*, v.37) and 'ever tranquil' (*nityaṃ śamātmakaḥ*, v.38), and it is his sons alone who start the feud by stealing Jamadagni's cow without his knowledge (v.40). At several points in the wider epic narrative also, Arjuna Pāṇḍava is compared in might to Arjuna Kārtavīrya which would again suggest an ambivalent attitude to Paraśurāma's rival. Scheuer comments on this comparison, suggesting that the two Arjunas represent the dharmic and adharmic king (1982:166). For a fuller discussion of the dharmic and adharmic aspects of Kārtavīrya's characterization, see Biardeau 1970.

overlaps with two other important avatars, participating in the consecutive periods allotted to them.

Intervention in *Rāmāyaṇa* Events

Paraśurāma's appearance in the affairs of Rāma Dāśarathi is perhaps the better known and I shall treat it briefly here, returning to it in more detail below.[4] Paraśurāma appears shortly after Rāma's wedding to Sītā, as the party is returning to Ayodhya. He presents a Vaiṣṇava bow to parallel the Śaiva one strung by Rāma to win his bride, and challenges him to string this too.[5] Rāma Dāśarathi does so effortlessly and Paraśurāma, recognizing him to be Viṣṇu, honours him and returns to Mount Mahendra:

> Then, while the world was stunned, ... Rāma Jāmadagnya, his power gone, gazed at Rāma.
> Stunned by the destruction of his strength by the other's fierce energy, Jāmadagnya spoke very faintly to Rāma, whose eyes were like the petals of the lotus...
> 'By your bending of this bow I know you to be the imperishable slayer of Madhu and Lord of the gods. Good fortune to you, enemy burner.'[6]

Although it is not made explicit in the text, where Paraśurāma does not himself appear as a form of Viṣṇu, this episode is traditionally taken as representing the passing of the avatar status from Paraśurāma to Rāma Dāśarathi, and two commentators on verse 11 cite a passage from the *Nṛsiṃhapurāṇa* to illuminate it:

> Then the power of Viṣṇu passed from the body of Paraśurāma, right before the eyes of all the gods, and entered Rāma.[7]

---

[4] The account is taken from *Rāmāyaṇa* 1.73.6 ff. Here and elsewhere *Rāmāyaṇa* references are to the critical edition edited by G.H. Bhatt and V.P. Shah. The encounter with Paraśurāma does not appear in the *rāmopākhyāna* episode in the *Mahābhārata* and the critical edition does not know it. It is, however, mentioned in some northern recensions (critical edition 3, Appendix 1.14).

[5] Biardeau has discussed the odd mixture of Vaiṣṇava and Śaiva associations carried by Paraśurāma (1976:183 ff.).

[6] *jaḍīkṛte tadā loke.../ nirvīryo jāmadagnyo 'sau rāmo rāmam udaikṣata// tejobhir hatavīryatvāj jāmadagnyo jaḍīkṛtaḥ/ rāmaṃ kamalapatrākṣaṃ mandaṃ mandam uvāca ha...// akṣayyaṃ madhuhantāraṃ jānāmi tvāṃ sureśvaram/ dhanuṣo 'sya parāmarśāt svasti te 'stu paraṃtapa//* Rām.1.75.11,12,17.

[7] The translation is Goldman's (1984:395, note on 1.75.11). The account of Paraśurāma's myth in the *Brahmāṇḍapurāṇa* reinforces this point: Kṛṣṇa tells the Bhārgava he will give him part of his energy but take it back again when he incarnates as Rāma Dāśarathi, after the breaking of the bow (3.37.29-33).

Intervention in *Mahābhārata* events

Paraśurāma's participation in the *Mahābhārata* events is less immediately obvious but far more pervasive, and I shall begin by simply presenting the material before going on to discuss my own and others' interpretations of it. Paraśurāma's presence is marked in the epic in two ways: in his involvement in the narrative events themselves; and in the importance that his previous deeds seem to carry for the text, where his massacre of *kṣatriyas* is referred to so frequently that Goldman can call it 'a sort of trademark stamped across the face of the vast epic' (1977:140).

Although references to Paraśurāma's deeds are indeed scattered throughout the text, they are also mentioned at some specific points in the narrative which are worth noting here as I shall come back to them later. His actions are first recounted at the very beginning of the epic, where the Kaurava battlefield, Kurukṣetra, is identified as Samantapañcaka, the scene of Paraśurāma's massacre and lakes of blood:

> At the juncture of the *tretā* and *dvāpara yugas* Rāma, the best of warriors, repeatedly destroyed the royal *kṣatriyas*, urged on by his anger.
> When he, radiant as the fire, had destroyed the *kṣatriyas* in their entirety by his own strength, he made five lakes of blood in Samantapañcaka.
> And when the juncture between the *kali* and the *dvāpara* arrived, the battle between the armies of the Kurus and the Pāṇḍavas also took place at Samantapañcaka.[8]

The identification of Kurukṣetra with Samantapañcaka is again made towards the close of the epic when, the fighting over, Kṛṣṇa leads the Pāṇḍavas over the battlefield now strewn with the dead and points out the lakes while telling them Paraśurāma's story (12.48.7 ff.). As well as this spatial juxtaposition of the scene of the Bhārata war with the scene of Paraśurāma's massacre, the *Mahābhārata* also states in several places that the warriors taking part in the war are descended from the remnant of *kṣatriyas* that Paraśurāma left.[9] Finally, Paraśurāma's deeds are further juxtaposed with the *Mahābhārata* events when

[8] *tretādvāparayoḥ saṃdhau rāmaḥ śastrabhṛtāṃ varaḥ/ asakṛt pārthivaṃ kṣatraṃ jaghānāmarṣacoditaḥ// sa sarvaṃ kṣatram utsādya svavīryeṇānaladyutiḥ/ samantapañcake pañca cakāra rudhirahradān.../ antare caiva samprāpte kalidvāparayor abhūt/ samantapañcake yuddhaṃ kurupāṇḍavasenayoḥ//* Mbh.1.2.3, 4, 9.

[9] Descended, that is, from those who were born from the widows of *kṣatriyas* and the brahmins who impregnated them. For the identification with the *Mahābhārata kṣatriyas*, see for example 2.13.2, 12.49.79.

Vaiśampāyana narrates the tale at the start of his account of the incarnations of the epic's protagonists (1.58.4).

Whatever significance his previous deeds may have for the *Mahābhārata*, however, Paraśurāma is not simply presented as a figure from the past, but also takes a more immediate role in the events of the epic as a living character. He is present at several crucial points in the narrative, such as the royal consecration of Yudhiṣṭhira (2.49.11), for example, and at Kṛṣṇa's peace embassy to Hāstinapura, where it is he who identifies Kṛṣṇa and Arjuna as Nara and Nārāyaṇa and says it is futile to fight them (5.94.3 ff.). Interestingly, he is not at Draupadī's marriage contest (*svayaṃvara*), but his presence is significantly echoed when Karṇa asks Arjuna, who is disguised as a brahmin and fighting the assembled kings, if he is another Paraśurāma (1.181.16). As well as being present at these important episodes, Paraśurāma is also depicted as the weapons' master of three central warriors: Droṇa (1.121.16 ff.), Bhīṣma (5.178.17) and Karṇa (3.286.8). This has some significance for future events in the epic narrative: as Droṇa's teacher, he becomes indirectly responsible for the martial knowledge of the principal warriors on both sides of the war; and as Karṇa's, he is directly responsible for one of the curses which incapacitates the warrior at a crucial moment and allows Arjuna the victory.[10]

The Battle with Bhīṣma

Paraśurāma's most detailed and significant intervention in the *Mahābhārata* narrative, however, and the one I would like to look at in detail, is the battle with Bhīṣma where he champions the rejected bride, Ambā (5.174.23 ff.).[12] As with Paraśurāma's original massacre of *kṣatriyas*, this episode is again closely connected with the Pāṇḍava/Kaurava battle, and forms a clear prelude to it, recounted just before the two armies march out. Like the main battle, it takes place at Kurukṣetra (5.178.31) and is similarly presented as a reluctant battle between a disciple and his teacher, with Bhīṣma asking for Paraśurāma's

---

[11] For the main account of Paraśurāma's curse, see Mbh.12.2-3; and for its application in the battle, specified only in variants to the critical edition, see 8.1123.

[12] Ambā and her two sisters had been abducted by Bhīṣma at their *svayaṃvara* as brides for his half-brother Vicitravīrya, who was then the king at Hāstinapura. The abduction had been carried out according to *kṣatriya dharma* but Ambā, being secretly promised to another king, Śālva, begged to be released. Bhīṣma agreed, but when she returned Śālva rejected her, saying she was now Bhīṣma's. Not wanting to return to either Hāstinapura or her father's house in shame, Ambā vowed revenge on Bhīṣma and asked Paraśurāma to champion her. Although the battle between Paraśurāma and Bhīṣma is recounted just before the Bhārata war, it had in fact taken place many years previously, and Ambā herself, reborn as Śikhaṇḍin, goes on to fight in the war and is the cause of Bhīṣma's eventual death.

	Rāmāyaṇa 1.73-5	*Mahābhārata* 5.178-87
1.	RD meets PR after his wedding to Sītā (which occurs at 1.72.8 ff.)	Bhīsma's battle with PR follows his abduction of Ambā at her *svayaṃvara* (recounted at 5.170.9 ff.)
2.	PR's appearance is accompanied by evil omens and imagery of the end of the world (*pralaya*; 73.9-19)	The battle is accompanied by *pralaya* imagery and upheaval (182.5-10; 183.21-4; 185.15-21)
3.	The connection is made with PR's massacre of the *kṣatriyas* (73.20)	The connection is made with PR's massacre (178.33-5 and *passim*)
4.	RD's father tries to dissuade PR (74.5-9)	Bhīṣma's mother tries to dissuade PR (179.22 ff.)
5.	RD expresses his respect for PR and says that he does not want to kill him (75.2,6)	Bhīṣma honours PR as his teacher and says he does not want to fight with him (178.15-16)
6.	Gods, *ṛṣis*, etc. witness the battle (75.9,10,18)	Gods, *ṛṣis*, etc. witness the battle (179.19)
7.	The world 'stood stunned' (75.11)	The world 'cried alas' (185.22)
8.	PR loses his strength to RD (75.11,12)	PR reaches the limit of his strength against Bhīṣma (187.3)
9.	PR admits defeat, acknowledges RD as Viṣṇu and honours him (75.12-23)	PR honours Bhīṣma (186.35)

Table 3. Parallels between the confrontation between Paraśurāma (PR) and Rāma Dāśarathi (RD) in the *Rāmāyaṇa* and the battle between Paraśurāma and Bhīṣma in the *Mahābhārata*.

blessing before he fights, as Yudhiṣṭhira will in turn ask for his (5.180.14). The connection back to Paraśurāma's extermination of the *kṣatriyas* is repeated again at this point, and Bhīṣma boasts that Paraśurāma could only accomplish that deed because there were no *kṣatriyas* like himself alive then (5.178.36-7). After a battle lasting for a great many days, Paraśurāma reluctantly admits defeat and is persuaded by his ancestors to give up the fight:

> Child, this is far enough in the battle with Bhīṣma. Desist Great-Armed One: withdraw from this battle.
> This is enough, bless you, of your bearing a bow: relinquish it, O terrible Bhārgava, and practise austerities.[12]

This battle is important for our understanding of Paraśurāma's role, both in the *Mahābhārata* and beyond. When it is compared in detail with his confrontation with Rāma Dāśarathi in the *Rāmāyaṇa*, it becomes apparent that the two accounts bear striking similarities. I shall present these first in tabular form, to give a clearer overview of the parallels (see Table 3).

It can be seen from this table that each stage of the *Rāmāyaṇa* account (which is presented chronologically) finds a parallel in the longer *Mahābhārata* episode, even down to the connection with a *svayaṃvara* or wedding and the intervention of the protagonists' parents. Three areas are particularly significant for our understanding of the two conflicts, however: first, the eschatological emphases found in each narrative (stages 2,6,7); second, the link with Paraśurāma's own avatar deed (stage 3); and third, the manner of his defeat and his attitude to the vanquisher (stages 8,9). I shall look at each of these more closely.

Eschatological Emphases

In both accounts, the battle is witnessed by representatives of most of the world's inhabitants (gods, *ṛṣis*, etc.) and the cosmic signifiance of this not uncommon phenomenon is emphasized by phrases which suggest that the fate of the world is in the balance: the world was stunned (*jaḍīkṛte loke,* Rām. 75.11); the world cried 'alas' *hāhākṛte loke,* Mbh.185.22). Both epics reinforce this sense of cosmic crisis by their use of the imagery of world destruction and other similarly appropriate descriptions. In the *Rāmāyaṇa*, heralding the

---

[12] *vatsa paryāptam etāvad bhīṣmeṇa saha saṃyuge/ vimardas te mahābāho vyapayāhi raṇād itaḥ// paryāptam etad bhadraṃ te tava kārmukadhāraṇam/ visarjayaitad durdharṣa tapas tapyasva bhārgava//* Mbh.5.186.13-4.

appearance of Parásurāma,

> .. a wind arose shaking the whole earth and uprooting the beautiful trees.
> The sun was engulfed by darkness and nothing could be seen in any direction. Everything was covered in ash and the army seemed stupefied.
> Then, in that horrible darkness, the ash-covered army saw a man of terrible appearance, wearing a knot of matted hair.
> Inviolable as Mount Kailāsa, irresistible as the fire of time, he seemed to blaze with fiery energy.[13]

In the *Mahābhārata*, Bhīṣma describes his battle with Paraśurāma:

> Then, beseiged by my arrows, great-souled Jāmadagnya discharged a terrible spear like a blazing meteor let loose by time, its burning tip filling the worlds with fiery light.
> With blazing arrows I cut in three that spear which was approaching, brilliant as the sun at the final hour, and made it fall to the earth.
> When it was severed, Rāma, blazing with anger discharged twelve other terrible spears...
> ... variously formed, blazing with terrible splendour like twelve suns at the end of the world.[14]

Or again, further on in the account:

> Then Rāma of great vows, revived and filled with anger and impatience, manifested the supreme *brāhma* missile.
> Thereupon, in order to counteract it, I (too) employed the supreme *brāhma* missile and it blazed out as if it was showing the end of the *yuga*.
> Then nothing but fire appeared in the sky and all beings became pained, O King.

---

[13] *vāyuḥ prādur babhūva ha/ kampayan medinīṃ sarvāṃ pātayaṃś ca drumāñ śubhān// tamasā saṃvṛtaḥ sūyaḥ sarvā na prababhur diśaḥ/ bhasmanā cāvṛtaṃ sarvaṃ saṃmūḍham iva tad balam// tasmiṃs tamasi ghore tu bhasmacchanneva sā camūḥ/ dadarśa bhīmasaṃkāśaṃ jaṭāmaṇḍaladhāriṇam// kailāsam iva durdharṣaṃ kālāgnim iva duḥsaham/ jvalantam iva tejobhir//* Rām.1.73.13-14, 16-17.

[14] *tataḥ śaktiṃ prāhiṇod ghorarūpām astrai ruddho jāmadagnyo mahātmā/ kālotsṛṣṭāṃ prajvalitām ivolkāṃ saṃdīptāgrāṃ tejasāvṛtya lokān// tato 'haṃ tām iṣubhir dīpyamānaiḥ samāyāntīm antakālārkadīptām/ chittvā tridhā pātayām āsa bhūmau// tasyāṃ chinnāyāṃ krodhadīpto 'tha rāmaḥ śaktīr ghorāḥ prāhiṇod dvādaśānyāḥ...//...nānārūpās tejasogreṇa dīptā yathādityā dvādaśa lokasaṃkṣaye//* Mbh.5.182.5.8.

> And the *ṛṣis*, *gandharvas* and gods suffered greatly, O Bhārata, tormented by the force of the weapons.
> Then the earth with her mountains, forests and trees trembled, and beings, tormented by heat, greatly despaired.
> The sky was blazing, King, the ten directions smoked and the birds were not able to remain in the sky.[15]

Connections with Paraśurāma's Previous Deeds

The connection with Paraśurāma's annihilation of the *kṣatriyas* is made in the *Rāmāyaṇa* account by Rāma Dāśarathi himself:

> I have heard of that deed you performed, Bhārgava. We honour it, brahmin, for you were acquitting your debt to your father.[16]

The link is also made in several other places (73.20; 74.6-8, 23-5). In the *Mahābhārata* account, the connection is even stronger. It is referred to several times during the conflict and is emphasized by the fact, already mentioned, that the duel is fought in the same place as Paraśurāma's previous slaughter, which will be the site of the greater battle to come:

> [Bhīṣma speaks] Go, then. Return to Kurukṣetra, O you who love war. I will go there to fight you, strong-armed ascetic.
> There where you previously performed the purification for your father, I, too, having killed you, will perform your purification, Bhārgava.[17]

---

[15] *samāśvastas tadā rāmaḥ krodhāmarṣasamanvitaḥ/ prāduś cakre tadā brāhmaṃ paramāstraṃ mahāvrataḥ// tatas tat pratighātārthaṃ brāhmam evāstram uttamam/ mayā prayuktaṃ jajvāla yugāntam iva darśayat// tato vyomni prādur abhūt teja eva hi kevalam/ bhūtāni caiva sarvāṇi jagmur ārtīṃ viśāṃ pate// ṛṣayaś ca sagandharvā devatāś caiva bhārata/ saṃtāpaṃ paramaṃ jagmur astratejobhipīḍitāḥ// tataś cacāla pṛthivī saparvata/ vanadrumā/ saṃtaptāni ca bhūtāni viṣādaṃ jagmur uttamam// prajajvāla nabho rājan dhūmāyante diśo daśa/ na sthātum antarikṣe ca śekur ākāśagās tadā//* Mbh. 5.185.15,16,18-21. *Pralaya* imagery is also used of Paraśurāma at 5.174.23 when his name is first suggested to Ambā and he is described as 'radiant as the fire of time' (*kālāgnisamatejasam*).

[16] *śrutavān asmi yat karma kṛtavān asi bhārgava/ anurundhyāmahe brahman pitur ānṛṇyam āsthitaḥ//* Rām.1.75.2.

[17] *sa gaccha vinivartasva kurukṣetraṃ raṇapriya/ tatraiṣyāmi mahābāho yuddhāya tvāṃ tapodhana// api yatra tvayā rāma kṛtaṃ śaucaṃ purā pituḥ/ tatrāham api hatvā tvāṃ śaucaṃ kartāsmi bhārgava//* Mbh.5.178.33-4.[18]

In both accounts, therefore, the present crises are presented in relation to the crisis that precipitated the slaughter in Paraśurāma's own avatar period.

Manner of Defeat

In the *Rāmāyaṇa* narrative, as was shown, Paraśurāma's defeat can be understood in terms of the power of the avatar passing from him to Rāma Dāśarathi: when Rāma Dāśarathi picks up Viṣṇu's bow, Paraśuramā's strength leaves him, destroyed by the power emanating from Rāma (1.75.11-12). Once defeated, Paraśurāma relinquishes the one-sided belligerence which triggered the confrontation and acknowledges Rāma his superior: both his power and his position have been handed over. In the longer epic, although it cannot be a question of passing the power of the avatar – that would have to be to Kṛṣṇa or, by extension, Arjuna – the parallels with the *Rāmāyaṇa* account suggest that a similar sort of 'handing over' is being presented, whatever this may mean in the *Mahābhārata* context. Thus, once again, Paraśurāma provokes the conflict with his intransigence in the face of Bhīṣma's arguments and seems certain of victory:

> There your mother the Jāhnavī may see you, Bhīṣma, filled with hundreds of arrows by me, slain and fodder for vultures, herons and crows.[18]

When he is finally forced to admit defeat, however, his truculence once more evaporates and he greets Bhīṣma's victory with pleasure:

> . . . and Rāma, the great ascetic, smiling affectionately said to me:
> In this world there is no *kṣatriya* walking the earth equal to you.
> You may be gone, Bhīṣma: you have greatly satisfied me in this battle.[19]

---

[18] *tatra tvāṃ nihataṃ mātā mayā śaraśatācitam/ jāhnavī paśyatāṃ bhīṣma gṛdhrakaṅkabaḍāśanam//* Mbh.5.179.3. Bhīṣma only reluctantly agrees to fight after all attempts at pacifying the Bhārgava have failed (5.178.10-33). In the *Rāmāyaṇa*, Paraśurāma similarly refuses to be conciliated by Daśaratha's pleas for his son (1.74.5-10). Although Paraśurāma's challenge to Bhīṣma in the *Mahābhārata* episode is caused by the fact that he is championing Ambā, it is a rather dubious point of *dharma* whether Bhīṣma is in fact the cause of her predicament: see 5.173.1 ff. and 176.1 ff., where the text discusses the issue; and 1.98.50-1, where Bhīṣma consults with brahmins before reaching his decision to release Ambā. Gail (1977:36-7) and Scheuer (1982:138-42) both discuss this issue.

[19] *rāmaś cābhyutsmayan premṇā mām uvāca mahātapāḥ// tvat samo nāsti loke 'smin kṣatriyaḥ pṛthivīcaraḥ/ gamyatāṃ bhīṣma yuddhe 'smiṃs toṣito 'haṃ bhṛśaṃ tvayā//* Mbh. 5.186.34-5.

Moreover, he goes on to apologize to Ambā with the words:

> I am not able to surpass Bhīṣma, best of warriors, in battle, even though fully displaying my best weapons.
> This is the limit of my power; this is the limit of my strength. You may go as you wish, good woman – or what else can I do for you?[20]

As with Rāma Dāśarathi, he must acknowledge that he has met his match and reached the limit of his supremacy.

Analysis of Paraśurāma's Role

How then are the similarities in these two accounts to be explained? Indeed, how are we to understand Paraśurāma's intervention in the events of the two epics at all, set as they are so far apart and so long after his own lifetime? Other scholars addressing this question have answered it quite simply, and it is important to assess the strengths and weaknesses of the answers they provide before going on to look at alternative interpretations.

The first person to look in any detail at Paraśurāma's involvement in the *Mahābhārata* was Sukthankar (1936), who considered it as part of a broader concern: Bhṛgu myths in the *Mahābhārata* and the evidence they provide for an extensive Bhārgava redaction of the text. Sukthankar's work has been very influential for subsequent interpretations of Paraśurāma's role and I shall therefore look at it in some detail.

Sukthankar proceeds by working through the epic, section by section, commenting on the various signs of Bhārgava influence he comes across. In the process, he notes all of Paraśurāma's main interventions in the epic and, one by one, dismisses them as irrelevant to the narrative action. Of Paraśurāma's mention at the start of the narrative, he says: 'Strangely enough, already in the second chapter of the Ādiparvan . . . we make our acquaintance with one of the Bhārgavas, the most famous of them, Rāma Jāmadagnya . . . a character which *in reality* has no connection whatsoever with the action of the sublime tragedy which is going to be unfolded in the epic' (p.4, Sukthankar's emphasis). The Bhārgava's role as Droṇa's teacher is dismissed as 'only symbolic', on the grounds that Paraśurāma lived at the *tretā/dvāpara* juncture and thus could not have lived at the time of the *dvapāra/kali* juncture as well. He is represented as alive in the *Mahābhārata* simply because 'once the symbol is accepted, it is

[20] *na caiva yudhi śaknomi bhīṣmaṃ śastrabhṛtāṃ varam/ viśeṣayitum atyartham uttamāstrāṇi darśayan// eṣā me paramā śaktir etan me paramaṃ balam/ yatheṣṭaṃ gamyatāṃ bhadre kim anyad vā karomi te//* Mbh.5.187.2-3.

treated as real, and the myth is worked out in great detail' (p.13). Paraśurāma's appearance with other sages at Yudhiṣṭhira's consecration is viewed as incidental: 'These static figures are like mural decorations, and of no special interest to us. We shall therefore ignore them.' (p.17). His intervention at Kṛṣṇa's embassy is 'an unnecessary digression' (p.35). References to Paraśurāma's massacre at crucial moments are also dismissed. Kṛṣṇa mentions it at the consecration 'quite irrelevantly' (p.17), and its recounting on the battlefield after the war is simply because the incident 'affords an easy opportunity for another repetition of the legend of Rāma's heroic exploit' (p.42). The encounter between Paraśurāma and Bhīṣma is likewise rejected: 'In another context Rāma is said to have fought with Bhīṣma, a fight which lasted for twenty-three days but was absolutely barren of any consequence' (p.25). [21]

For Sukthankar, therefore, the answer to the puzzle of Paraśurāma's involvement in the *Mahābhārata* is straightforward: he is there largely as the result of Bhārgava interpolation and neither he nor his story have any genuine significance for the textual narrative.

Goldman, in his continuation of Sukthankar's inquiry, *Gods, Priests and Warriors: The Bhṛgus of the Mahābhārata*, further develops these points. However, his understanding of the *Mahābhārata* material remains basically the same for our purposes: Paraśurāma's participation in epic events is the result of anachronism and interpolation, and accounts of his massacre of the *kṣatriyas* serve primarily to emphasize the Bhārgavas' control of the epic itself (1977:138 ff.).

In a later work (1984), Goldman goes on to discuss Paraśurāma's involvement in the *Rāmāyaṇa*. Once again, he argues that the episode is an interpolation, forming part of 'a certain amount of originally unrelated and almost certainly later material [which] has been juxtaposed with the central part of the *Bālakāṇḍa*' (p.79). Conceding the psychological and literary importance of the story in the text, he continues (p.80):

> Nonetheless, it is clearly a later interpolation, for the figure of Rāma Jāmadagnya is proper to the *Mahābhārata* in its expanded form and was a product of the Bhārgava redactors of that work. Since the older portions of the *Rāmāyaṇa* are older than the *Mahābhārata* and the development of the figure of Rāma Jāmadagnya belongs to a relatively late stratum of the Bhārata corpus, it would follow that the episode of the encounter of the two Rāmas must be a late development in the *Bālakāṇḍa*.

---

[21] Again, Sukthankar makes no connection between Paraśurāma's role in this episode and his confrontation with Rāma Dāśarathi, even in the vulgate *āraṇyakaparvan* (Sukthankar is working from the vulgate). He describes the latter as a 'grotesque story' involving disrespect for a character held in esteem by the *Mahābhārata*; as such it belongs to legends 'quite inharmonious with the *Mahābhārata* context' (p. 21).

Other scholars concur with these points. Brockington, for example, argues that both the *Rāmāyaṇa* and the *Mahābhārata* versions of the conflict with Rāma are interpolations (1984:315, 231). Karve agrees with Sukthankar about Paraśurāma's involvement in the *Mahābhārata*, and goes on to call the *Rāmāyaṇa* account 'a grave anachronism... a forced unnatural entry for the double purpose of retrieving the honour of the *kṣatriyas* and to declare to the world the godliness of Rāma [Dāśarathi]' (1932:129-30).

It would appear, then, that any attempt to invest Paraśurāma's interventions in the affairs of Rāma or the *Mahābhārata* with a genuine narrative significance has to fly in the face of a substantial body of opinion. The different components of the myth have been severally examined and dismissed as a set of discrete incidents bearing no meaningful relationship either to each other or to the narrative of the texts which contain them. Paraśurāma's appearance in the *Rāmāyaṇa* is seen as a later addition with little relevance to the story. His appearance as a living character in the *Mahābhārata* is deemed the result of anachronism and Bhārgava enthusiasm. His conflict with Bhīṣma is again an irrelevant interpolation, and the accounts of his own massacre of the *kṣatriyas* is no more than a Bhārgava 'trade-mark' (Goldman 1977:140) with no real significance for the story unfolding around it.

The arguments put forward in each of these instances certainly appear to hold some force, and to provide a substantial barrier to any narrative, rather than textual, explanation of Paraśurāma's role. However, their strength relies largely on the various instances being taken separately. When these elements are taken together and placed more firmly against their narrative background, the overall conclusions begin to look less convincing.

The role played by Paraśurāma's own story in the *Mahābhārata* narrative is the best illustration of the importance of context and juxtaposition. While Bhārgava enthusiasm for the story may indeed explain the sheer frequency with which it is told, when the context of these tellings is taken more carefully into account, it becomes apparent that Paraśurāma's past exploits are being presented as a deliberate backdrop to the Bhārata battle. As demonstrated above, Paraśurāma's story is not merely situated haphazardly in the more accommodating parts of the epic, which would have been sufficient for Bhārgava purposes, but rather is consistently found at highly significant points in the narrative: at the opening of the epic, repeated at the start of the list of incarnations which begins the narrative account proper; immediately before the battle begins (in the encounter with Bhīṣma); and immediately after the battle has ended, retold over the bodies of the slaughtered combatants. In other words, the story is told precisely where one would expect to find it if the narrators wanted to draw out a resonance with the events unfolding in the epic. Moreover, the connection is made explicit, especially in the first reference considered (1.2.3-9) where the battlefield for the current action is identified as the scene of Paraśurāma's previous slaughter. That the two elements should be read in context, therefore, could hardly be made more obvious.

It is not surprising that the narrators should think to juxtapose Paraśurāma's slaughter of the *kṣatriyas* with the Bhārata battle in this way: at the very least it stands as an indication of the severity of the massacre about to take place, a severity seen only before at the hands of Paraśurāma. However, other similarities also exist which the juxtaposition could well be intended to highlight. Not only is the scale of the carnage comparable, but so too is its purpose: a removal of the overabundant and adharmic kings who are oppressing the earth and threatening cosmic stability. That this process has some eschatological significance in each case is again made clear by the passage setting the two events at consecutive *yugāntas* (1.2.3-9); and I shall return to the implications of this below.

I shall now turn to the general question of Paraśurāma's depiction as a living character so long after his original actions. Sukthankar's argument on this point runs as follows: Paraśurāma cannot be alive at the time of the epic, therefore he is not alive at the time of the epic; the fact that he appears to be alive can only be explained by Bhārgava enthusiasm. This clearly begs the question. Once the circular reasoning is removed, a more straightforward reading of the material as it stands suggests that Paraśurāma's portrayal as still alive is quite deliberate, and that this preternatural longevity is an essential part of his make-up. This is reflected in the epic's use of the epithet *cirajīvan* ('long-lived') which implies an indefinitely extended life-span, well in excess of the generally elongated but finite terms of existence usually allotted to mythical characters. It is also reflected in the fact that accounts of Paraśurāma's earlier deeds are left inherently open-ended: he is simply banished to Mount Mahendra with no mention made of an eventual demise. Purāṇic accounts of the banishment reinforce this continued existence, and the *Bhāgavatapurāṇa* is quite explicit about the possibility of future action:

> Lotus-eyed Rāma, the illustrious Jāmadagnya, will promulgate
> the Vedas in a future period.
> He is dwelling even now on Mount Mahendra.[22]

It is interesting to note, moreover, that this odd relationship with time, and the periods of 'dormancy' before future action which it involves, occur in another aspect of Paraśurāma's myth, namely the circumstance of his birth. As was mentioned earlier, Paraśurāma's conception comes about through an accidental mixture of *brahman* and *kṣatra* power, a mixture which endows him with a fierce nature more suitable to a warrior than a brahmin. Bhṛgu, the

---

[22] *jāmadagnyopi bhagavān rāmaḥ kamalalocanaḥ/ āgāminy antare rājan vartayiṣyati vai bṛhat// āste 'dyāpi mahendrādrau//* *Bhāgavatapurāṇa* 9.16.25-6.

sage whose boon inadvertently led to this, explains the situation to Paraśurāma's intended mother Satyavatī:

> Your son shall be a brahmin with the conduct of a *kṣatriya*; your mother's great son will be a *kṣatriya* with the behaviour of a brahmin.[23]

Satyavatī pleads that it should be her grandson rather than her son who is the war-like brahmin, and thus Paraśurāma's birth is set in motion, but delayed a generation.

Once we accept the possibility that Paraśurāma's longevity is deliberate, one of the major barriers to a meaningful exploration of his role in the epics is removed. However, another still remains: the objection that the various Paraśurāma episodes are mere interpolations to the main narrative. This objection is particularly hard to refute in relation to the *Rāmāyaṇa* episode where the evidence of interpolation is particularly strong. Although a recognition of this fact may be useful in determining the genesis and development of the episode, however, it remains largely irrelevant for an understanding of the role that the encounter plays in the narrative as a whole. Returning again to the importance of context, I would argue that the place of interpolation is at least as important as the fact of interpolation and it cannot be overlooked that the episode now forms the culminating event of the *Bālakāṇḍa* and marks the end of Rāma's boyhood. That the conflict with Paraśurāma should make narrative sense in this situation has always been maintained by the tradition itself, which has come to view it as the highly significant moment when Rāma fully becomes the avatar.[24]

The arguments against Paraśurāma's appearances in the *Mahābhārata* are also weaker than they at first appear. If we accept that Paraśurāma can indeed be alive at this time, it is no longer so fanciful to see him involved in epic events *per se*. Furthermore, his involvement is again not as haphazard as Sukthankar

---

[23] *brāhmaṇaḥ kṣatravṛttir vai tava putro bhaviṣyati/ kṣatriyo brāhmaṇācāro mātus tava suto mahān//* Mbh.3.115.25-6.

[24] There are, of course, many issues involved in the status of interpolations in a text such as the *Mahābhārata*. Not only does its oral origins make the whole question of what is and what is not an interpolation a tricky one, but its character as a narrative also affects the way we view it. Considerations applicable to texts made up of collections, such as the *Ṛgveda* or the Hebrew Bible are less relevant to narrative literature, where any skilful addition becomes part of the continuous flow of the story. As such it is reasonable to ask what relevance it has to the story, that it should have been inserted at that particular point in the narrative and not another. Of course, considerations of textual expediency and narrative relevance tend to overlap in many cases, as when myths are told at the end of a book or episode, which is at once an easy place for interpolation and a highly charged moment in the story.

suggests. His role as weapons' master is fairly consistently maintained, as is his attendance at the various turning-points in the narrative, even to the extent of tangential reference being made to it at one of the few important events he misses.[25] Nor are his appearances on these occasions merely ones of static decoration. In at least one example he plays a more active and surely important role: when he recognizes the divine identities of Arjuna and Kṛṣṇa at their peace embassy, a role reminiscent of his recognition of Rāma's true identity in the *Rāmāyaṇa* episode.

Having overcome some of the underlying objections to a meaningful analysis of Paraśurāma's role in the epics, I shall now consider the most complex and puzzling aspect of his involvement there, namely the parallels between his conflict with Rāma in the *Rāmāyaṇa* and that with Bhīṣma in the *Mahābhārata*. As demonstrated, the two incidents show marked similarities, both in their constituent elements and in their underlying concerns. These were too consistent to be explained by simple coincidence. Yet it would be difficult to find any historical explanation which would adequately account for them, without having recourse to a scenario of textual borrowing that is both convoluted and chronologically unlikely. This leaves us, therefore, with the likelihood that the similarities in the two accounts arise from the fact that they are fulfilling similar functions.

One possible functional similarity emerges from the work of Adalbert Gail, one of the two people who have looked at Paraśurāma's conflict with Bhīṣma in any detail (1977:35-9). Gail provides a more sophisticated version of the argument that Paraśurāma's defeat indicates a reassertion of *kṣatriya* supremacy, an argument encountered earlier in relation to the *Rāmāyaṇa* episode. He argues that what the conflict and its outcome in Bhīṣma's favour represent is not so much a reassertion of *kṣatriya* values as a reassertion of the values of a clearly demarcated *varṇadharma*. Paraśurāma could not defeat Bhīṣma as he could the other *kṣatriyas* because the story is being told against a different ethos where it is no longer appropriate for a brahmin to take up arms, even in the cause of *dharma*. Thus Paraśurāma, a brahmin, cannot defeat and kill Bhīṣma, the best *kṣatriya* of his generation: only another *kṣatriya*, Arjuna, can do that.

Gail's arguments are attractive and certainly throw light on some aspects of the account. However, there are also problems with his interpretation. Bhīṣma's

---

[25] In the shape of Karṇa asking Arjuna whether he is another Paraśurāma as he fights the kings at Draupadī's *svayaṃvara* (see above). The other episode where Paraśurāma is absent is the dice game and here there is no mention made of him during the specific events involved. However, it is perhaps worth noting that the reference to his presence at the royal consecration occurs not in the original account of that event, but in Duryodhana's disgruntled description of its grandeur which forms the immediate preamble to the dicing.

own rather dubious relationship to *dharma* (as a *kṣatriya* who has made a vow of celibacy more appropriate to a brahmin) makes him an unlikely vehicle for reasserting the importance of *varṇadharma*. Nor is it strictly correct to counterbalance Paraśurāma's defeat with Arjuna's victory, for although it may well be the *kṣatriya* Arjuna who will be the immediate cause of Bhīṣma's death as the text here states (5.186.19), in practice he can only achieve this with the help of the highly ambivalent figure, Ambā-Śikhaṇḍin. More important in this context, however, is the fact that Gail's reading of the conflict fails to take into account several elements which are significant both here and in the conflict with Rāma. In particular, it offers no explanation for the eschatological emphases, nor for the manner of Paraśurāma's defeat. Gail's analysis in terms of *varṇadharma*, therefore, can only go part of the way towards finding a similarity of function between the two accounts.

Scheuer has more to say about the eschatological significance of the story and thus comes closer to my own concerns. Arguing that Paraśurāma's defeat by Bhīṣma is not there simply to highlight Arjuna's later achievement, Scheuer goes on to analyse it in terms of Paraśurāma's own avatar deed and the greater battle which is about to take place. Paraśurāma's involvement at this juncture tells us that once again the world is in a situation of dharmic crisis where the relationship between the top two *varṇas* is distorted. His defeat, however, tells us that the proper battle to re-establish dharmic balance is yet to come. The fight between Paraśurāma and Bhīṣma 'n'est qu'un prologue de la grande guerre des Bhārata, sur le même champ de bataille' (1982:141). Scheuer's analysis of the function of this event thus helps both to account for the eschatological emphasis in the episode – it heralds the crisis of *dharma* in the world which will call for the intervention of an avatar – and also to highlight its role in the wider narrative context. However, Scheuer's concern is primarily with the *Mahābhārata*, and consequently he draws no parallels between this episode and the confrontation with Rāma in the *Rāmāyaṇa*.

I shall now turn to my own analysis of the two conflicts. Several different strands emerge from the material under consideration, and I shall look at each of these in turn before attempting to draw them all together. I shall focus on the following elements of the myths: first, the conflict with Rāma in the *Rāmāyaṇa*; second, the variation on this found in the vulgate *Mahābhārata*, with some considerations that arise from this; and third, the conflict with Bhīṣma in the *Mahābhārata*.

The conflict with Rāma Dāśarathi in the *Rāmāyaṇa* is the simpler of the two episodes and introduces the basic themes to be explored, namely, the manner of Paraśurāma's defeat and the eschatological emphases in the accounts. Several elements of the story feed into these themes and their significance will become clearer as I proceed. As was demonstrated, the conflict with Paraśurāma comes at an important point in Rāma's life, with his boyhood over and the events leading up to his own avatar deed about to begin. It was also shown that the encounter is significant in the affairs of the world, and is eschatologically fraught. Further on in the account, the manner of Paraśurāma's defeat was seen to be distinctive, involving a ready capitulation and reverence for the victor. The ostensible function of this in the text is to allow Paraśurāma to recognize Rāma as Viṣṇu and to acknowledge him as such to the world. When the defeat is considered more from Paraśurāma's perspective, however, a different emphasis emerges, namely, that he is meeting with his own limitation: prior to the challenge, he was feared as the invincible scourge of warriors; after it, he feels his strength destroyed and must acknowledge that his days of supremacy are over. Thus, in the *Rāmāyaṇa* account, both protagonists meet at a threshold in their own lives, a moment which is in turn seen as eschatologically charged and therefore crucial to the world. Little surprise, then, that the tradition should have interpreted this threshold as that between one avatar and another.

An interesting variation on this idea of limitation emerges from the version of the episode found in the vulgate *Mahābhārata*, where the idea of threshold is expressed in spatial terms. In this account, the two Rāmas meet at a physical boundary, the borders of Daśaratha's domain, where the power of Rāma will restrict the Bhārgava:

> Hearing that Rāma [Bhārgava] had arrived at the border of his domain, Daśaratha sent his son Rāma to honour him.[26]

The word used for 'domain' here (*viṣaya*) also highlights the interplay between spatial and existential threshold found in these two versions of the myth, as it means both sphere of influence or action as well as physical territory. The word appears elsewhere in Paraśurāma's story, at the end of his slaughter of *kṣatriyas*, when he is banished by Kaśyapa. It is found in the *Śāntiparvan* version of the tale where Kaśyapa says:

> Rāma, you must not remain here in my domain at any time.[27]

It is used again in the *Rāmāyaṇa* when the story is retold by Paraśurāma:

> When previously I gave the earth in gift to Kaśyapa, he said to me, 'You should not stay in my domain.[28]

---

[26] *taṃ vai daśarathaḥ śrutvā viṣayāntam upāgatam/ preṣayām āsa rāmasya rāmaṃ putraṃ puraskṛtam//* Mbh.3. Appendix 1.14.29-30. The idea of physical boundary is present in the *Rāmāyaṇa* account but not emphasized.

[27] *na te mad viṣaye rāma vastavyam iha karhicit//* Mbh.12.49.58. Kaśyapa banishes Paraśurāma in order to preserve a remnant (*śeṣa*) of *kṣatriyas* (v.57).

[28] *kāśyapāya mayā dattā yadā pūrvaṃ vasuṃdharā/ viṣaye me na vastavyam iti māṃ kāśyapo 'bravīt//* Rām.1.75.13.

Here again, then, at an earlier stage in his life, Paraśurāma encounters a physical and functional boundary which he must not transgress.

Accounts of Paraśurāma's banishment by Kaśyapa highlight another noteworthy feature: Paraśurāma's unusual relationship to space. Kaśyapa banishes the Bhārgava after being given the earth as his sacrificial fee, and some accounts make it clear that the extent of this gift leaves nothing remaining:

> He gave the eastern region to the *hotṛ*, the southern region to the *brahman*, the western to the *adhvaryu*, the northern region to the *udgātṛ*.
> He gave the intermediate directions to the others and the middlemost space to Kaśyapa.[29]

In the *Rāmāyaṇa* version, Paraśurāma himself states that after his banishment he no longer has a place on earth:

> Acting on the words of my teacher Kaśyapa, I promised that I would not spend a night on earth.[30]

This suggests that Paraśurāma's banishment must be to some kind of spatial no man's land. This haziness of location can also be found in the regional variations of the myth which have grown up in West and South West India. In most of these, Paraśurāma is said to have reclaimed land from the sea for his place of exile. This idea is also found in the epic, where the ocean gives him a place to dwell after his banishment from the earth; that is to say, a place whichis again outside the normal categories of space.[31] While this connection with reclaimed land may well reflect historical and geographical considerations, as

---

[29] *dadau prācīṃ diśaṃ hotre brahmaṇe dakṣiṇāṃ diśam/ adhvaryave practīcīṃ vai udgātre uttarāṃ diśam// anyebhyovāntaradiśaḥ kāśyapāya ca madhyataḥ// Bhāgavatapurāṇa* 9.16.21-2.

[30] *so 'haṃ guruvacaḥ kurvan pṛthivyāṃ na vase niśām/ iti pratijñā kākutstha kṛtā vai kāśyapasya ha//* Rām.1.75.14. Some accounts run counter to this trend and make Mahendra an earthly retreat, as is obvious from the fact that the Pāṇḍavas visit it and meet Paraśurāma there in the tour of the sacred fords (3.115-17). This visit is the occasion for the first long account of Paraśurāma's complete story and it is interesting to note that in this version Kaśyapa does not banish him, but rather the Bhārgava simply goes to Mahendra after his gift. This could suggest that the spatial anomaly grew up alongside the idea of banishment, both gaining strength as the myth developed.

[31] Rām.12.49.49. For regional versions, see Karve 1932:115 ff., 136 ff.; Janaki 1966: 59 ff.; and Charpentier 1935:12 ff.

has been argued,[32] it also serves to reinforce the idea that Paraśurāma's exile and continued existence involves him in an anomalous relationship not only with time but also with space.

Finally, I shall consider the more complex interaction with Bhīṣma in the *Mahābhārata*. The two main themes introduced by the *Rāmāyaṇa* episode are even more pronounced here: the eschatological import of the conflict is emphasized more frequently, and the change in Paraśurāma after his defeat is more marked. The *Mahābhārata* account also reinforces the idea that Paraśurāma's defeat involves a boundary or limitation to his powers which he cannot go beyond. This is made clear in his words to Ambā:

> I am not able to surpass Bhīṣma in battle...
> This is the limit of my power; this is the limit of my strength...'[33]

Paraśurāma's acceptance of the defeat is also more strongly emphasized in this account, where he greets Bhīṣma's victory with positive pleasure.

In my preliminary discussion of the episode, these similarities were taken to suggest that the conflict with Bhīṣma was still essentially a process of 'handing over'. The question was raised, however, of what this could mean in the context of the *Mahābhārata* account. If the Bhārgava's opponent in this conflict were Kṛṣṇa or Arjuna, the similarities between the two episodes would be so marked that we could answer this simply: Paraśurāma is once again handing over the avatar status to the appropriate person for the current crisis. Thus his role would become clear as being some sort of guardian figure for the avatar power. However, his opponent is neither Kṛṣṇa nor Arjuna, but Bhīṣma, and I shall now explore what this choice could signify.

One clue lies in the episode's narrative context. The conflict with Bhīṣma is recounted on the very eve of the Bhārata battle and serves in many ways as a smaller model for the great war to come. The Bhārata battle is the result of the earth seeking relief from her oppression by over-abundant and adharmic inhabitants[34] and is clearly presented as the crisis which marks the juncture of the *dvāpara* and *kali yugas*, the outcome of which will determine the world's fate and its safe passage from one period to the next.[35] Such a situation of

---

[32] According to Karve, for example, it is used as a charter myth to explain the physical characteristics of the Konkan (1932:116 ff.), while Charpentier argues that the stories reflect the historical process of brahminization in the South (1935:15 ff.). In relation to Paraśurāma's connection with the sea in these myths, it is interesting to note that in the epic his main enemy, Kārtavīrya, is called 'King of the Marshlands' (*ānūpapatir*, Rām.3.116.19).

[33] *na... yudhi śaknomi bhīṣmaṃ...viśeṣayitum...// ...me paramā śaktir...me paramaṃ balam//* Mbh.5.187.2-3.

[34] See, for example, Mbh.1.58.25 ff.

[35] See, for example, Mbh.1.2.9 cited above and 12.337.42-3.

dharmic and eschatological crisis is typically the point when the avatar intervenes to restore order and thus allow the cycle of the *yugas* to continue. If the conflict between Paraśurāma and Bhīṣma is read against this background, as its place in the narrative suggests it should be, it would appear that although the avatar of the period may not be directly involved, the struggle with the Bhārgava is nevertheless once again taking place in a situation closely involved with the avatar's essential work: the restoration of cosmic order at the critical 'joints of time'.

In the *Mahābhārata* account, therefore, I would argue that it is principally the context of the conflict rather than the protagonist which lends it meaning. However, the choice of Bhīṣma for protagonist is by no means unsuited to this interpretation. Bhīṣma is the chief warrior among the Kaurava forces and will lead them into the battle to come. He is the common elder of the warring cousins and honoured by both sides as the grandfather of the tribe. Furthermore, he is also the person who is ultimately most responsible in human terms for the current crisis, for the very reasons which made him unsuitable for Gail's purposes: his vow of celibacy results in the disputed succession which leads to the war. It could be argued, therefore, that to some extent Bhīṣma represents the Bhārata situation itself. His role as protagonist serves to highlight the context of the conflict, namely the inauguration of the battle which marks the turning-point of the *dvāpara/kali yugānta*,[36] with all that this may imply for the significance of Paraśurāma's defeat.

Conclusions

It is now possible to begin drawing together the different strands that have emerged from this analysis. First, the story of Paraśurāma's own avatar deed does in fact have genuine significance for the narrative around it: it brings into focus the scale of the massacre about to take place; and suggests that the reasons for it are similar, namely, to relieve the earth of her burden of adharmic *kṣatriyas*. In addition, Paraśurāma's appearances after this original *geste* are not simply the result of textual accident. This is borne out not only by the consistently significant points at which they occur in the narratives, but also by the fact that this extended existence is implicitly or explicitly written into accounts of his earlier life. The unusual nature of Paraśurāma's relationship to time, therefore, is an essential part of his characterization, reinforced and paralleled by a similar relationship to space.

[36] See, for example, Mbh. 5.47.59;140.6-15. Elsewhere, both the dice game and the death of Kṛṣṇa are given as the moment of the turning.

Moreover, a logic has emerged in the temporal pattern of Paraśurāma's appearances which can now be unpacked. The date of the Bhārgava's slaughter of *kṣatriyas* is rather vague in the classical texts which usually place it at an unspecified time in the past, or early in the *tretāyuga*.[37] However, there is evidence from the regional variations to suggest that he came to be associated more precisely with the *kṛta/tretā yugānta*. Babb, for example, working with villagers in Madhya Pradesh, notes that the agricultural festival of *akti* is associated both with the birthdate of Paraśurāma and with the commencement of the *tretāyuga* (1975:141). According to Karve, the *śākta*-influenced Marathi version of the *Mahābhārata* puts Paraśurāma's mother Reṇukā at the *kṛta/tretā yugānta*, to parallel Sītā at the *tretā/dvāpara* and Draupadī at the *dvapāra/kali* (1932:138).[38] As the avatars seem to be associated fairly consistently with the *yugānta* junctures, and as that between the *kṛta* and *tretā yugas* is the only one not firmly occupied by another avatar, it is not surprising to find Paraśurāma popularly located here in this way and doubtless other instances could be found in support of this. Paraśurāma's next appearance comes in the conflict with Rāma, clearly situated at the start of the crisis of the *tretā/dvāpara yugānta*. He then reappears at the time of the Bhārata events which culminate in the conflict with Bhīṣma on the eve of the battle marking the *dvāpara/kali yugānta*. The only *yugānta* where we do not find him, therefore, is that between the *kali* and *kṛta yugas* and there he is replaced by a similar figure, the brahmin warrior Kalkin.[39] Paraśurāma's appearances, therefore, are by no means temporally haphazard but rather, they consistently occur at the critical junctures between the *yugas*.

Finally, the idea of limitation and boundary has been demonstrated in each of these instances. Paraśurāma acts in a clearly demarcated arena, reaches the limits of his task, and then disappears back to the spatial and temporal sidelines, where he will wait until his reappearance at the next *yugānta*.

---

[37] See, for example, Mbh.13.4.1 which simply sets it in olden times (*purā*) and Mbh. 12.326.77 which sets in in the *tretā* (*tretāyuge bhaviṣyāmi rāmo bhṛgukulodvahaḥ*). In the *Purāṇas* a similar picture emerges: the *Brahmāṇḍa* (2.3.73.90) sets Paraśurāma in the nineteenth *tretāyuga* (with Rāma Dāśarathi in the twenty-fourth), while the *Bhāgavata* comes closest to the *yugānta*, putting his birth fourteen generations from the dawn of the *yuga* (9.14.49-15.5). As I have shown, one *Mahābhārata* reference places Paraśurāma's actions at the *tretā/dvāpara yugānta* (1.2.3), but the evidence is much stronger for allocating this *yugānta* more consistently to Rāma Dāśarathi.

[38] *kṛte ca reṇukā kṛtyā tretāyāṃ jānakī satī/ dvāpare draupadī kṛtyā kṛtyā mlecchagṛhe kalau//* Karve 1932: 138.

[39] This connection is strengthened by a reference in the *Kalkipurāṇa* to Kalkin learning at the feet of Paraśurāma (2.1-5, cited Janaki 1966:73). Scheuer discusses the similarities between Paraśurāma and Kalkin (1982:329-31). The importance of the mixture of *brahman* and *kṣatra* power found in these brahmin warrior figures for our understanding of the essential nature of the avatar has been discussed by Biardeau (1976:182 ff.).

Taking all these steps together, therefore, I would argue that it is possible to arrive at an interpretation of Paraśurāma's role in which, as I suggested earlier, he does indeed stand as a guardian, supervising a 'passing-over'. However, rather than simply involving the power of the avatar, as was seen in the *Rāmāyaṇa* episode, comparison with the conflict in the *Mahābhārata* indicates that Paraśurāma's stewardship is temporal, and that what he is guarding is, in fact, the end of the *yuga*, ensuring its passage into the crisis of the *yugānta* which will mark its turning. The logic of his presence in the *Mahābhārata*, therefore, becomes clearer: he stands there as one of the many *yugānta* 'motifs' which supply the epic with the eschatological context for the human tragedy unfolding.

Abbreviations

Mbh.	*Mahābhārata*
Rām.	*Rāmāyaṇa*

References

Babb, Lawrence A. 1975. *The Divine Hierarchy: Popular Hinduism in Central India.* New York: Columbia University Press.
Bhatt, G.H. and Shah, V.P., gen. eds. *The Vālmīki-Rāmāyaṇa: Critical Edition.* Baroda: Oriental Institute, 1960-75.
Biardeau, Madeleine. 1970. 'The Story of Arjuna Kārtavīrya Without Reconstruction.' *Purāṇa* 12.
—. 1976. 'Études de Mythologie Hindoue II: Bhakti et Avatāra.' *Bulletin de l'École Française d'Extrême-Orient LXIII.*
Brockington J.L. 1984. *Righteous Rāma.* Delhi: Oxford University Press.
Charpentier, J. 1935. 'Paraśurāma: The Main Outlines of his Legend.' *Kuppuswaṃi Shastri Commemorative Volume*, 9-16.
Gail, A. 1977. *Paraśurāma: Brahmane und Krieger.* Wiesbaden: Otto Harrasowitz.
Goldman, R. 1972. 'Some Observations on the Paraśu of Paraśurāma.' *Journal of the Oriental Institute of Baroda XXI:* 153-65.
—. 1977. *Gods, Priests and Warriors: The Bhṛgus of the Mahābhārata.* New York: Columbia University Press.
—, ed. tr. 1984. *The Rāmāyaṇa of Vālmīki, vol. I: Bālakāṇḍa.* Princeton: University Press.
Janaki, K.S.S. 1966. 'Paraśurāma.' *Purāna* 8:52-82.
Karve, I. 1932. The Paraśurāma Myth.' *Journal of the University of Bombay* 1:115-39.

Mahābhārata. Critical edition by V. S. Sukthankar *et al.* Pune: Bhandarkar Oriental Research Institute, 1933-70.

Rāmāyaṇa. The Vālmīki-Rāmāyaṇa: Critical Edition. General editors, G.H. Bhatt and V. P. Shah. Baroda: Oriental Institute, 1960-75.

Scheuer, J. 1982. *Śiva dans le Mahābhārata*. Paris: Presses Universitaires de France.

Sukthankar, V.S., *et al. Mahābhārata*. Critical edition. Pune: Bhandarkar Oriental Research Institute, 1933-70.

Sukthankar, V.S. 1936. 'The Bhṛgus and the Bhārata: A Text Historical Study.' *Annals of the Bhandarkar Oriental Research Institute* 18:1-76.

Thomas, Lynn. 1987. 'Theories of Cosmic Time in the *Mahābhārata*.' Unpublished DPhil thesis, University of Oxford.

5

Menstruation Myths

Julia Leslie

Introduction

Sudhir Kakar, the Indian psychoanalyst, argues that for the majority of Indian women female sexuality is 'a utilitarian affair', its primary value lying in 'its capacity to redress a lopsided distribution of power between the sexes' (1989:3). Since ancient times, however, that unequal distribution of power has been explained by the dominant (and predominantly male) ideology in terms of the inherent nature of women. This traditional view of women may be found encapsulated in myths and stories, or it may be confronted directly in treatises on the proper behaviour of men and women according to sacred norms (*dharma*). At its simplest, this view maintains that women are inherently wicked, that they are possessed of an uncontrollable and threatening inborn sexuality, and that they are innately impure.

I shall explore the link between notions of female sexuality and the idea of an inherent nature of women, within the narrower context of traditional Indian discourses on menstruation. First, I shall set the scene with a brief sketch of the debate on the inherent nature of women. I shall then relate two epic stories about female sexuality (one positive, one negative), and the dominant myth about the origins of menstruation. Finally, I shall look at the discourse on menstruation, and its implications for female sexuality, within three different indigenous frameworks. A reasonably objective, if not entirely accurate, account of

---

This chapter first took shape as 'Menstruation and Sexuality', a paper delivered at the Wellcome Symposium on the History of Medicine entitled The History of Medical Attitudes to Sexuality, held at the Wellcome Institute, London, on 28th June 1991. It was subsequently published as 'Some Traditional Indian Views on Menstruation and Female Sexuality' in *Sexual Knowledge, Sexual Science: The History of Attitudes to Sexuality*, ed. R. Porter and M. Teich, pp. 63-81 (Cambridge University Press, 1994).

menstruation may be found in the medical treatises of *āyurveda*, the 'science of life'. Revulsion for the female body is the keynote of the ascetic discourse, exemplified here by the debate on women in the texts of Jainism. The third framework is that provided by the religious ideology of orthodox Hinduism (that is, according to *dharmaśāstra*, 'the science or discipline of what is right'). While this last is the dominant voice of the culture, it is important that one does not generalize from it. Since Indian culture contains many subcultures, male and female, dominant and 'muted',[1] the frame of reference is vital.

The Inherent Wickedness of Women

There is plenty of evidence in Sanskrit literature for the perceived inherent wickedness of women. Much of it is reproduced in the *Strīdharmapaddhati*, an eighteenth-century Sanskrit treatise on the proper behaviour of women.[2] The author, Tryambaka, concedes that women are indeed inherently wicked. However, he goes on to argue that they are not beyond religious instruction: they can learn how to behave. His scriptural proof is the famous saying, 'good conduct destroys inauspicious marks'.[3] These 'marks' include the inauspicious potential of female nature. Tryambaka's meaning is clear. Women who listen to pandits like himself can learn to behave according to the codes of conduct (*dharma*) laid down for women. They should transform themselves into devoted wives in order that the inherent evil of their female natures may be annulled.[4] The rest of Tryambaka's treatise explains how this may be done.

The Inherent Sexuality of Women

The sexuality of women is closely related to the notion of inherent female nature. However, the familiar Indian equation between the inherent weakness and wickedness of women on the one hand and their inborn sexuality on the other is by no means obvious. For the sexuality of women is not invariably negative. In that same treatise on the perfect wife, Tryambaka recommends a 'bold confidence in sexual matters' (*prāgalbhyaṃ kāmakāryeṣu*).[5] His subsection on going to bed in the evening stresses her sexual initiative:

[1] For the classic statement on dominant and 'muted' groups see E. Ardener, 1975.

[2] An analysis and partial translation of this work is presented in Leslie 1989. All references to the *Strīdharmapaddhati* are to the reconstruction of the text in this work.

[3] *ācāro hanty alakṣaṇam*. Cf. *Manusmṛti* 4.156; *Vasiṣṭhadharmasūtra* 6.8; *Viṣṇusmṛti* 71.91 (V. Krishnamacharya edition, Adyar 1964, Mysore MS).

[4] For an analysis of Tryambaka's discussion on this topic see Leslie 1986 and Leslie 1989:246-72.

[5] *Strīdharmapaddhati* 22v.3-5; Leslie 1989:274.

> After paying homage to her husband's feet, she should go to bed. Treating her beloved in a way that gives him pleasure (*āhlādasaṃyuktaṃ kṛtvā*), she should engage in sexual intercourse (*saṃyogam ācaret*; i.e. she should make love to him).[6]

In another section, he instructs the good wife to 'make sexual advances' (*upasarpati*) to her husband at the appropriate time.[7]

Further evidence both for and against female sexuality may be found in India's great epic, the *Mahābhārata*. This vast poem, which probably evolved between 400 BCE and 200 CE, is primarily an exposition on *dharma*. The well-known story of Bhaṅgāśvana (13.12) is told in support of female sexuality; the equally well-known tale of Aṣṭāvakra and the female ascetic (13.19 ff.) takes a negative stance.

Bhaṅgāśvana is a childless king who, in order to obtain children, performs a fire sacrifice disliked by the god Indra. Bhaṅgāśvana obtains a hundred sons but, in doing so, he enrages Indra who transforms him into a woman. Abandoning both family and kingdom, the female Bhaṅgāśvana retires to the forest. There she meets a male ascetic with whom she has another hundred sons. Her ability to thrive infuriates Indra. This time, he causes the two sets of children to fight and kill each other. The carnage complete, Indra appears to Bhaṅgāśvana and (to cut a long story short) grants her a wish. Without hesitation, Bhaṅgāśvana asks the god to bring back to life the children she produced as a woman – on the grounds that the love of a woman is greater than that of a man (13.12.42). Indra revives both sets of children, and grants Bhaṅgāśvana the further wish of choosing which sex he/she would like to remain for the rest of his/her life. Bhaṅgāśvana chooses to remain a woman – on the grounds that women experience greater pleasure in sexual intercourse than men (13.12.47). This story makes a virtue of the much-maligned sexuality of women.

The fact remains, however, that most statements relating to female sexuality take the opposite view. The classic story in support of this view is that of the youth Aṣṭāvakra and the elderly female ascetic to whom he is sent in preparation for his marriage. Despite her age, the ascetic repeatedly attempts to seduce the young man, assuring him that for women there is no greater delight and no more destructive urge than sex (13.20.59-60, 64-7); that even very old women are consumed by sexual passion (13.22.4-5); and that a woman's sexual desire can never be overcome in all the three worlds (13.22.9). In the *Mahābhārata*, this story is told by the revered elder statesman, Bhīṣma, to demonstrate the true nature of women. His point is that even after the taking of

---

6 *Strīdharmapaddhati* 20r.6-7; Leslie 1989:237.

7 *Strīdharmapaddhati* 40r.1; Leslie 1989:286.

ascetic vows, even in extreme old age, a woman cannot overcome her lustful nature, and therefore one should always beware of the sexuality of women.

Similar evidence can be found elsewhere. In one of the oldest and most important collections of myths and legends, the *Mārkaṇḍeyapurāṇa* (compiled about 300 to 600 CE), we learn that sex, described as the cause of death in the world, is also the direct result of the passionate nature of women (49.28-9). The *Mahābhārata* links the origin of evil directly to the sexual passion of women (13.40.5-12). The best-known work of *dharmaśāstra*, the *Manusmṛti* (compiled between 200 BCE and 200 CE), provides the familiar saying that women are innately promiscuous, fickle-minded, lacking in love, and unfaithful to their husbands even when closely guarded; indeed, they have been possessed of an indiscriminate sexual desire since time began (9.15). This is certainly the more common prejudice.[8]

The Innate Impurity of Women

The third point in the theory of inherent female nature is provided by the allegation of innate impurity. There are two main arguments in support of this view. First, woman's lack of access to initiation and religious education means that they are unable to use sacred mantras to purify themselves.[9] Second, menstruation pollutes. Indeed, menstruation is perceived as the visible sign both of a woman's sexual appetite and of her innate impurity – and thus, arising from the combination of these two, of her propensity for evil.

At one level, of course, menstruation is simply one of the impurities of the body. The traditional list includes semen, blood, urine, faeces, ear-wax, nail-parings, phlegm, tears, dandruff, and sweat.[10] One might therefore assume that menstrual blood is no more polluting for women than, for example, semen is for men. But this is not the case. According to the powerful mythic context, menstrual blood is far more than a physical impurity; it is the inescapable reminder of women's collective guilt.

The story of Indra's brahminicide is told in a range of texts, one of the earliest and most authoritative accounts being that in the *Taittirīyasaṃhitā* (a liturgical text compiled between 800 and 500 BCE).[11] When the universe is threatened by Viśvarūpa, Indra destroys him. But Viśvarūpa is a brahmin and

[8] In this context, it is no surprise that the independent or 'fierce' (*ugrā*) goddesses are perceived as 'wild destructive females associated with rampant appetite and sexuality, and the blood of battlefield, sacrifice and menstruation' (Leslie 1989:320).

[9] Some of the causes of this historical development are discussed in Leslie 1989:36-8.

[10] See, for example, *Manusmṛti* 5.135.

[11] *Taittirīyasaṃhitā* 2.5.1 ff. For a discussion of the myth in the context of Vedic *śrauta* ritual, see Smith 1991.

Indra is condemned as a brahmin-killer. To escape the consequences of this particularly dreadful crime, Indra persuades the earth, the trees and women to assume one-third of his guilt each. In return, he grants each a wish: the earth, when dug, will heal within one year; trees, when cut, will grow again; and women, unlike all other creatures, will enjoy sexual intercourse at any time, even in advanced pregnancy. In several variations on this theme in other texts, Indra distributes his brahminicide in four parts: among rivers, mountains, earth and women in one text (Mbh.5.10.13); among fire, trees, cows and women in another (Mbh.12.329.28-41); among trees, earth, water and women in a third (*Bhāgavatapurāṇa* 6.9.6-10). In all versions, however, one recipient is constant: women. In some texts, Indra's sin causes the recipients to become impure; in others, the recipients are already impure. According to one source, Indra's guilt is offloaded onto 'foetus-killers'.[12] According to another, it is given to sinful brahmins whose crimes include such things as serving low-caste *śūdras*.[13] In yet another, it falls to those who kill brahmins.[14] In this somewhat confused context, the issue of which came first – the impurity of women or the assumption of Indra's guilt – is blurred.

Either way, the mark of Indra's guilt has two crucial implications: a cyclical fertility and a recurrent power to pollute. In the case of the earth, Indra's guilt takes the form of fissures in the ground during the dry season, the sign of an infertile (and hence inauspicious) land prior to the release of the monsoon rain. During this time, the earth should not be 'ploughed', an obvious metaphor for sexual intercourse. In the case of trees, Indra's guilt takes the form of sap, the vital juice that signals the fecundity of plant life and without which there can be no growth, no fruit; yet the not uncommon ruling that one should avoid the 'red secretions' and resin from cut trees demonstrates a power to pollute.[15] In the case of rivers, the swirling mud-red waters of the rainy season are described in terms of a symbolic menstruation: they are *rajasvalāḥ*, 'full of dirt' or 'full of passion', a word also applied (in both senses) to menstruating women. Such waters should not be entered for fear of pollution: a ruling that applies equally to muddy monsoon rivers and menstruating women.[16]

In women, Indra's guilt takes the form of menstrual blood. Menstruation is thus the sign of a woman's participation in brahmin-murder. It marks her innate impurity, her cyclical fecundity, her uncontrollable sexuality, and, by extension, the inescapable wickedness of her female nature. This is the mythic dimension of what we might call the socio-religious politics of menstruation. Before I elaborate on this further, I shall outline my three frameworks for the discourse on menstruation.

---

12 *Atharvaveda*, p.522.
13 *Skandapurāṇa* 5.3.118.141.
14 *Rāmāyaṇa* 8.86.10-16.
15 See, for example, *Manusmṛti* 5.6, *Taittirīyasaṃhitā* 2.5.4.
16 For a discussion of this point, see Salomon 1984.

Menstruation in the Context of Medical Discourse

The earliest fully developed āyurvedic work, the *Carakasaṃhitā* (probably composed in the first or second centuries BCE, and further redacted over subsequent centuries), explains that there are four criteria of truth: scriptural testimony, direct observation, inference, and reasoning. Anything contrary to reason, we are told, should be rejected as untruth.[17] To these four may be added two more: tradition and analogy.[18] According to *āyurveda*, the human body is a microcosm of the universe. The aim of *āyurveda* is to provide information about the parts and functions of that microcosm.

According to Caraka, conception occurs inside the womb as a result of the union of three things: the mail seed (*bīja*; or semen, *śukra*), the female seed (*strībīja, śoṇita*), and the descending spirit (*jīva, cetanādhātu*) impelled by the *karma* of former lives.[19] If the spirit does not descend, no life can be created and so conception does not occur. In medical texts, the 'female seed' is usually equated with the uterine blood of the mother (*śoṇita* means 'red'), and hence with menstrual blood.[20] The most common terms used to denote menstrual blood are: *ārtava*, described by Bose *et al* as 'a special and fiery variety of blood' (1971:242); and *rajas*, defined as 'the blood of a woman that appears at the time of puberty'.[21] Sexual intercourse enables the man's semen to enter the woman's uterus where it is united with her menstrual blood. The sex of the child depends on the preponderance of either semen or menstrual blood: the former produces a son, the latter a daughter; if the two exist in equal quantity, the resulting offspring is sterile, impotent, or hermaphrodite (*napuṃsaka, klība*). We are also told that conception occurring on odd days of the menstrual cycle produces females because menstrual blood increases in quantity on those days (Jolly 1977:63).

In order to create a normal foetus, both the man's semen and the woman's menstrual blood must be pure. Pure semen is described as transparent, fluid, glossy, sweet-smelling like honey, and like oil or honey in appearance. Pure menstrual blood resembles hare's blood or the colour of lac, and it leaves no stains in washed clothes.[22]

All the medical texts agree that the first three days and nights of the menstrual flow are unsuitable for conception: for then the semen is like an

---

[17] *Carakasaṃhitā, sūtrasthāna* 11.17-26.

[18] *Carakasaṃhita, vimānasthāna* 8.33.

[19] *Carakasaṃhitā, śarīrasthāna* 4.5.

[20] Mention is also made of the 'semen' of women but, according to the *Aṣṭāṅgasaṃgraha* 2.1, this plays no part in the formation of the foetus. Cf. Jolly 1977:61.

[21] *Suśrutasaṃhitā* 1.14.2.

[22] *Suśrutasaṃhitā* 3.2.17-18; *Aṣṭāṅgasaṃgraha* 2.1.96 ff.; *Aṣṭāṅgahṛdaya* 2.1.10-19.

object cast into fast flowing water and swept away by the stream.[23] During these three days, the menstruating woman should follow a strict regimen designed to encourage a successful pregnancy, a regimen deriving both from notions of health and from magical correlations relating to the future foetus. For example, she should not indulge in sexual intercourse.[24] She should eat only easily digested milk-based foods. She should not sleep too much, laugh too much, hear loud noises, and so on. Breaking these guidelines may injure the unborn child.[25]

At the end of the three days and nights, she should take a cleansing bath, put on fresh clothes and ornaments, and go to her husband. The following twelve days (or, according to some authorities, sixteen) are suitable for conception. This is the period when the woman is deemed to be in 'season' (*ṛtu*). After this period, her womb will not allow the man's semen to enter, just as the lotus closes itself at the end of the day.[26]

The resulting embryo inherits from its mother the soft parts of the body (skin, blood, flesh, fat, heart, liver, lungs, spleen, kidneys, stomach, intestines, and so on), and from its father the hard parts (bones, teeth, veins, tendons, ligaments, arteries, semen, hair and nails).[27] In particular, the child's heart is directly linked to its mother's through the umbilical cord and the placenta. Indeed, medical texts derive *dohada*, the term denoting the cravings of the pregnant woman, by folk etymology from *dvaihṛdaya*, meaning 'two-hearted', on the grounds that the hearts of the mother and child are linked in this way. Hence the ruling that one should never deny the cravings of the pregnant woman.[28] For in indulging the mother-to-be one is in fact indulging the child who still craves for the experiences of its former life.

After conception, the channels carrying the menstrual blood are obstructed by the foetus, which explains why pregnant women no longer menstruate. When a woman's blood is 'obstructed below' in this way, apart from flooding

---

[23] *Suśrutasaṃhita* 3.2.31.

[24] Somewhat at odds with this idea is the wish Indra granted to women. There are evidently two ways of approaching the question. As a general rule, *āyurveda* stresses the medical aspects and thus the prohibition on sex during pregnancy. *Dharmaśāstra* seems undecided. Some texts follow the myth, insisting that if a woman wants to make love, her husband should not refuse, right up to the delivery of her child (e.g. the *Mitākṣara* commentary on *Yājñavalkyasmṛti* 1.81; *Taittirīyasaṃhitā* 2.5.1.4-5). Others rule that she should avoid sex (e.g. *Strīdharmapaddhati* 41r.3-4 in the section on the duties of the pregnant woman; Leslie 1989:289).

[25] *Suśrutasaṃhitā* 3.2.25 ff.

[26] *Suśrutasaṃhitā* 3.3.9; *Astāṅgasaṃgraha* 2.1.198.

[27] *Carakasaṃhitā, śarīrasthāna* 3.6-7. According to this view, a child may be born of the combined seed of two women, but it will be a deformed child without bones etc., for these are provided by the seed of the male (*Suśrutasaṃhitā* 3.2.47).

[28] *Aṣṭāṅgahṛdaya, śarīrasthāna* 1.52-3: cf. *Strīdharmapaddhati* 41r.9-41v.2 (Leslie 1989:289-90).

the placenta to nourish the foetus, it also moves up to her breasts where it forms the future mother's milk.[29] This point deserves emphasis. What in religious and mythic contexts is seen as the most polluting of all substances (i.e. menstrual blood) is transformed into what in those same contexts is one of the purest (i.e. breast-milk).[30] In the context of *āyurveda*, both blood and milk are perceived simply as sources of maternal nourishment, and the process of transformation from one to the other is a physical one.[31] For *āyurveda* is concerned primarily with what are perceived to be the physical facts. While āyurvedic texts inevitably reflect to some extent the assumptions and prejudices of the culture, there is little evidence of an ulterior motive of socio-religious control. Hence the view of menstrual blood and breast-milk as nourishment for the foetus, and the stress on the mechanics of conception. Sermons on the inherent wickedness of women, on the consequences of her innate sexuality, and the polluting powers of menstrual blood, are conspicuously absent.[32]

Menstruation in the Context of Ascetic Discourse

A totally different view of both menstruation and female sexuality is provided by the ascetic mode. In the case of Indian Buddhism, Prince Siddhārtha's transformation into Śākyamuni Buddha is marked by the sensitive young man's revulsion for the sweaty sexuality of dancing girls:

> And the Future Buddha awoke, and ... perceived these women lying asleep, ... some with their bodies wet with trickling phlegm and spittle; some grinding their teeth ...; some with their mouths open; and some with their dress fallen apart so as plainly

[29] *Suśrutasaṃhitā* 3.4.24.

[30] For the symbolism of blood and milk in Purāṇic mythology, see O'Flaherty 1980:40-3. For related ethnographic material see Jeffery, Jeffery and Lyon 1989:76: 'The mother's contribution to the baby's development, then, is towards its growth rather than its essential make-up – and that, too, using defiling blood (*ganda khūn*). ... Early in pregnancy, preparations begin for nurturing the baby after birth: some blood is believed to congeal into breast milk, which remains in the breast and becomes heavy or solidified and yellow in colour ("like pus").'

[31] 'The developing foetus takes its strength from the mother's retained menstrual blood' (Jeffery, Jeffery and Lyon 1989:76).

[32] This is not the only instance in which *āyurveda* stands out against the normative tradition. Remedies are often prescribed without regard for the expectations of Hindu orthodoxy, and without either apology or explanation for breaking normative rules. For example, the wholesome properties of meat and alcohol are discussed without reference to the religious context (e.g. *Carakasaṃhitā, sūtrasthāna* 27.311; *cikitsāsthāna* 24.61). These are not the texts of unbelievers (atheists, *cārvākas*): the authors are pious enough, but their first allegiance is to the 'science of life' (*āyurveda*).

> to disclose their loathsome nakedness.[33]

A second-century retelling of the same episode describes how, when the prince saw these women lying dishevelled and twitching in their sleep, he was moved to scorn. This, he concluded, is the nature of women (*svabhāva*): 'impure and monstrous (*aśucir vikṛtaś ca*) in the world of living beings'.[34] Here is the standard (or male) ascetic identification of the phenomenal world with sensual pleasures, typified by women as essentially worldly and sexual beings. The future Buddha's aversion for the female body constitutes a step forward on his path to enlightenment.

The aversion displayed by Jain ascetic discourse is even more striking. The issue is this. The last great teacher of the Jains was Mahāvīra who may have lived around 599 to 527 BCE. He was a naked ascetic (*acelaka śramaṇa*). There is no disagreement on this point; disagreement arises only in the interpretation to be put upon this fact. Is nakedness an essential prerequisite of renunciation? Or is it merely an optional, if commendable, practice? Broadly speaking, by about 300 BCE, Jainism had split into two camps: on the one hand, the naked or 'sky-clad' Digambaras for whom nakedness was an essential part of the renouncer's path; and on the other, the 'white-clad' Śvetāmbaras for whom it was not. However, both sides agreed that women should never be naked in public – on grounds ranging from the fact of menstruation to the inherent sexuality of women, and even to their vulnerability to sexual harassment. Thus this major split came to focus on the question of whether or not women can attain salvation. For the Śvetāmbaras, initiation into the monastic life is sufficient proof of renunciation, both for men and for women (although it is conceded that the life of the renouncer is especially hard for women). For the Digambaras, the wearing of clothes (whether by men or by women) signals an incomplete renunciation, while the female body is itself proof of inadequate spiritual advancement. According to the Digambaras, then, it is impossible for a woman to attain liberation; to be more precise, the (non-gendered) individual self cannot attain salvation immediately after a lifetime as a woman. However pious she may be, the most that a woman can hope for is to be reborn in a male body; only then will she have access to the true path of renunciation (that is, the path of the naked male ascetic). This is the path which culminates in *mokṣa*, release from the cycle of rebirth.

The arguments for and against the likelihood of women attaining salvation are catalogued in the Jain texts.[35] Some of these arguments are familiar, even predictable: the male ascetic's rejection of the social and physical world; his

---

[33] From the introduction to the *Jātaka* or 'Birth stories' of the Buddha (Warren 1896:60-1).

[34] *Buddhacarita* 5.63-4. See Cowell 1894.

[35] See Jaini 1991.

contempt for women as the symbols of sexuality, procreation, and society in general; and so on. What is startling, however, is the unbridled disgust for women's bodies and, in particular, for that most physical (and, according to tradition, essentially sexual) process, menstruation. The latest contribution to the debate is found in the *Yuktiprabodha* ('Teaching Through Arguments') by the seventeenth-century Śvetāmbara author, Meghavijaya. In this work, Meghavijaya sets out to demolish eighty-six points of Digambara doctrine, including their much-disputed views regarding the salvation of women (*strīmokṣa*). *The Yuktiprabodha* includes the following statements of the Digambara point of view:

> Women, namely, those beings who have the physical sign of the human female, do not attain mokṣa in that very life for their souls do not manifest that pure transformation which is called "a Perfected Being" (Siddha).[36]
>
> ... the biologically female is distinguished ... by the fact that she has an impure body, as is evident by the flow of [menstrual] blood each month.[37]
>
> Moreover, it is said in the scriptures that on account of the constant flow of the menstrual blood, various types of minute beings are generated in the genitals of women; this also occurs on other parts of her body, such as the breasts.[38]

This picture of women's genitals and breasts as prime sources of impurity, swarming with microscopic creatures, may be contrasted with the matter-of-fact āyurvedic statement that menstrual blood and breast-milk are sources of maternal nourishment. For the Jain theologians, however, menstruation is a

---

[36] *Yuktiprabodha* 1 (Jaini 1991:162). The commentary explains: 'The specific use of the word "*dravyataḥ*" [i.e. biologically] indicates that males who possess the female libido (*bhāvataḥ*) [and thus can be considered psychologically female] are not inherently opposed to the attainment of mokṣa.' As the ensuing discussion makes clear, the Digambaras do not deny the possibility of salvation to men who are 'psychologically female' (i.e. homosexual) nor do they allow it to women who are 'psychologically male' (i.e. lesbian). The issue is not sexual or psychological orientation, or even spiritual advancement, but simply a matter of physical fact: the female body demonstrates the impurity of the soul within. The Digambara position on this point concludes: 'We therefore maintain that there is no mokṣa possible for those persons who are biologically female, because crookedness (kauṭilya) is their very nature. ... As it is often said in the world: "Falsehood, rashness, deceitfulness, foolishness, excessive greed, lack of affection and pitilessness are the innate faults of women".' (*Yuktiprabodha* 2-8).

[37] *Yuktiprabodha* 10 (Jaini 1991:166).

[38] *Yuktiprabodha* 12 (Jaini 1991:166).

form of violence (*hiṃsā*): the flow of blood destroys countless minute living beings (*aparyāpta*). Moreover, as a result of these bodily secretions and their inhabitants, women suffer from a constant itching which gives rise to continuous and uncontrollable sexual desire. This leads to the further violence of sexual intercourse. The *Yuktiprabodha* provides quotations to this effect:

> The Omniscients have said that when a man is overcome by sexual passion and engages in sexual activity, he kills 900,000 minute beings [i.e, the sperm cells in the ejaculate]...
>
> In the vagina of a woman also, beings ... are born, numbering ... up to ... 300,000.
>
> When a man and a woman unite sexually, these beings in the vagina are destroyed, just as if a red-hot iron were inserted into a hollow piece of bamboo [filled with sesame seeds].[39]

The logic is clear. How can woman become renouncers when they are never free of sexual desire and when their very bodies form the site and sources of violence against living beings?

Nor is menstruation condoned as an involuntary process. On the contrary, it is perceived as the consequence of 'a sexual volition... comparable to a man's emission of semen in a dream'.[40] As a result, menstruation – together with its underlying cause, female sexuality – creates in women two powerful emotional forces; a deep sense of shame (which compels them to wear clothes in order to hide their bodies from men); and a constant fear of sexual assault (perceived as the male response to the sexually active woman). The constant presence of these powerful emotions of shame and fear (from which men by the very nature of their bodies are deemed to be free) renders women unfit to take the higher vows of the religious mendicant.

Now this is far more than the usual negative view of menstruation, the taboo that can be observed in so many traditional cultures all over the world. It constitutes an elaborate phobia about the reproductive process and a radical contempt for women's bodies. But perhaps we need to be reminded of the context of this alarming centuries-long debate. The issue of nakedness is part of an interminable battle of wits between two opposed sects. Given the attitudes towards women in Indian literature in general, and in ascetic discourse in particular, it is unlikely that any of the male debaters cared very deeply about the salvation of women. It is far more likely, as Goldman suggests, that the

---

[39] *Yuktiprabodha* 69 (Jaini 1991: 179). These statements are presented by the *Śvetāmbara* spokesman who, while evidently accepting their validity in the case of ordinary women, argues that they do not apply to nuns who refrain from all sexual activity and who 'maintain extreme skillfullness and presence of mind'.

[40] Jaini 1991:13-14. Cf. *Yuktiprabodha* 89 and Jaini 1991:192-3, note 49.

debate was 'a kind of protracted metaphor for a struggle over the spiritual validity of the two paths of Jaina mendicancy'.[41] This is the hidden agenda. For the Digambaras, this obsessive picture of menstruation and female sexuality is a vital part of their argument that their white-clad rivals are at the same secondary level of spiritual advancement as their own pious but white-clad Digambara women. By describing the female body, and menstruation in particular, in terms calculated to disgust, and by simultaneously equating these physical processes with the need to wear white garments, the Digambaras intended to tar the Śvetāmbaras with the same polluting brush.

Menstruation in the Context of Normative Discourse

I shall now turn to *dharmaśāstra* and, in particular, to Tryambaka's views on menstruation in the *Strīdharmapaddhati*. Under the general heading of 'duties common to all women' (*strīṇāṃ sādhāraṇā dharmāḥ*), Tryambaka groups together a variety of rulings to form nine sections, one of which details 'the duties of the menstruating woman' (*rajasvalādharmāḥ*).[42] This is a loosely structured section that touches on most of the points normally made on the subject in *dharmaśāstric* texts.

The woman herself is described in a number of different ways that together demonstrate the ambivalent attitudes towards her. For example *puṣpiṇī* and *puṣpavatī* (meaning 'bearing flowers' or 'in bloom') are positive terms of almost horticultural heartiness.[43] In contrast, there is the blunt *malavadvāsas* ('she whose clothes are stained'), or the graphic *ārtavābhiplutā* ('overflowing with menstrual blood'). More euphemistic terms include *rajasvalā* ('full of impurity, or dirt, or passion'; recalling the mud-red monsoon rivers) and *strīdharmiṇī* ('she who has the duty or condition of women'). These last two terms manage to encapsulate within the definition of the menstruating woman our three themes of the inherent nature of women, sexual passion, and innate impurity.

The first point that Tryambaka makes is that 'the menstruating woman is impure for three (days and) nights'.[44] According to a famous quotation:

> On the first day, she is declared to be [as polluting as] an untouchable; on the second, [as polluting as] a brahmin-killer;

---

[41] Foreword by R. P. Goldman, in Jaini 1991:xx.

[42] Leslie 1989:283-8.

[43] The implications of these terms may not be wholly positive. In *Bhagavadgītā* 2.42, for example, the adjective *puṣpita* ('flowered'; in this context, 'flowery' speech) suggests something without substance, bearing flowers but not the all-important fruit. I am grateful to Tuvia Gelblum for this suggestion.

[44] *Strīdharmapaddhati* 33v.8-9 (Leslie 1989:283).

> on the third, [as polluting as] a washerwoman; on the fourth, she is purified.[45]

I have already discussed the significance of this impurity, and the traditional tracing of its origins to the story of Indra's brahminicide.

Equally predictable are the innumerable prohibitions relating to the menstruating woman. Some of these demonstrate her impure state: for example the ruling that she should not touch (i.e. pollute) fire; that is, she should not cook.[46] Some strive to avoid deepening that state of impurity still further: for example, she should not cut her nails. Others demand that she should not make herself attractive: for example, she should not use collyrium for her eyes, comb her hair, take a bath, or massage her body with oil.[47] Nor should she in any way suggest that she is sexually available: for example, she should not eat from her husband's plate; she should not even look at her husband. In effect, she is in no fit state to do anything.

These prohibitions are reinforced by the threat of defects accruing to the unborn child. As in the āyurvedic context, the link often reflects a magical correlation. For example, if she uses collyrium, her child will be blind in one or both eyes. If she combs her hair, he will be bald. If she massages her body with oil, he will have a skin disease. If she takes a bath, he will die by drowning. If she cleans her teeth, his teeth will be discoloured. If she cuts her nails, his nails will be diseased. If she plaits rope, her child will hang himself. If she laughs, his palate, lips and tongue will be discoloured. If she talks a lot, he will be a chatterbox. If she hears a loud noise, he will be deaf. If she runs, he will be unstable. If she roams about, he will be insane. And so on.

The most important prohibition of all is the ban on sex. If a menstruating woman makes love during the crucial three days, her child will be an untouchable, or cursed. Hence the detailed prohibitions to ensure that she is neither available nor attractive to her husband at this time.

Next come the rulings regarding the ritual bath of purification. Towards the end of the morning on the fourth day, she should cleanse herself with sixty lumps of earth (the high number indicating the depths of her impurity).[48] Then she should clean her teeth, and take a ritual bath. Pure once more, she should gaze at the sun, pray for a male child, and attend to her 'women's duties'. According to one quotation:

---

[45] *Strīdharmapaddhati* 36r.2-3 (Leslie 1989:283).

[46] Leslie 1989:284.

[47] For some of the implications of rulings relating to a woman's appearance, see Leslie 1992:198-213.

[48] This high number is exceeded by that stipulated for the polluting and inauspicious menstruating widow (Leslie 1989:286).

> When she has bathed properly, she should look at her husband's face..., or (if he is away) she should look at the sun while meditating on her husband in her mind.[49]

That evening, she should make sexual advances to her husband. A second quotation is more explicit:

> Anointed with unguents of ground turmeric and saffron, wearing bright garments, thinking of her husband's lotus foot, gazing at her own toes [i.e. keeping her eyes cast down], not looking at other men, thinking only of her husband, thinking of him as light itself..., beautifully dressed and ornamented and anointed with perfume, and in good spirits, she should go to bed.[50]

This is an entirely positive (if male-oriented) image of female sexuality. Within the framework of marriage, and in the wider context of the dharmaśāstric norm of the householder, sex in pursuit of progeny is appropriate. Within that context, female sexuality as an expression of fertility is highly auspicious.

But what if the menstrual flow does not cease on the morning of the fourth day? Tryambaka is quite clear. If bleeding continues after the fourth day, she is considered 'fit to be touched' by her husband and therefore pure with regard to sexual intercourse with her husband, that is, she should still make love to him. Until her menstrual flow has ceased altogether, however, she is not held to be 'of pure conduct' and therefore she is not 'fit to perform the ritual worship of the gods'.[51]

We may speculate on the hidden agenda here. I suggest that a number of issues are at stake. First, there is the overriding importance of establishing a pregnancy in the hope of producing sons. A blanket prohibition on sexual intercourse during the menstrual flow might prevent a couple from taking advantage of the woman's 'season'. Second, there is perhaps the desire to take the initiative out of the hands of women. A woman who does not wish to have sex, or who is anxious not to conceive, might use persistent bleeding as an excuse. Finally, vaginal bleeding remains a bodily impurity that requires some form of purification before any religious ritual. A ruling attributed to the *Smṛticandrikā*, a thirteenth-century collection of rulings on *dharma*, makes this clear:

---

[49] *Strīdharmapaddhati* 37v.3-4 (Leslie 1989:286).
[50] *Strīdharmapaddhati* 37v.5-7 (Leslie 1989:287).
[51] *Strīdharmapaddhati* 36r.6-8 (Leslie 1989:287).

> For women (who continue to bleed from the fourth) until the twelfth day, the purification (appropriate) for urine is required; a ritual bath is (prescribed for those who bleed from the twelfth) until the eighteenth day; after that, she is (again) impure for three days (i.e. it is assumed that another cycle has begun).

The distinction between vaginal bleeding and menstrual blood proper is a nice one: it gives a man maximum access to his wife's body; it makes the greatest possible allowance for pregnancy; and yet it continues to protect religious ritual from pollution.

This point is taken further. Still using the *Smṛticandrikā* as his source, Tryambaka explains that the menstruating woman loses two kinds of blood:

> That which occurs to women at the wrong time (i.e. outside the crucial three days) men call 'blood' (*raktam*); that which occurs at the right time (i.e. within those three days) is called 'menstrual blood' (*rajas*); as a result of the latter alone, she becomes impure.[52]

The distinction being made here is evidently not the āyurvedic one between pure and impure substances, between healthy and sickly menstrual blood: the consistency and colour of the blood is not discussed. Nor does it reflect the phobic response of the Jain ascetic to all female fluids. Rather it represents a clash of dichotomies. According to the pure/impure dichotomy, all impurities of the body (blood, semen, sweat and so on) render a person impure. According to the auspicious/inauspicious dichotomy, menstruation bears the added weight of two quite different elements: the mythological burden of Indra's sin of brahmin-murder, and the extreme inauspiciousness of infertility. On those first three days of her menstrual cycle, a woman is temporarily barren and, as in the case of the cracked dry earth before the monsoon rains, infertility makes her inauspicious. But on the fourth day of the menstrual cycle, whether or not the flow of blood has ceased, women are deemed to be in 'season' once more, both fertile and auspicious. Here auspiciousness overrides impurity, not entirely, but with crucial effect: 'menstrual blood' (*rajas*) is redesignated '(ordinary) blood' (*raktam*). Fertility wins the day.

Another quotation provides a more detailed definition:

> The best of wise men know that the menstruation of women is of four kinds: that which is due to illness; that which is due to (a disturbance of) the emotions; that which is due to (an imbalance

[52] *Strīdharmapaddhati* 35v.6-9 (Leslie 1989:283-4).

> of) the humours; and that which occurs at the right time (of the monthly cycle, i.e. during the crucial three days).[53]

Tryambaka concludes that only the fourth type of bleeding makes a woman ritually impure.

Finally, there are the rulings concerning the importance of making love at the proper time. These take the form of penalties or atonements enjoined for those husbands and wives who fail to take proper advantage of the opportunity to conceive. For example,

> A man who fails in his duty to his wife should put on the skin of a donkey with the hair turned outwards and go to seven houses calling (out to each in turn): '(Give) alms to a man who has failed in his duty to his wife!' And this should be his livelihood for six months.[54]

In fact, this ruling is normally cited in the context of adultery. A variety of penalties may be imposed on the wife who refuses to make love; and again, these are penalties usually associated with adultery. For example, according to one authority, she should perform a severe twelve-day penance every month for six months. According to another, she should be abandoned. According to a third, she should be devoured by dogs in a public place. An anonymous source maintains that she will be reborn as a bitch, a she-wolf, a female jackal or a female hog. Yet another authority enjoins that her husband should proclaim her publicly to be a foetus-killer and drive her out of his house. Tryambaka concludes by demonstrating that the woman who leaves her husband's house, even to return to her natal home, is assumed to be unfaithful.[55]

These rulings bring us full circle. The woman who refuses to make love with her husband at the auspicious time of her fertile season is demonstrating (albeit by implication) the promiscuity or negative sexuality commonly cited in discussions of the inherent wickedness of women. Sudhir Kakar describes this type of discourse as 'the cornerstone of the culture's official view of women', thereby acknowledging its power. These rules and images, which Kakar refreshingly dismisses as 'a collective fantasy of the wife' (1989:18-19), focus on the possible sexual abandon of adult women, and the implications of that abandon for a culture that depends upon its stability to control the sexuality of women.

In contrast, the woman who makes sexual advances to her husband at the proper time makes both herself and her sexuality auspicious. For the

---

[53] *Strīdharmapaddhati* 35v.3-4 (Leslie 1989:284).
[54] *Strīdharmapaddhati* 37v.7-9 (Leslie 1989:287).
[55] Leslie 1989:287-8.

auspiciousness of a wife lies in the gift of her fertility (and thus of progeny) to her husband and her husband's family. Puberty marks the onset of that fertility; hence the celebrations of the first menstruation in many parts of India. For the wife, the blood that signals the start of another menstrual period means several things: temporary impurity, certainly; but also proof of pregnancy lost, and thus of a temporary but exceedingly inauspicious barrenness. On the fourth day of the cycle, however, after her bath of purification, both fertility and auspiciousness return, and the scales tip the other way. Indeed the start of a woman's fertile 'season' is so powerfully auspicious that Tryambaka can write in his section on the inherent nature of women that menstruation is the mark of an all-encompassing purity unique to women:

> Women are incomparably pure; at no time are they defiled; for menstruation sweeps away their sins month after month.[56]

Conclusions

So what conclusions can we draw? For *āyurveda*, the issue is the pragmatic one of healthy versus unhealthy substances. For the male ascetic, the motive force is renunciation of the physical and sexual world, and hence contempt for women's bodies as the epitome of both. For *dharmaśāstra*, dominated by the householder code with the reproductive power of women at its core, bodily fluids are impure but fertility is auspicious. This is the dominant voice of a culture that both controls and depends upon the sexuality of women. Furthermore, as each of my three different frameworks demonstrates, fascination, disgust and fear all relate directly to the power of women to create and nourish life from the substance of their own bodies. The particular substance that serves to focus this confused attention is the essentially sexual fluid of menstrual blood.

---

[56] *Strīdharmapaddhati* 21v.9-10 (Leslie 1989:254). In fact, this is the standard argument not for the purity of women *per se*, but for the proper treatment of the wife who has been raped or abducted, or who has temporarily left her husband. When the next menstrual period demonstrates that she is not carrying another man's child, she may once more be accepted into the marital home. For some writers on *dharmaśāstra*. menstruation purifies a woman of 'mental adultery' such as impure thoughts but not of 'physical adultery'; for others, the issue is whether or not she conceives (see Leslie 1989:254-5).

References

Ardener, E. 1975. 'Belief and the Problem of Women.' In *Perceiving Women*, ed. S. Ardener. London: Dent.

Aṣṭāṅgahṛdaya, ed. Kunte and Navre. Bombay, 1939.

Aṣṭāṅgasaṃgraha, ed. Āṭhavale. Pune, 1980.

Atharvaveda, ed. S.D. Satvalekar. Bombay, 1957.

Bhāgavatapurāṇa, ed. E. Burnouf with French translation. Paris, 1840-1898.

Bose, D.M., S.N. Sen, and B.V. Subbarayappa, eds. 1971. *A Concise History of Science in India*. Delhi.

Carakasaṃhitā, ed., tr., P.V. Sharma. Varanasi 1981-1985.

Cowell, E.B., ed., tr., 1894. *The Buddha-Karita or Life of Buddha by Asvaghosha*. Oxford, 1894.

Jaini, P.S. 1991. *Gender and Salvation: Jaina Debates on the Spiritual Liberation of Women*. Berkeley: University of California Press.

Jeffery, P., R. Jeffery, and A. Lyon. 1989. *Labour Pains and Labour Power: Women and Childbearing in India*. London: Zed Books.

Jolly, J. 1977. *Medicin*. Strassburg.

Kakar, S. 1989. *Intimate Relations: Exploring Indian Sexuality*. Delhi: Penguin Books (India).

Leslie, I.J. 1986. '*Strīsvabhāva:* The Inherent Nature of Women.' In *Oxford University Papers on India: Volume 1, Part 1*, ed. N.J. Allen, R.F. Gombrich, T. Raychaudhuri, and G. Rizvi, 28–58. Delhi: Oxford University Press.

—. 1989. *The Perfect Wife: The Orthodox Hindu Woman according to the Strīdharmapaddhati of Tryambakayajvan*. Delhi: Oxford University Press.

—, ed. 1991. *Roles and Rituals for Hindu Women*. London: Pinter, 1991.

—. 1992.'The Significance of Dress for the Orthodox Hindu Woman.' In *Dress and Gender: Making and Meaning in Cultural Contexts*, ed. R. Barnes and J.B. Eicher, 198-213. Oxford: Berg Press.

Mahābhārata. Critical edition by V.S. Sukthankar *et al.* Pune: Bhandarkar Oriental Research Institute, 1927-66.

Manusmṛti, ed. V.N. Mandlik. Bombay, 1886.

Mārkaṇḍeyapurāṇa, ed. K.M.Banerjea. Calcutta, 1862.

O'Flaherty, W.D. 1980. *Women, Androgynes, and Other Mythical Beasts*. Chicago: University Press.

Rāmāyaṇa, ed. S.K. Śāstrigal. Madras, 1958.

Salomon, S. 1984. 'Legal and Symbolic Significance of the "Menstrual Pollution" of Rivers.' In *Studies in Dharmaśāstra*, ed. R.W. Lariviere, 152-78. Calcutta: Firma Klm Private Limited.

Skandapurāṇa. Veṅkateśvara Press edition. Bombay, 1909-11.

Smith, F.M. 1991. 'Indra's Curse, Varuṇa's Noose, and the Suppression of the

Smith, F.M. 1991. 'Indra's Curse, Varuṇa's Noose, and the Suppression of the Woman in the Vedic *Śrauta* Ritual.' See Leslie 1991: 17-45.
Strīdharmapaddhati. See Leslie 1989.
Suśrutasaṃhitā, ed. Jādavaji Trikamji. Bombay, 1915.
Taittirīyasaṃhitā. Pune: Ānandāśrama, 1900-08.
Vasiṣṭhadharmasūtra, ed. A.A. Führer. Pune, 1905.
Viṣṇusmṛti, ed. V. Krishnamacharya. Adyar, 1964.
Warren, H.C. 1896. *Buddhism in Translations: Passages from the Buddhist Sacred Books and Translated from the Original Pali*. Cambridge, Mass.
Yājñavalkyasmṛti, ed. Nārāyan Rām. Bombay, 1949.

6

The Struggle for Salvation in the Hagiographies of Ravidās

Peter Friedlander

Introduction

This chapter is an examination of the ways in which the hagiographies of Ravidās depict the struggle for salvation. In common with other Indic hagiographic materials these stories may be seen to function on many levels. On one level, they depict the social context of the struggle between the heterodox communities and the orthodox brahminical tradition. On the second level, they delineate the intercommunal relationships of different heterodox traditions. And on a third level, they may be seen to function as didactic tales relating to the individual spiritual struggles of Ravidās. These three levels may also be seen to represent three phases, or aspects, of the struggle itself: opposition, reconciliation and resolution.

The Sources

There are a number of textual sources which contain hagiographic material related to the life of Ravidās. Ravidās, also known as Raidās or Rohidās, was a fifteenth-century poet-saint of the *camār* community of Varanasi.[1] On the basis of the comparative study of these accounts, I propose that they may be regarded as textual exemplars of three oral traditions which underlie the extant textual traditions. The three traditions are: first, a Hindu tradition current amongst the

[1] For a detailed study of the life and works of Ravidās, see Callewaert and Friedlander 1992.

kathāvācaks who performed the *Bhakta-māl* texts; second, a Sikh tradition related to the telling of tales concerning the lives of the *bhagats*, or precursors of the Sikh gurus; and third, an oral tradition current amongst followers of Ravidās.[2]

The *Kathāvācak* Tradition

The term *kathāvācak* ('teller of tales') can be used to refer to the traditional expositors of the *Bhakta-māl* cycle of stories. The earliest textual version of this work was composed around 1600 CE by Nābhādās at Raivasa in Rajasthan. It is generally accompanied by a commentary called the *Bhaktirasabodhinī* composed in 1712 by Priyādās, a disciple of Nābhādās. These texts contain accounts of over two hundred different subjects and figures related to the Vaiṣṇava devotional movement. Included in them are references to Ravidās as a disciple of Rāmānand and a cycle of stories concerning the life of Ravidās.[3]

Another important early textual source from this tradition is the *Bhakti-ratnāvalī* of Anantadās. A collection of hagiographies of devotees composed in 1588 CE. The stories in this text and in Priyādās's work are substantially the same.[4]

Later textual exemplars of this tradition include the Rajasthani Dādūpanthī *Bhakta-māl* of Raghavadās (c.1713) and its late eighteenth-century commentary by Caturdās (see Nāhaṭā 1965). The *Pad-prasaṅga-mālā* of Nagarīdās, composed in the first half of the eighteenth century also contains an interesting short account of an incident from the life of the Ravidās belonging to this tradition (Gupta 1965:2, 360-1).

All these textual exemplars of this tradition share a common core of stories. The central episode concerns a contest before a king of Varanasi to see whether the brahmins or Ravidās have closer access to divine power. Other episodes include: first, that in a past life Ravidās was a brahmin who was reborn as a *camār* due to an error in his conduct; second, a test of Ravidās in the form of the gift of a philosopher's stone; third, Ravidās's construction of a temple; fourth, his acceptance of a Rajasthani princess as a disciple; fifth, a visit to Chittorgarh and his conflict with the brahmins there; and sixth, his final revelation of a subtle sacred thread within his own body, and his disappearance.

---

[2] These sources are cited in the order of their first written textual forms.

[3] For a description of this work, see McGregor 1984: 108-9; and for the text of its section on Ravidās, see Rūpakalā 1962:470-9.

[4] For a published version of this text, see Śarmā 1982; and for a study of its contents, see Dīkṣit 1957.

The Sikh Tradition

There are a number of references to Ravidās and his life in the Ādi Granth (1603-4) and in other Sikh works.[5] The most substantial seventeenth-century Sikh account of the life of Ravidās is found in the work called the *Premaṃbodha* ('The Ocean of Love') which was composed in 1693 by an unknown author who probably presented it at the court of the tenth Sikh Guru, Gobind Singh. This work contains accounts of the lives of seventeen *bhagats* including Ravidās.[6] All these sources include materials relating to the life of Ravidās which appear to revolve around a common core of episodes. This common core of Sikh Ravidās hagiography is probably substantially the same as the version in the *Premaṃbodha.* It contains the following episodes in its hagiography of Ravidās: first, a vision of God seen by Ravidās in a dream; second, the story of the coin and the bracelet; third, the initiation of Mīrābāī; fourth, the contest with the *śālagrāms*; and fifth, Ravidās's final vision and disappearance.

The Ravidāsī Traditions

There are no early textual sources from the followers of Ravidās for either his works or his hagiography. The earliest textual source from the Ravidāsī tradition appears to be a work called the *Ravidās-rāmāyaṇ* composed in the early twentieth century by an author from Meerut called Bakhśīdās (1911?). This is a long account of the life of Ravidās and clearly draws upon numerous sources, none of which is named in the work. It contains all the episodes mentioned above as found in the other traditions, and numerous other episodes. These include: Ravidās and the daughters of Kabīr; Ravidās and the reversal of the current of the Ganges; Ravidās and the humbling of Gorakhnāth; and Ravidās and his trials by Sikander Lodi. The range of stories in this work is very wide indeed due to the fact that, unlike in the Hindu and Sikh traditions, Ravidās is here the central figure of the work.

It is unfortunate that no earlier textual exemplars of this tradition exist, as this makes it hard to establish its relationship to the other traditions. It is possible that it represents the late nineteenth-century form of a tradition that originated with Ravidās himself and which was the source for other traditions' accounts of Ravidās's life. However, it is possible that it represents a new late nineteenth-century tradition synthesized from other traditions. In the absence of further evidence on this subject, I shall not debate it here.

---

[5] For details of these references, see Callewaert and Friedlander 1992:11-13.
[6] For the text of this story of Ravidās, see Sābar 1984:69-81.

The Social Context of the Stories

The first level of conflict which these stories depict is that of the struggle between the heterodox traditions and the brahminical orthodoxy. In this they are heir to an ancient Indian tradition of such stories, dating back at least to the time of the *śramaṇa* ascetics' opposition to Vedic orthodoxy and Buddhist conflicts with brahminical Hinduism.

Indeed it is striking that many of the themes met with in Ravidās's hagiography are also found in the lives of the Buddhist *siddhas*, the perfected masters of the late Indian Tantric Buddhists. Accounts of their lives were recorded on the basis of Indian traditions by the Tibetan Tāranāth in approximately 1600 CE. In these stories a key element is the conflict between *tīrthakas* (here signifying non-Buddhists) and the heterodox *siddhas*. There are numerous stories of conversions and contests, debates and tests before kings, and the demonstration of miraculous powers as testimonies to the validity of the *siddhas*' attainments.

The Contest Before the King

An instance of the similarity of themes in *siddha* and *sant* hagiographies, such as that of Ravidās, is shown by the central episode of the *kathāvācak* tradition, which concerns a contest before the king between Ravidās and the brahmins.

The context of this story is this. Once the brahmins became annoyed that the low-caste Ravidās was worshipping a *śālagrām*, an aniconic symbol of Viṣṇu in the form of a round black fossil from the Himalayas. The brahmins complained to the king and Ravidās was summoned to the royal court to justify his actions. It was then decided that, in order that justice should be seen to be done, a contest, or test, should be held before the king. The image, or *śālagrām*, would be placed in the centre of the court and Ravidās would sit on one side of the court, presumably with his followers, and the brahmins would sit on the other side. The test was to see who could miraculously make the *śālagrām* come to them.

The core of the episode is the contest itself. As described by Anantadās, the brahmins recited Vedic mantras all day to no avail: the *śālagrām* would not move. Then came Ravidās's turn. He began to sing a song with the refrain: 'I have come, I have come, to take refuge with you Lord'.[7] For three watches, around nine hours, he sang this song until at last he was so overcome by emotion that his eyes filled with tears and the Lord was so touched by his devotion that the *śālagrām* moved and settled in Ravidās's lap.

---

7 *āyo ho āyo dev tumh saranāṃ//* Callewaert and Friedlander 1992:184 (*pad* 8).

As a postscript to the story, in some versions, it says that it had been agreed beforehand that whoever was the victor would be carried on a palanquin through the streets of Varanasi by the losers. And so it was that the brahmins carried Ravidās through the streets with a canopy over his head on a palanquin.

It is interesting to compare this story with that of the *siddha* Kāṇhapā and Lalitacandra, king of Bengal, as told by Tārānāth. Once there was a minister of the Hindu king Lalitacandra called Kuśalanāth who was a Buddhist. He used to worship in his own home an image of a deity who was trampling on Hindu deities. When this became known to the king, his ministers urged that Kuśalanāth should be executed at once. But the king said, 'I, as a king, am obliged to investigate things more thoroughly.' He then set about discovering the truth and decided that, in order to test the powers of his own Hindu deities and Kuśalanāth's deity, there should be a test. Two paintings were made: one of Heruka (Kuśalanāth's deity) trampling on Mahéśvar (Lalitacandra's deity), and one of Maheśvar trampling on Heruka. The paintings were installed in a locked room and each party began to make offerings to their respective deities.

For seven days neither party gained any advantage. So Kuśalanāth went to his guru Kāṇhapā and asked for help. But Kāṇhapā told him nothing needed to be done; he continued to sing and dance in the cemetery where he was residing.

On the eighth day, when both parties went to look at the paintings, they saw that Heruka's image had grown larger and that Maheśvar's image had been transformed into a second image of Heruka. The king admitted defeat and allowed Kuśalanāth to continue to worship Heruka (see Templeman 1989:34-6).

Contests before kings, the embodiment of justice, are an excellent metaphor for the conflict between the brahminical orthodoxy and the heterodox traditions. It is therefore only natural that they should appear in the context of Buddhist hagiography and in the case of *sants* such as Ravidās. However; in the *siddha* stories the victory in such contests also normally transfers royal patronage to the Buddhists, whereas in Ravidās's story there is no direct statement that this occurred, only that his own right to worship as he wished was vindicated and the right of the brahmins to control him was denied by the king.

The displays of miraculous powers that form the heart of such episodes also demonstrate a continuity in the tradition of heterodox versus brahmin as a theme in Indic hagiography. It is Ravidās's absorption in his singing that moves the deity in his favour, just as it is Kāṇhapā's continued singing and dancing that accompanies (and perhaps precipitates) his devotee's victory. In both instances, it is self-abandonment that distinguishes the devotee from the calculating brahmins' blind performance of Vedic rituals and mantras. Moreover, the fact that the final miracle in Ravidās's story occurs when his eyes fill with tears recalls the *siddha* theme of 'ritual gazes' through which many of their own miracles are accomplished. The notion of vision is central to Indic mythology and the ability of perfected individuals to have visions and to create visions is a vital testimony to their exalted state. It is therefore no accident that at the moment when Ravidās's emotions reach such a level that his vision is affected, and at that moment alone, God is moved to grant his vision to his devotee.

This conflict of the brahmins and the heterodox is irreconcilable. The brahmins in these tales can never accept the right of others to worship according to their own beliefs. Thus in the tests that resolve this conflict in heterodox hagiography there can only be one outcome: the humbling of the brahmins before the power of the devotee to manifest his direct connection to the divine.

Ravidās and the Princess

A second episode in the hagiography of Ravidās which focuses on caste conflict also concerns both royalty and brahmins.

Once a Rajasthani princess came to Varanasi and, when she begged Ravidās to allow her to be his disciple, he accepted her. She then returned to her own home, Chittorgarh, and invited Ravidās to come and visit her. On his arrival, she resolved to hold a feast in his honour but her family brahmins objected and said that she could only do so if she fed them first at the feast. This is, of course, an inversion of normal precedence in which the guru should be fed first; it was also a calculated slight to Ravidās who, as an untouchable, the brahmins could not accept as the guru of their princess. She then consulted with Ravidās as to how she should act and he told her that she should feed the brahmins first as they requested. She then made all the arrangements for the feast. But when the brahmins sat down to eat they found that between every two brahmins there was a miraculous manifestation of Ravidās. They then set a messenger to Ravidās's camp and found that he was seated in meditation there. Humbled by this display of miraculous power, they then invited him to the feast and gave him a place of honour.

This theme of miraculous duplication is also found in a similar form in a story concerning Ravidās's contemporary, Kabīr. Once Kabīr was in Puri in Orissa and wished to see inside the Jagannath temple but the priests of that place would not admit him because he was an untouchable Muslim weaver, not a Hindu. However, after they sent him away and he had returned to his encampment by the seashore, the priests found that all the images in the temple had been transformed into images of Kabīr himself. Humbled by this they then had to go to him to beg his forgiveness and plead for the restoration of the statues to their former likenesses.[8]

---

[8] Based on an interview at the Kabīr *maṭh* at Puri in 1987.

Unlike the contests before the king, here the conflict is directly between the brahmins and the heterodox. The miraculous vision reveals the truth that there can be no caste purity for, by reduplicating themselves, Ravidās and Kabīr demonstrate that they cannot be excluded from any place. Moreover, the ability of the perfected disciple to reduplicate his bodily form testifies to his accomplishment. It is found as a theme in *siddha* and *sant* hagiographies and to this day is often found in the hagiographies of modern Hindu saints testifying to their greatness.

Brahminical Trickery

A third episode that focuses on caste conflict also introduces the popular theme of the attempts by brahmins to falsify miracles.

On another occasion the brahmins again complained to the king that Ravidās was worshiping a *śālagrām* and demanded a test before the king of their relative rights to worship a *śālagrām*. However, this time they thought of a way in which they felt they must be able to defeat Ravidās: they made a wooden *śālagrām*, painted it to look like a real one, and challenged Ravidās to see whose *śālagrām* could float on the Ganges. Needless to say, the brahmins' trickery was to no avail: their wooden *śālagrām* sank while Ravidās's stone *śālagrām* floated on the surface of the river 'like a duck swimming around in circles'.[9]

Another interesting parallel is found in *siddha* hagiographies where the *siddha* Saraha is challenged by brahmins about his beer drinking. Saraha throws a great stone onto the surface of the lake and says that, if it floats, it will prove that there has been no beer-drinking, and the rock duly floats (Templeman 1983:2).

In these episodes there is no possibility of a peaceful resolution of the conflict between the brahmins and the heterodox. Here Ravidās and Saraha manifest their powers over the spirits of the water, an ability which the brahmins utterly lack. This theme relates to the second level of the struggle in these stories to which I will now turn.

The Communal Context

At the second level of struggle in these stories, the struggle is between the different heterodox communities rather than with the brahmins. Here there are four possible outcomes: assimilation, exclusion, amalgamation, and inclusion.

[9] This version of the story is as told in the *Premaṃbodh*.

Each of these aspects of Ravidās's hagiography is clearly shown in the following episodes.

Assimilation

The assimilation of other belief systems into Ravidās's hagiography is apparent in his relationships with the goddess of the Ganges, Gaṅgā. Several episodes depict a close relationship between Ravidās and Gaṅgā. The most striking of these stories is first referred to in the Sikh sources and is told at length in the *Premaṃbodh*. It is also found in the Ravidāsī tradition's materials.

The context of the story is that once a brahmin was going to the Ganges to bathe and perform rituals and on the way he stopped to have his shoes mended by Ravidās. After Ravidās had mended his shoes, he gave the brahmin a coin and asked him to give it as an offering from him to the Ganges. The brahmin agreed and went to the river where he bathed and performed his own rituals, then just before he left he remembered Ravidās's coin and tossed it into the Ganges. To his astonishment, the goddess Gaṅgā manifested herself, took the coin and gave in return a beautiful gold bracelet which she told him to give to Ravidās. The brahmin, however, was overcome by greed and took it home with him instead. When his wife saw it she said to him that, when there was no food in the house, gold bracelets were useless and it would be better to sell it. So the brahmin went to the market to do so. But when he tried to sell it to a jeweller, the latter became suspicious, wondering how a poor brahmin could have such a costly bracelet, and summoned the magistrate to investigate the matter. The brahmin was then brought before the king and accused of being a thief, to which he replied that it had been a gift from Gaṅgā. But then the queen saw the bracelet, took a liking to it, and demanded that the brahmin should ask Gaṅgā for a second bracelet, or he would be executed as a thief. So the brahmin went to the Ganges and prayed to Gaṅgā to give him another bracelet, but to no avail. Eventually, he had to admit to the king that the bracelet was a gift from Gaṅgā to Ravidās. The king and his courtiers and the brahmin then all went to Ravidās's place and asked him to go with them to the Ganges to get a second matching bracelet. Ravidās replied that he was a poor working man who had no time to go to the river, but that he would get them another bracelet at once. He then prayed to the water in a vat he used for steeping leather and, as he did so, Gaṅgā raised her arm out of the vat and gave him a matching bracelet. At this the brahmin was humbled and the king and queen became the disciples of Ravidās.

In this story, there are various elements which have appeared before: the test before the king, and the struggle between Ravidās and the brahmins. What is distinctive here is that the miracle that resolves the struggle is a gift by the goddess of the waters. From the theological viewpoint of the medieval devotional movement, the intensity of Ravidās devotion moves the goddess to protect her devotee. However, from the viewpoint of the power relationship in the story, it is equally true that Ravidās is demonstrating his power over the goddess. His actions therefore testify to his assertion of power over the goddess as the spirit of the water.

There are many other close links between Ravidās and the goddess. According to Anantadās, Ravidās was born into a family that worshipped the goddess and only after his birth became worshippers of Viṣṇu. Anthropological data also shows that Ravidās's community had a world view in which the power of the goddess was central (see Briggs 1920). It is because of this importance of the goddess for his community that Ravidās must come to an accommodation with her, and this he does by asserting his authority over her and incorporating her power into his own. Another instance of this is his relationship with Lonā Camārin, a kind of magical woman who shifts in stories from human to witch to goddess, and is often regarded as Ravidās's wife.

A further striking collection of Ravidās and Gaṅgā stories is found in the Vernacular Census of Marwar for 1895 (Singh 1891:528 *passim*). These stories were all then current in Mandu, in Dhar district of Madhya Pradesh. One of the stories relates how once Gaṅgā was living with Ravidās in Mandu in the form of his beautiful daughter. A king saw her beauty and wanted to abduct here. She was then pursued by the king and his soldiers but, as they were about to catch her, she dived into a well and, as she did so, a torrent issued forth from it and drowned the king and his men.

In a sense, whether Ravidās is conceived of as conquering the goddess by his devotion or by his spiritual power amounts to the same thing: the goddess as protector, wife or daughter is always depicted as under his control. Ravidās's relationship to the Gaṅgā is thus one in which he assimilates her hagiography into his own by establishing authority over her.

Exclusion

A second struggle within the heterodox community depicted in the hagiography is that between Ravidās and the Nāths, normally personified as Gorakhnath himself. The conflict between the Nāths and other heterodox communities is an ancient theme and can be found in the Buddhist *siddha* literature. An important tale on this theme concerns the imprisonment of Jalandharipā by Gopicand, king of Bengal and devotee of Gorakhnāth, and the revenge of Jalandharipā's disciple, Kāṇhapā, upon the king for his insult to his guru and to the Buddhist *dharma*.[10] It is thus apparent that stories of Nāths

10 See the fourth instruction lineage in Templeman 1983.

versus other heterodox groups go back at least as far as the tenth century.

While none of the early hagiographies of Ravidās include any such material, later Ravidāsī sources include a wealth of Ravidās and Nāth stories. A typical modern Ravidāsī story on this theme is as follows.[11]

Once Gorakhnāth came to visit Ravidās and asked him how to attain perfection. Instead of telling him the answer, Ravidās merely offered him a drink of water from his vat for steeping leather. Gorakhnāth did not want to drink the polluted water, so he pretended to do so but spilled it on his cloak instead. When he went home he gave his cloak to Kabīr's daughter, Kamalī, to wash. As she was washing it she found the water's stain would not come out in the wash so she started to suck at it to try and loosen it; and as she did so she attained accomplishment. When Gorakhnāth saw what had happened, he went back to Ravidās to beg for a drink of this water, but Ravidās refused saying he now had no such water to give to Gorakhnāth.

Here it is notable that the conflict is depicted in a context where Gorakhnāth comes to visit Ravidās to ask something of him. This is clearly the influence of the sectarian context of the story as normally, in Nāth hagiography, Gorakhnāth is depicted as a perfected being in his own right who would have no need to ask such a question of anyone. Despite this the core of the story contains an inherent conflict, two figures disputing over who knows best about perfection, and a resolution that involves a miracle. Interestingly again, it also involves water from the leather-steeping vat, a female figure, and a concern with ritual purity – all themes already encountered in other stories too. Here, as in the stories of Ravidās and brahmins, it seems no reconciliation is possible. But it is indicative of the different relationship between the communities that the brahmins assert authority over Ravidās and are defeated by him, while Gorakhnāth asks a boon from him but fails to get it due to his caste prejudice and is thus excluded from the circle around Ravidās.

The relationship of Kamalī, the daughter of Kabīr, and Ravidās in these stories is also an indicator of the close relationship between the hagiographies of the two men. Moreover Kabīr stories often include conflict with Nāths. For instance, once Kabīr was walking on the shore of the Ganges and saw Gorakhnāth there. Gorakhnāth challenged Kabīr to a contest of miraculous powers. Gorakhnāth thrust his trident into the ground, rose up in the air, and sat in the lotus posture on its prongs. In response, Kabīr tossed his shuttlecock up so that it hung in mid-air at a higher level than Gorakhnāth, whereupon Kabīr rose up and sat on it.[12] Here the conflict is straightforward and the result different. Kabīr asserts the superiority of his doctrine over Gorakhnāth's, and demonstrates greater power, yet still acknowledges that his rival has some

[11] Based on an interview at the Ravidās temple at Rajghat, Varanasi, in 1991.
[12] Based on an interview at Kabīr Caura *maṭh*, Varanasi, in 1987.

ability. Thus Kabīr's relationship to Gorakhnāth is one of competition. However, Ravidās's relationship is one of simple exclusion: Gorakhnāth has no power and cannot obtain any. Two interesting parallels can be drawn here. First, while Kabīr's verses include much material that is closely related to Nāth yogic techniques, Ravidās's include very little indeed. Second, while Kabīr's followers have traditionally had close links with the Nāths, Ravidās's followers have always had much closer links with Vaiṣṇava devotees.

Amalgamation

Another mode of relationship between heterodox communities demonstrated by these hagiographies takes the form of an amalgamation of hagiographies. A relationship of this kind is apparent in the stories of Ravidās and Mīrābāī. The period during which this connection developed must have been prior to 1693 when, in the *Premaṃbodh*, the Rajasthani princess is identified as Mīrābāī. Indeed, a link between them appears in both its account of Ravidās's life and in its account of her life. Contemporary Ravidāsī tradition also asserts that Mīrābāī was his disciple and, to support their claim, quotes songs attributed to Mīrābāī in which she describes him as her guru. This relationship is also supported by the fact that low-caste followers of Mīrābāī in Saurashtra sing songs in the form of dialogues between Mīrābāī and her guru Ravidās (Mukta 1994).

However, it is hard to say whether this relationship dates back earlier than the mid-seventeenth century: the oldest textual sources all call the princess 'Jhālī', and it is not until the late seventeenth-century *Premaṃbodh* that she is named 'Mīrābāī'. Moreover it is not possible to date the connection back to Mīrābāī herself through her songs, as the age of these songs (rejected by some scholars as inauthentic) is unclear. Printed versions go back only to the nineteenth century and, even in manuscripts, there is little evidence that her songs appear much before the eighteenth century.

In this regard, it is also notable that the account of Mīrābāī's visit to Varanasi in the sectarian Ravidāsī work of the *Bhagavān Ravidās kī satyakathā* ('The True Story of Ravidās'; see Kurīl 1941) appears to be a reworking of Anantadās's version of the story of Jhālī, but with the name changed to Mīrābāī. However, in earlier sectarian Ravidāsī works such as Bakhśīdās's *Ravidās Rāmāyaṇ* (1911?), Mīrābāī appears only in the context of one story involving Kamalī and another relating her trials by the Rāṇā.

In the first of these stories, Ravidās was wandering in the east and he came to Multan. At a well outside the town, Mīrābāī and Kamalī were drawing water. Seeing a holy man they offered him water, and both took him as their guru and were blessed with enlightenment. Yet again this story shows the three features typical of Ravidās hagiography: water, women and miraculous realization. Due to their selfless offering of water and implied rejection of caste rules on purity, they both became part of the realized company of Ravidās's community.

Regarding the story of Kamalī, little is known other than odd references to her in the stories of the *sants*,[13] but there is a wealth of information on Mīrābāī due to her contemporary popularity. Most of this contemporary body of material does not include Ravidās in it at all, which probably indicates the context of its literature amongst caste Hindus, for where it does occur in a low-caste context, as in Saurashtra, the connection of guru and disciple is attested.

In the sectarian Ravidāsī hagiographies, there is a marked difference between Ravidās's relationship to Mīrābāī and his relationship to Gaṅgā. For Mīrābāī is never the servant of Ravidās, but rather his disciple; Ravidās is protected by Gaṅga, but he protects Mīrābāī. This then is a relationship in which the two hagiographies are fused through the device of making one devotee the disciple of another and thus empowering the devotee.

Inclusion

The fourth kind of relationship apparent in the hagiographies of Ravidās is his own inclusion into a greater hagiography. In this his greatness is subordinated to his role in a pantheon of saints. The best examples of this are his inclusion as a disciple of Rāmānand in the *kathāvācak*'s story cycles, and as a precursor of the Sikh gurus in the Sikh tales of the *bhagats*' lives.

Ravidās's inclusion in the kathāvācak *tradition*

The *Bhakta-māl* ('Garland of Devotees') by Nābhādās is an important textual landmark in the tradition of telling tales about the lives of the Vaiṣṇava devotees. Composed in about 1600, it is now often viewed as the well-spring of this tradition. However, it is not the first such hagiographical encyclopaedia as it is predated by Jain and Buddhist works, and it seems almost certain that both it and its commentaries were composed by drawing on a stock of oral traditions current at that time.

One cycle of stories within this tradition concerns the disciples of Rāmānand who are said to be twelve in number and include Kabīr, Ravidās, Pīpā and others. Whether this tradition has any historicity has been hotly debated. The traditional acceptance of this lineage as a historical as well as a hagiographic truth has been challenged by Western scholars on the grounds that the dates of Rāmānand and Kabīr are too far apart. However, recently Lorenzen has argued that the conflict can be resolved (1991:9-18). I do not propose to examine this debate here; instead I would like to stress that, whether or not the

[13] Some details are found in Lorenzen 1991.

lineage is a historical fact, it is central to the inclusion of Kabīr and Ravidās in the *Bhakta-māl* tradition that it is true in hagiographic terms. Indeed it is only due to their relationship with Rāmānand that they can be included in this cycle of stories at all. For part of Rāmānand's greatness in the stories comes from the way that, despite being an orthodox high-caste Vaiṣṇava, he converted low-caste followers in the north of India. From the viewpoint of the tellers of the *Bhakta-māl* cycle of stories, what is important about describing the *sant*s as devotees of Rāmānand is that this establishes their legitimacy as member of the lineage and, in so doing, includes them in the company of Vaiṣṇava devotees. From the viewpoint of the struggle amongst heterodox groups, it represents Rāmāsand's assertion of authority over them. Just as Ravidās himself asserts authority over Mīrābāī by accepting her as his disciple, so Rāmānand asserts his authority over Ravidās. Yet there are certain oddities about the story which are of note and indicate the problems felt by high-caste devotees, however liberal, in accepting an untouchable saint into their community.

In these stories about Ravidās, there is an apparent need to account for his caste status which is envisaged as inherently degraded. Both Anantadās and Priyādās tell how Ravidās was a brahmin disciple of Rāmānand in a previous life who due to an error in conduct related to eating meat, or accepting offerings touched by untouchables, was cursed by Rāmānand to die and be reborn as an untouchable.

Two things are notable about this. First, this story is patently of high-caste origin as its attitudes to meat-eating and untouchability are not those of the Ravidāsī community itself. Second, it does not appear to contain the element of struggle or conflict which typifies Ravidās's hagiography. It might also be viewed as an explanatory tale inserted into the cycle of stories to explain away his caste status. A similar device is employed in the case of Kabīr, who has to trick Rāmānand into becoming his guru by hiding on some steps and causing Rāmānand to trip over him and cry out 'Ram! Ram!' and, in so doing, to initiate him. Both these tales depict how Rāmānand, despite reluctance due to the origins of these disciples, is forced to initiate them.

Ravidās's inclusion in the Sikh tradition

In contrast to the evident problems encountered by the *kathāvācak*s in including Ravidās in their cycle of stories, for the Sikh tellers of the tales on which the *Premaṃbodh* is based there were no such problems. For them caste purity was not an issue and caste had no bearing on salvation, so his low-caste origins were irrelevant. Nor does the issue of the guru of Ravidās seem to have been important for them for Ravidās is depicted as having had no human guru at all. What mattered in that context was direct revelation through love alone.

The theme that runs through the whole of the *Premaṃbodh* is that of the power of love and how it manifests in the world as the link that binds the lover, love and the beloved; all of which are only aspects of one divine reality. The primary metaphor that is used to express this is that of the ocean of love. Rather than seeing the world as *saṃsār*, the ocean of suffering, the world is seen as an ocean of love that is the divine *līlā*. All that is needed is for the devotee to dive into the ocean of love and accept this view of the world.

The linking episode that relates Ravidās to this cycle of stories is a simple one. One night the devotee Ravidās dreamed that he dived into the ocean of love itself and so merged with the divine that he become a *divānā*, one intoxicated with divine love who appears like a madman to the world. It is a neat and simple manner of including Ravidās and one not incompatible with Ravidās's own hagiography. For it includes two typical Ravidāsī themes, water and revelation. Moreover, it includes a power relationship in that Ravidās when he dives into the water becomes 'under the sway of love'. In other words it subordinates Ravidās's power to the greater power of the ocean of love itself.

Thus the Sikh cycle of stories includes Ravidās by making him part of the lineage of those who are absorbed in the ocean of love, while the *kathāvācak*s include him by making him part of the lineage of Vaiṣṇava saints. The strategies for including him are thus different, and each is based upon the dominant ideologies of the host tradition.

The Personal Context

The third level at which struggle is inherent in these stories is the personal level. This can be interpreted both as representing Ravidās's own struggle for liberation and as a metaphor for the personal struggles of his devotees. To illustrate this level of struggle, it is appropriate to give three examples: Ravidās and the philosopher's stone, Ravidās and the miracle at Chittorgarh, both of these stories being from the *kathāvācak* cycle, and Ravidās's final realization from the Sikh cycle. These episodes all concentrate on the struggle between Ravidās and the divinity itself and function as testimonies to the inner strength of Ravidās as a realized spiritual teacher.

Ravidās and the Philosopher's Stone

This story was popular in the *kathāvācak* tradition and is found in various versions by Anantadās and Priyādās; it is, however, not found in the *Premaṃbodh*.

Once Ravidās was visited by someone who appeared in the guise of a holy man and offered him the gift of the philosopher's stone. He spoke to Ravidās of the poverty he lived in and showed him how with the philosopher's stone he could become wealthy; he even demonstrated this by touching Ravidās's knife with it and turning it into gold. But Ravidās was not interested: he said he preferred a steel knife to a gold one and had no use for worldly wealth, but if the stranger insisted on leaving the stone then he should tuck it under the eaves of the thatched roof. This the visitor did before he left.

A year later the visitor returned to see what Ravidās had done with the stone. To his surprise he found everything just as it had been and Ravidās no richer than when he had visited before. So he asked after the philosopher's stone and Ravidās told him that it was still where he had left it in the thatch of the hut and he was welcome to take it back now. Ravidās told the visitor that he had no use for it because he already had the true philosopher's stone: the name of Rām.

The keynote of this story is that it is a test of Ravidās. It is conflict not between Ravidās and the brahmins, or other heterodox groups, but between Ravidās and the divine. He is offered a choice between the spiritual wealth he already possesses and limitless material wealth. Unmoved by this, Ravidās shows that he values spiritual above material wealth. In terms of the power relationship here, it is of note that by refusing the gift Ravidās asserts his power over the visitor, interpreted by the tellers of this tale as God in disguise. He thus obliges God to continue to protect him and asserts his right to possess the true philosopher's stone.

It is also significant here that the form of limitless wealth offered is a philosopher's stone. Such stones are intimately connected with the alchemical traditions of the Śaiva Nāths and Buddhist *siddhas* of medieval India. That Ravidās should be offered one at all points to his connections with these communities. But that he should turn it down in favour of the Vaiṣṇava supreme treasure of the name of Rām is also significant. It is another indication of Ravidās's rejection of the Nāth path and his assertion of his authority.

As a metaphor for the personal struggle of Ravidās, the story relates to his struggle with himself rather than with God. For by rejecting the material philosopher's stone, he is asserting authority over his own material self which he sees as serving a higher purpose. Ultimately all of the other levels – communal, social and spiritual – can mean nothing if the stories do not assert that Ravidās had conquered his mind and established authority over his own nature. For the well-spring of all spiritual authority in hagiography is the individual's own realization.

Ravidās and the Miracle at Chittorgarh

The climax of the *kathāvācak* cycle of Ravidās stories occurs at the feast in his honour at Chittorgarh. Having humbled the brahmins by reduplicating his form, he is invited back to the feast. There he teaches that caste has no relationship to realization. Finally, he tears apart his own chest to reveal a luminous sacred thread that runs through his body. With this revelation of his true nature, he merges into the light and the story ends. There is a slight ambiguity in the story as it is told: it is not clear if this is merely the end of the episode, or the end of Ravidās's life. I interpret it as representing the final act of Ravidās's life and think that it should be understood to imply that Ravidās's physical form merges into the light and disappears.

This episode contains a number of elements which may have accumulated around the core image of the episode over a period of time .

The first element is the well-known theme of tearing apart the chest to reveal the heart. Probably the most famous version of this story is that of Hanumān who tears his chest open to reveal that Rām and Sītā are in his heart. It is a vivid symbol of giving testimony by the self-sacrifice of tearing open one's chest – suicide unless one has a divine protector.

The second element is the revelation of a luminous sacred thread. Within the framework of the *kathāvācak*'s story, this seems to represent Ravidās's claim that he was a brahmin in a previous lifetime. As such it acts as a mirror in the story to the first episode, Ravidās's previous birth as a brahmin. But as a symbol viewed from the point of view of the spiritual struggle, it stands not for his assertion of brahmin status but as a witness to the fact that he possesses the true sacred thread, the thread of life itself. Just as the material philosopher's stone is of no value compared to the name of Rām, so the material sacred thread is of no value to Ravidās compared to the real subtle thread of life.

This story then is again a metaphor for Ravidās's complete authority over himself. He is willing to sacrifice his physical form in order to testify to what for him is the ultimate truth. This episode is a final resolution to all the struggles in the hagiography of Ravidās. For this episode asserts that all dualities – brahmin and heterodox, Ravidās and other heterodox communities, Ravidās's material and spiritual manifestations – are in the end illusions; the only reality is the one light into which Ravidās is absorbed.

Ravidās's Final Realization in the *Premaṃbodh*

The final realization as envisaged in the *Premaṃbodh* is rather different from its *kathāvācak* parallel. In the *Premaṃbodh*, the final realisation is a private affair between God and Ravidās and occurs when Ravidās is old and at home. This echoes the way that Ravidās's original revelation in this tradition also occurs when Ravidās is alone. It recounts how, after many years of devotion, the supreme spirit finally granted Ravidās a vision of itself and offered Ravidās the gift of all the wealth in the world that he desired. Ravidās was overjoyed by the vision but had no interest in the worldly wealth he was offered. He replies that, as there was nothing that was not part of the supreme spirit, so nothing could be given or taken away: it was all one. And with this utterance the physical form of Ravidās was transformed into light and merged into the supreme light, and Ravidās's earthly existence came to an end.

It is interesting to note that the themes of testing with material wealth and merging into the light occur here together in one episode, whereas in the *kathāvācak* stories they form two separate episodes. But most striking of all is that the theme of merging into the light is common to both story cycles. In both, Ravidās's final struggle is with himself: he transcends his physical body to attain a luminous form and union with the supreme spirit.

Conclusion

In this chapter I have argued that Ravidās' hagiography should be interpreted as a multi-levelled depiction of a spiritual struggle. At a first (social) level, it belongs to the Indic tradition of stories depicting the conflict between the heterodox and the brahminical traditions. At a second (communal) level, it depicts how Ravidās coexists with other heterodox communities. On a third (personal) level, it shows how he gained mastery over his own self.

All three cycles of stories also vividly depict one of the central mysteries or paradoxes of refuge. Ravidās may be lowly and the divine all-powerful but, by taking refuge with the divine, Ravidās puts the divine into a position in which it is obliged to protect him. Thus his hagiographies serve as vehicles for a teaching that stresses that the powerless may gain supreme power if in their struggles they take refuge in the divine alone.

The evident importance of the goddess and of water in the stories is a remarkable feature of Ravidās's hagiographies. It testifies to the manner in which these Vaiṣṇava hagiographies viewed the powers of the goddess as underlying the attainments of their own pantheon of saints, and how they therefore had to incorporate her into their own cycles of stories. It is also of note that each tradition – *kathāvācak*, Sikh, and Ravidāsī – developed its hagiography of Ravidās by incorporating him as a figure of power within a spiritual lineage, a context that simultaneously endowed him with power and allowed him to empower the tradition.

Finally, it is significant that each tradition also shaped his story to fit a particular context – a Vaiṣṇava universe, a Sikh universe, or a Ravidāsī universe – but that, despite the varying contextualizations of the story and the different selections of episodes presented in each tradition, a common theme emerges from all the versions of his hagiography. For Ravidās's hagiography is centred on a life in the world that is a constant struggle: in a social context, he struggles with and defeats the brahmins; in a communal context, he struggles with other heterodox traditions and either absorbs, excludes or coexists with them; and, at a personal level, he grapples with his own nature and attains mastery over it.

References

Bhakśīdās. 1911(?). *Ravidās rāmāyan*. Meerut: Pathak Printing Press.

Briggs, G.W. 1920. *The Chamars*. Calcutta: Association Press.

Callewaert, W.M., and Friedlander, P.G. 1992. *The Life and Works of Raidās*. Delhi: Manohar.

Dīkṣit, T.N. 1957. *Paricayī sāhitya*. Lucknow: Viśvavidyālay Hindī Prakāśan.

Gupta, Kiśorīlāl, ed. 1965. *Nāgrīdās granthāvalī*. Varanasi: Nāgrīpracāraṇī Sabhā.

Kuril, Rāmcaraṇ. 1941. *Bhagavān Ravidās kī satyakathā*. Kanpur: Kṛṣṇa Press.

Lorenzen, D.N. 1911. *Kabīr Legends and Ananta-Das's Kabīr parachai*. New York: State University of New York Press.

McGregor, R.S. 1984. *Hindi Literature From its Beginnings to the Nineteenth Century*. Vol. VIII, fasc. 6 of *A History of Indian Literature*. Wiesbaden: Otto Harrassowitz.

Mukta, P. 1994. *Upholding the Common Life: The Community of Mirabai*. New Delhi: Oxford University Press.

Nāhāṭa, A., ed. 1965. *Rāghavadāskrit bhaktamāl*. (With commentary by Caturdās.) Jodhpur: Rajasthan Oriental Research Institute.

Rūpakalā, S.B., ed. 1962. *Śrībhaktamāl*. (With commentaries by Priyādās and Rupākalā.) Lucknow: Navalakiśor pres.

Sābar, J.S. 1984. *Bhagat Ravidās srodh pustak*. Amritsar: Gurū Nānak Dev University Press.

Śarmā, B.P., ed. 1982. *Bhakti-ratnāvalī*. Chandigarh: Viśva bhārtī Prakāśan.

Singh, Hardayal (Superintendent). 1891. *Maraduśumārī rāj ṃāravāḍ* Jodhpur: Johdpur State.

Templeman, D., tr. 1983. *The Seven Instruction Lineages*. Dharmsala: Library of Tibetan Works and Archives.

—. tr. 1989. *Tārānātha's Life of Kṛṣṇācāryā/Kāṇhapāda*. Dharmsala: Library of Tibetan Works and Archives.

7

Reconstructuring Spiritual Heroism: The Evolution of the Swadeshi Sannyasi in Bengal

Indira Chowdhury-Sengupta

Introduction

The central theme of this chapter is the shift that took place within the conceptualization of Hinduism in nineteenth-century Bengal. Although an outcome of interactions with Orientalist ideas, this shift was nevertheless a significant attempt at a nationalist self-portrayal. Orientalist scholarship had by this period envisioned for India a glorious past locating it on a continuum of great civilizations that shaped the world. The indigenous understanding of the Orientalist perception comprised a complex interactive process through which knowledge about the self was renegotiated. It was such a negotiation that underlay the fashioning of a nationalist identity. In this chapter, I shall explore the overlaps between, on the one hand, confrontations with colonialism and more generally the West and, on the other, the definition of an oppositional identity which set itself up through the reinterpretation and reconstruction of Hinduism by concentrating on the icon of the sannyasi[1] and the accretions it came to acquire. In order to do this, I shall first take up features that informed the redefinition of the icon of the sannyasi within the context of nineteenth-century Bengal, and then briefly consider Swami Vivekananda and the appeal of this icon to the Swadeshi[2] activists. The icon of the sannyasi, its appeal to the Bengali middle-class, and its role in constructing a nationalist identity have not

[1] Sanskrit: *sannyāsin*, *-sī*.

[2] The nationalist movement that followed in the wake of Curzon's partition of Bengal between 1903 and 1908.

been adequately explored in existing studies of nationalism in Bengal.

The resurgent nineteenth-century Hinduism described variously as Neo-Hinduism or Hindu revivalism has been the subject of many studies. Such studies, however, have generally not only neglected the multiple strands within what they define as Neo-Hinduism but they have also left unasked questions about both the social delineations of such articulations and the features which make space for a political dimension. *Europe Reconsidered*, Tapan Raychaudhuri's subtle study of three key figures within the nineteenth-century Bengali intelligentsia (1988), has contributed to our understanding of the interactions between European notions and traditional Indian ones in defining powerful trends in nineteenth-century Bengal. However, while Raychaudhuri's book focuses on perceptions of Europe, it does so in such detail that it is difficult to place the three figures within the more general context of nineteenth-century religious ferment. On the other hand, Sumit Sarkar's study of Ramakrishna Paramahamsa within the context of *bhadralok*[3] religiosity in nineteenth-century Bengal (1985a) has contributed to historically contextualizing the saint from Dakshineswar. Despite these two fine studies, the need remains to study the emerging Hindu discourse of the nineteenth century, not as a revivalism, but as a reconstruction which took over notions from the religious sphere and translated them into principles that were perceived as permeating every aspect of a national culture. I shall argue that, in nineteenth-century Bengal, the components of Hinduism that were employed to define a national culture transcended accepted religious precepts, making Hindu spirituality a mode of resistance for the middle-class Bengali élite as it framed its own identity within the colonial ambience.

The Physical/Spiritual Dichotomy

Early Orientalist scholarship, which claimed to discover ancient Indian culture, had set up the dichotomy between the supposedly eternal spiritual values of the East and the materialistic values of the West. While Orientalist discourse abstracted the imagined essences of Indian culture, the missionary effort grappled with the meaning of the various religious practices encountered. These confrontations threw up questions that were carried over from the Enlightenment, questions that differentiated what was deemed civilized and cultured from the barbaric and primitive. Such interactions brought into Orientalist debates a dichotomy between the ancient practices which were perceived to be pure and thus closer in essence to 'Hinduism', and present-day customs which

[3] A Bengali term meaning literally 'respectable' but in colonial India denoting the English-educated middle-class Bengali.

were dismissed as debased. This stance resulted in an important link being established between the glorious Aryan past and what was believed to be true Hinduism. It was in fact this new wave of Orientalist findings that gave the nineteenth-century reconstruction of Hinduism its drive and direction. That is not to say that the reconstructed Hinduism defined itself in Orientalist terms. While Orientalist scholarship evolved a redefinition of what was Hindu, these notions were evaluated and appropriated at various levels of meaning. The Orientalist dichotomy between the gentle Hindu and the barbaric Muslim (with the underlying emphasis on civilized Christian attempts to understand the Hindus) was appropriated by the Hindu discourse and reallocated with a different set of dichotomies. In Bengal at least, this shift was informed by the colonial emphasis on the physical debility of the Bengalis and by the elaboration of the theory of the martial races that excluded Bengalis. A report in the *Amrita Bazar Patrika* on 4 February 1875 (RNPB 1875(6):3) typifies this appropriation:

> (During the Mahomedan period) ... we kept our political privileges – we were allowed to march to battle – ... and gymnastic exercises were in vogue ... These all produced cheerfulness in our hearts, gave strength to our bodies and kept disease at a distance.

While the Muslim ruler is seen as comparatively unselfish, what is perceived as the direct and confrontational Muslim style of functioning is set up as another dichotomy. A report in the Dacca *Saraswat Patra* on 27 September 1890 (RNPB 1890(40):944) warns of the insidious nature of friendships which plant anti-Hindu ideas in Hindu minds:

> Hinduism is now under greater danger than it was in any former time, because anti-Hindu ideas do not now try to *force* themselves upon the minds of the Hindus as in the days of the Mussulman rule, but seek entrance into their hearts in the seductive garb of friends. And whereas all enemies of Hinduism in former times were outside the pale of Hindu society, there are amongst its enemies at the present time misguided Hindus themselves who are working the ruin of their own society and religion.

The nineteenth-century discourse of a reconstructed Hinduism attempted to build on these dichotomies in order to create a cohesive group which could shield and protect from colonial intervention. At the ideational level, it both valorized the qualities that the Hindu was said to possess in the past and emphasized with renewed vigour the integration of the physical with the mental.

Bankim Chandra Chattopadhyay, writing *Dharma-Tattva* in 1888, gives the notion of *dharma* such a consolidated definition. In Chapter V (entitled *Anuṣīlan*, literally 'Practice'), he defines this concept incorporating positivistic, Western notions as well as indigenous ones that had been invoked in the debate. In Bankim, as also in other participants in such debates, there is an anxiety to draw the boundaries of the discourse carefully, so that the end-product is a recognizable attempt at self-definition. *Dharma-Tattva* is cast in the form of a dialogue between a guru and a disciple. When the disciple imputes to the guru an appropriation of Western notions in his definition of *dharma*, the latter replies:

> I am not exactly following the ways of the Occident and I trust that I am not bound to. Indeed, my purpose would find fulfilment in following Truth. We have now categorized all the faculties of man into four: 1) Physical, 2) Intellectual, 3) Executive, 4) Aesthetic. The just development and growth of all these and their balance is humanism. (*Bankim Racanā balī* vol.2, p.595)

Bankim's definition of *dharma*, though framed in humanistic terms, is identified as something that pervades every aspect of a Hindu's life. He takes great pains to emphasize the importance of the physical and the need to cultivate bodily strength – a concern that includes diet. Interestingly, Bankim's guru draws upon the *Bhagavadgītā* to illustrate his point. 'The suitable diet of a righteous man', says he, 'is that which increases longevity, enthusiasm, health and strength; it is that which is palatable, cooling and heartening, above all nutritious and also looks appetizing' (p.60). Apart from its emphasis on the physical, the notion of *karma* embodied in the *Gītā* gained in significance during the nineteenth century in Bengal. The notion of *karma* shifts from the Orientalist understanding of it in terms of fate that is inescapable to a notion imbued with activism in work. Action and *karmayoga* became for the nineteenth-century Bengali intelligentsia the principle ethics of action. The space occupied by the *Upaniṣads* in the early nineteenth century – with Ram Mohun Roy and Debendranath Tagore basing their reinterpretation of Hindu principles on these texts – comes to be occupied by the *Gītā* in the late nineteenth and early twentieth centuries. The reasons for this have been variously attributed to the growth of nationalism (e.g. Ray 1986) and to the rise of the middle-class intelligentsia (e.g. Subramaniam 1987). In a recent study, Sudipta Kaviraj has analysed Bankim's concern with the figure of Krishna as an exemplary Hindu (1987:81). The notion of an ideal Hindu, and the qualities that defined him remained an important concern throughout the nineteenth century in Bengal. This translated itself, as will become clear, into the image of the ascetic or sannyasi. The interrogation of masculinity, prompted by the colonial scepticism about its existence among the Bengali Hindus, furthered the synthesis of a masculinity reformulated in terms of ascetic rigour. The image of the sannyasi itself implied a heroic capacity to bear hardships and undertake penance, but the integration of the notion of sacrifice in political terms – in terms of a selfless devotion to the cause of the shackled Motherland – endowed this figure with an increased resonance in nineteenth-century Bengal.

Reconstructing the Sannyasi Icon

The image of the wandering sannyasi was not created by the nineteenth-century Hindu discourse. It had its particular descriptive reverberation within the various Hindu sects. In scriptural constructions it was juxtaposed with the notion of *brahmacarya* and understood to be a stage or a choice available to the devout Hindu. In the context of the nineteenth century, however, the significance of the sannyasi figure was shaped as much by events in the recent past as by scriptural constructions. The menacing image of the sannyasi-fakir had been elaborately recorded in the official records of the 1770s. The Council had noted in 1773:

> A set of lawless banditti known under the name of Sanyasi or Faquirs, have long infested these countries; and under the pretence of religious pilgrimage, have been accustomed to traverse the chief part of Bengal, begging, stealing, and plundering wherever they go, and as it best suits their convenience to practice.[4]

While official discourse had perceived the sannyasis as threatening, by the early nineteenth century Orientalist discourse had methodically classified the numerous sects of sannyasis and fakirs. Of particular importance were H.H. Wilson's articles in the *Asiatick Researches* (1828) which apart from systematizing the various types of Indian ascetics also indicated the various kinds of austerities that were practised by them. Wilson's articles were important because of the influence they wielded when reproduced in Bengali by Akshyay Kumar Datta. Entitled *Bhāratvarṣer upāsak sampradāy*, these two volumes (1870, 1883) soon became models of historical research. According to Akshyay Kumar, they were not mere translations but contained additional notes on specific sects and religious practices. These various strands in the discourse on the Indian ascetic had, by the mid-nineteenth century, succeeded in endorsing India as a fixed society where every type of cultural practice was mapped and accounted for. John Campbell Oman (1973:15) gave the following

[4] Quoted in Hunter 1860:70.

reasons for the prevalence of asceticism in India:

> ... under the combined influence of the physical, political, and social conditions..., aided powerfully by the intellectual and moral peculiarities of the people, a dull stagnation has been for ages the unenviable lot of... the Indian people – a state very conducive to mental depression and gloomy religious speculations, leading naturally to abnegation and ascetic living.

This negative characterization of Hindu ascetics was appropriated and endowed with alternative significance by the nineteenth-century Hindu discourse, which devised the sannyasi as a free-floating agent containing threatening as well as virtuous aspects. The terms used for such definitions, however, were often the very categories that had denied the acceptance of Indian asceticism as a valid spiritual exercise. Nineteenth-century indigenous discourses often deflected meanings ascribed to Indian asceticism, thus redefining and often contesting the assumptions of the colonial discourses. Thus while the performance of peculiar penances is perceived by Orientalist classificatory schemes as being rooted in a false understanding of the Divine (with its promise of marvellous powers to weak mortals), the same terms were recast within the nineteenth-century discourse on Hindu asceticism. In this reverse discourse, the insistence on legitimacy involved certain incorporations. Sometimes, Christian notions of asceticism were transformed before being incorporated, while at other times the inclusion of terms from a totally disparate area evolved a different definition. I shall try to demonstrate that both kinds of incorporations were instances of redefinitions induced by a colonial context.

The privileging of the sannyasi that took place within this reconstructed Hinduism was aided by the debates that focused on what were perceived as debased marriage customs. The various reforms relating to marriage – the Age of Consent debates, the Restitution of Conjugal Rights, and the Marriage of Widows – had focused on the 'barbaric practices' of the Hindus, throwing up questions about the kind of married life that such unions encouraged. Sumit Sarkar has shown in a recent study that the contested notion of conjugality indicated 'acute problems of interpersonal adjustments within the family' (1985b, quoted Chatterjee 1989:235). However, insufficient attention has been paid to the concern with physical weakness. Anxiety was articulated specifically about practices that were designated as racially weakening. A report in the *Somaprakash* of August-September 1884 illustrates this. The report, entitled 'What are the present duties of the youth of our country?' (*āmāder jubakgaṇer ekhan karttabya kī*), focuses on the need to cultivate bodily strength:

> The main obstacle on the path of our bodily improvement is the practice of child marriage. A fragile seed is incapable of sprouting into a mature tree. This is not its only adverse result. If one marries early, then one is burdened with a number of children within a spate of a few years. Nor are these children well looked after. As a result they soon become emaciated and weak and disgrace the whole country.[5]

The 'emaciated and weak' Bengali – a disgrace to the whole nation – was a frequently deployed colonial notion. The indigenous reception of what was defined by the colonisers as a physical problem was often ambiguous. One aspect of this reception was in terms of a spiritual problem, transforming the sannyasi-figure into a spiritual hero and so avoiding charges of effeminacy. In the context of such anxieties, the notion of sannyas helped to deflect attention away from 'barbaric' marital practices towards a disciplined masculinity which, far from being passive, was conceptualized as an active living force. Moreover, celibacy promised an escape from the guilt and uneasiness that underlay marriage.[6] In nineteenth-century Bengal, anxiety about 'depraved conjugality' was especially a problem for the educated *bhadralok*: as a result of their own exposure to Western learning, their expectations of their child-wives (who had not been exposed to it) were disproportionately high. Perceiving themselves as leaders in a cultural revolt, they often looked upon incompatibility in marriage as an undesirable diversion from their public activities. This anxiety finds typical expression in the diary of Hemendra Prasad Ghose, later editor of the *Basumati* and a member of the Indian National Congress. Married at the age of twenty to a twelve-year-old, he advises a friend on 13 February 1897:

> I am not of the opinion that the institution of marriage should be dispensed with or that everybody should lead the life of a celibate. But there are men who are by nature fit to bear the heat and dust of a married life and, my lad, there are men who are by nature incapable to do so. Personally, I have no faith in the sex – rightly termed the weaker sex.

Married life thus held no hope and became sublimated to a desire for celibacy. Moreover, this combination of asceticism and celibacy enabled a shift in focus. Far from signifying any lack of responsibility, this combination implied a

[5] *Somaprakash*, 3 Bhadra 1291, 1884. In *Sāmayik patre bāṅlār samāj citra 1840-1905* [*The Picture of Bengali Society from Journals and Newspapers*], ed. Benoy Ghose, p. 317. Calcutta: Path Bhavan, 1966.

[6] An aspect of this anxiety is expressed in the cultural disease of *dhātu* or semen loss in Sri Lanka, as studied by Gananath Obeyesekere (1976:213).

heightened spirituality that emanated from the retention of semen. That leadership in the cultural revolt envisaged for itself by the middle-class was compatible with the notion of sannyas is demonstrated by the middle-class following of Ramakrishna Paramahamsa as well as by later Swadeshi activists – as I shall explain.

Another instance of incorporation resulted in the creation of the paradoxical image of the political sannyasi, an image which was to have a tremendous appeal for the participants in the Swadeshi movement of 1905. That the figure of the ascetic could also be threatening was borne out by the Sannyasi Rebellion. But in late nineteenth-century Bengal, this aggressive aspect of the sannyasi was consolidated by the assimilation of politics, a concept which lay outside the norms that defined the Hindu ascetic. This incorporation also erased aspects that had been designated as peculiar by the colonial discourse.

By the 1890s, the notion of a political sannyasi had gained unprecedented significance. On 19 January 1870, Nabagopal Mitra's *National Paper*, an organ of the Hindu Mela, an annual gathering sponsored by the Tagores of Jorasanko, published the obituary of a 'Sannyasi Political' in Kutch. The late Anandashram Swamy, 'a native of Bengal' who 'belonged to a mercantile family of Calcutta', was described as an exemplary modern-day rishi (*ṛṣi*) or sage (p.32):

> His moral and political aspirations were those of the educated native . . . he preached to crowds of men and women the duty of doing spiritual service to God and good to man . . . . His advice to native Princes was judicious and firm. He would never consent to their yielding a jot of their just right to the demands of the Political officers of the British Government, but he insisted also on the reforms of their administrations as a prime duty and function of their existence.[7]

What is of particular interest here is the attempt to fit the figure of the ancient rishi into a contemporary framework. Anandashram Swamy's political awareness is appreciated as a higher mode of knowing on account of such an awareness being separate from the everyday pleasures of life. A report on a comparable figure occurs in the Calcutta weekly *Sanjivani* in the 1890s. This political sannyasi intends to take petitions containing twenty-three complaints from Indians to the Secretary of State and the British Parliament in England. These complaints include 'the murder of natives by Europeans', 'the violation of chastity of coolie women', 'interference with religion', and 'a circular ordering a supply of prostitutes for the army'.[8] This construction in fact

[7] 'In Memoriam of a Sannyasi Political', *National Paper*, 19 January 1870, p.32.

[8] *Sanjivani*, 8 November 1890, RNPB 1890(46):1034-5. Details are published from the same issue of the *Sanjivani*, RNPB 1890(47).

relocated the sannyasi in the political present, while retaining his distinctive resonance. The political sannyasi became established as one who takes up the grievances of the people and thus claims more credibility for approaching the problems in a disinterested light.

The image of a socially committed sannyasi is also a fairly common theme during this period.[9] The best-known example is provided by the *santāns* (literally, 'children of the Motherland') of Bankim Chandra's *Ā nanda Maṭh*. First serialized in his journal *Banga Darshan* (1880-2), the novel was published as a book in 1882. With the famine of 1776 as its background, Bankim's *santāns* are celibate sannyasis. It was only in the third edition of the novel that he included extracts from Gleig's *Memoirs of the Life of Warren Hastings* and W.W. Hunter's *The Annals of Rural Bengal* to link his ascetics to the rebellious sannyasi-fakirs of 1773. Such a construction of asceticism affirms a heroic defiance of death. In a conversation between Bhabananda (the ascetic) and Mahendra (a wealthy villager), Bhabananda specifies that courage is a quality that has to be cultivated through asceticism:

> Bhabananda:...The final thing is courage – the cannon balls drop only in one place, so there is no need for two hundred people to run from one cannon ball. But the entire tribe of Muslims flee if they see one cannon ball and not one Englishman will flee in the face of scores of them.
>
> Mahendra: And do you have the same calibre?
>
> Bhabananda: Do you not see that we are Sannyasis? Our sannyas is for the cultivation of such virtues...[10]

At several points in the novel, the state of celibacy is stressed as a means of releasing potential strength. Thus Bankim points towards the possibility of using a known and accepted mode of resistance, a mode into which he incorporates the masculine English virtue of courage to face danger. If the insistence upon celibacy manifested a heroic masculinity that matched the admirably virile English, it also closed the space for women as women. It is worth recalling here the heroic Shanti of *Ānanda Maṭh*.[11] By transcending her sexuality and leading the life of a *brahmacāriṇī*, Shanti gives an added resonance and legitimacy to her status as Bhabananda's *sahadharmiṇī* (equal

---

[9] The anonymous sannyasi in Chandicharan Sen's novel *Jhānsir Rāṇī* [*The Queen of Jhansī*] transcends his caste identity and bears political messages across the land.

[10] Bankim Chandra Chattopadhyay, *Ānanda Maṭh*. Quoted from *Bankim Racanābalī*, vol. 1 (Calcutta: Sahitya Samsad) 1953:675.

[11] For a detailed discussion, see Bagchi 1986:59-76.

partner in *dharma*). The implication this is that if women insist on being included in this world of heroic celibacy, they must renounce their sexuality.

The notion of resistance through sannyas during the Swadeshi period was thus concerned with reasserting a wounded masculinity. However the lineage of the Swadeshi sannyasi, as set out in Aurobindo's *Bhavānī Mandir* of 1905, was not a simple descent from Bankim's *santāns* of *Ānanda Maṭh* of the 1890s and/or the rebellious sannyasi-fakirs of 1773. This masculinity, reappropriated in the face of charges of effeminacy levelled at the Bengalis, affirmed its strength by rejecting marriage and retained its heroic dimension by being dedicated to the cause of the country. The space between the *santāns* of Bankim and the Swadeshi sannyasis was occupied by an exemplary sannyasi figure, that of Swami Vivekananda. The Swami came to embody aspects of the sannyasi icon in a way that enhanced the appeal of this figure for early nationalists.

Masculinity Redefined

The sannyasi icon did not, however, appear as a monolithic and homogeneous figure in the 1890s. Reports about false sannyasis were fairly frequent in the print media in the 1890s. In his diary entry for 18 February 1897, Hemendra Prasad Ghose juxtaposes his views regarding false sannyasis with an appraisal of Vivekananda on his triumphant return to Calcutta:

> The talk of the town today is Swami Vivekananda. The Swami (Naren Dutt) returns to Calcutta tomorrow after an absence of more than 4 years I believe. The Hindoos – specially the followers of Ramakrishna will give him a reception.... The cause of the Hindoo preachers has suffered much by the case instituted against Krishnananda (Baboo Srikrishna Prasanna Rai) at Benares. He is charged of rape. I myself have not much faith of sannyasis.

The guile associated with the garb of the sannyasi had rendered it problematic. Hemendra Prasad also stressed that the sexuality implied by the image of the perverted celibate formed the basis of the sannyasi's credibility. The power of the sannyasi lay in his ability to transmute sexual energy into inner spiritual strength. It is with specific reference to this aspect of the sannyasi that I shall discuss Vivekananda.

Vivekananda's success at the World Parliament of Religions in 1893, and his subsequent efforts to set up Vedanta centres in New York and London, had been noted in the English and vernacular press. While Vivekananda's representation of Hinduism has multiple dimensions within its own historical context, I shall focus on the particular elements relevant to the construction of the sannyasi icon. While abroad, Vivekananda had constantly proclaimed his position as a sannyasi, a representative of Indian asceticism. This is clear from his earliest public appearance in America. In his first speech before the Parliament, he thanked the gathering 'in the name of the most ancient order of monks in the world' (CWSV 1:3), thus placing the order of the Ramakrishna monks he had founded in 1886 within the context of a given tradition of renunciation and spirituality which was much older.

Vivekananda's physical presence further contributed to the anchoring of the sannyasi icon. We read in S.N. Dhar's *Comprehensive Biography of Swami Vivekananda* that silk alkhallas (long flowing robes) were purchased for him by the Munshi of Khetri (1975:1.392). When he had to adapt his dress on account of the cold weather, he took particular care, as his letters to his followers in America demonstrate, to acquire the right colour of cloth for his coat.[12] The right colour in this case was saffron (*geruā*) which signified renunciation. He evidently considered this important since, when he summoned his fellow-disciple Swami Abhedananda to join him in 1895, he added: 'Gangadhar's Tibetan *choga* is in the Math; get the tailor to make a similar *choga* of gerua colour' (CWSV 8:352). This emphasis on the colour and the style of dress is particularly significant for the creation of the icon. The image of the sannyasi thus expressed the implicit spiritual abstractions in an intelligible form. In the process, this icon was fashioned into a recognizable symbol of renunciation that was also distinctly 'Indian'. This last notion also had its links with the debates concerning dress in the 1880s, when the wearing of European dress by 'natives' was complicated by notions of honour and dishonour.[13] In a letter to Swami Brahmananda in 1895, he writes: 'It sets my nerves on edge to look at those who don hats and pose as *Sahibs*! Black as chimney sweeps, and calling themselves Europeans! Why not wear one's country-dress, as befits gentlemen?' (CWSV 6:337). Vivekananda's reconstruction of the sannyasi icon fed into this debate by rendering the ascetic distinctively and visibly 'Indian'.

The virtues of asceticism had won for him a high degree of credibility in America. He revealed his awareness of this in a letter to Manmatha Nath Bhattacharya written in September 1894:

> Consider this: they have allowed me, an unknown young man, to live among their grown-up daughters, and when my own

---

[12] See his letter to Miss Mary Hale: 'By very good luck, I have found the orange cloth and am going to have a coat made as soon as I can.' CWSV 8: 375.

[13] As the *Sadharani* notes in a report dated 4 January 1885: '. . . the natives who come from England come to lose a very important quality, namely, the power of ascertaining what constitutes honour and what constitutes dishonour; otherwise they could have never come to believe that the wearing of English dress makes them respected' (RNPB 1885(2):56).

> country-man, Mazoomdar, says I am a rogue, they don't pay any attention! ... I am like a foster son to the American women; they are really my mother.
> Please don't make this letter public. You understand, I have to be careful about every word I say – I am now a public man. (CWSV 7:476-7).

There are several points of interest here: fear of misinterpretation and malice, the support system offered by his extended family in America (for he addresses all his disciples as 'mother', 'sister', 'brother'), and – of particular relevance – Vivekananda's depiction of his life as a sannyasi as an active public one as opposed to the traditional image of the world renouncer. The rendering of a space previously accessible only to initiates into something that would admit the general public was an attempt to redefine both the role of the sannyasi and the term 'public'. Vivekananda thus stands as an exemplary figure: a sannyasi whose mendicant way of life brought him to the West and – even more important – a sannyasi with a deep social commitment. Another letter, this time to Ramakrishnananda in 1894, illustrates this:

> Suppose some disinterested Sannyasins, bent on doing good to others, go from village to village, disseminating education and seeking in various ways to better the condition of all down to the Chandala, through oral teaching, and by means of maps, cameras, globes and accessories – can't that bring forth good in time? (CWSV 6: 254-5)

The innovative public role formulated for a sadhu is explained by his brother, Bhupendranath Datta (a Swadeshi activist), as a historically necessary departure from orthodox notions:

> He organized Sadhus recruited from the middle class for social service schemes that he put forth.... Formerly, the Christian missionaries did this work.... Lastly came Swami Vivekananda to mobilize young monks for social service. This new phase of Sadhu movement is in contra-distinction with the quietism and pietism of time-hallowed custom of recluse life. The Sadhu of the Ramakrishna order lives out of the society as well as in it. (Datta 1954:323)

The public role envisaged for the sannyasi was also infused with a different notion of masculinity which derived its strength from the state of celibacy. As I have explained, the notion of strength associated with celibacy within the nineteenth-century Hindu discourse draws on the idea of a sexuality which shares in the energy of the great cosmic power. Sannyas, however, means not a denial of this energy but rather a concentration of it by preserving the vital fluid that is analogous to cosmic energy, semen. In *Six Lessons on Raja-Yoga*, a series of talks given around 1896, Vivekananda explains:

> The great sexual force, raised from animal action and sent upward to the great dynamo of the human system, the brain, and there stored up, becomes Ojas or spiritual force.... This Ojas is the real man and in human beings alone is it possible for this storage of Ojas to be accomplished. One in whom the whole animal sex force has been transformed into Ojas is a god. He speaks with power, and his words regenerate the world. (CWSV 8:46)

This transformation of sexual energy grants the essential power to the heroic figure of the sannyasi. As Elisabeth Haich points out, 'as soon as he ceases to expend sexual energy, retaining it as a living fuel for himself, in order to stimulate and activate his nerve...centres...he attains mastery over the spiritual-magical powers and obtains the goal of his life, all consciousness in God' (1972:157-8). But in order to historicize Vivekananda's stress on the transformation necessary in the practice of Raja Yoga, we have to look more closely at the context within which he functioned. Vivekananda was in fact incorporating an idea that lay outside Hindu definitions: the vulnerability of the flesh which defines the austere bodily discipline of the Christian faith. Characteristically, Vivekananda deployed the counter-notion of the *ojas* or spiritual power. The fact that this power was not perceived as a stasis, but as a movement towards an equilibrium between the cosmic power and the power within, indicated the frailty of the flesh that had to be conquered.

Related to this transformation, and to the articulation of difference with reference to sannyas, is the delineation of the role assigned to the householder. According to traditional definitions there are four states or stages of life (*āśrama*). Of these, the state of the celibate student and the state of the forest hermit are similar to sannyas in that both lack the regular joys and responsibilities of the householder (Dange 1986(1):50-4). The category of hermit denotes a state of celibacy within marriage. While accepting the traditional idea of four stages, the nineteenth-century Hindu discourse in fact privileged certain aspects of the fourth stage or state of the sannyasi. It is this image which resonates within nineteenth-century Bengal and, later, in the context of the Swadeshi movement. The received image of the sannyasi as an ascetic detached from the world is recast. There is in Vivekananda's speeches and writings a conflation of meaning between sannyasi, sage and priest – all the figures visualized as bearing India's spiritual tradition. Progress is perceived as a return to the core of this tradition. An extract from *Lectures from Colombo to*

Almora (a work much celebrated by early Swadeshi nationalists of Bengal) illustrates this point:

> The Sannyasin, as you all know, is the ideal of the Hindu's life, and every one by our shastras is compelled to give up.... Therefore my friends, the way out is that first and foremost we must keep a firm hold of spirituality – that inestimable gift handed down to us by our ancient forefathers. Did you ever hear of a country where the greatest kings tried to trace their descent not to kings, not to robber-barons living in old castles who plundered poor travellers, but to semi-naked sages who lived in the forest? ... This is the land.... Therefore, whether you believe in spirituality or not, for the sake of the national life, you have to get a hold of spirituality and keep to it. (CWSV 3:150-3.)

The sannyasi becomes in Vivekananda's representation a bearer of a distinguishing culture – the culture of spirituality – and therefore has the capacity to deliver the nation from its present degenerate state. The sannyasi's presence within the everyday world is never denied, although he can engage with it only in certain ways. Adherence to this path requires strict self-discipline, and celibacy is conceived as an intrinsic part of that discipline.

Vivekananda elaborates this connection between celibacy and strength, in terms of discipline, in a letter written from America to his disciple Alasinga. While emphasizing the need for strong men, he defines this strength in terms of both renunciation of the world and celibacy. Although he sees 'Madrasis' as capable of carrying out this project, he regrets that 'every fool is married'.[14] The letter to Alasinga continues:

> Strength, manhood, Kshatra-Virya + Brahma-Teja. Our beautiful hopeful boys – they have everything, only if they are not slaughtered by the millions at the altar of this brutality they call marriage...Madras will then awake when...educated young men will stand aside from the world, gird their loins, and be ready to fight the battle of truth, marching from nation to nation. (CWSV 5:117)

It is possible to see in Vivekananda's equation of celibacy and strength a continuity with the prevalent Hindu notion that ejaculation (*bīryapāt*) weakens the male. The word *bīrya* in Bengali connotes bravery, courage, splendour,

[14] This incidentally is aligned with Vivekananda's views on the 'diabolical custom' of child marriage. See his letter to Saradananda, 23 December 1895 (CWSV 8:365).

strength as well as the semen which contains the seed of procreation. In addition, semen is traditionally associated with vitality and strength. In this context, the strength of the sannyasi is seen to derive from his celibate state. Sumit Sarkar (1985a:99-100) elaborates on Ramakrishna's view that ejaculation enervates the male while continence in the midst of temptation is a potent source of spiritual energy:

> Ramakrishna stood four-square within this tradition when he condemned repeatedly any contact between *sannyasis* and women: they must not see pictures of the latter, or come near them physically in any way.... The standard is naturally different for householders – ...but they too were urged by Ramakrishna to abstain from intercourse after one or two children, and to live henceforward as brothers and sisters.

Vivekananda's ideas derive from the same basic premise, although at one remove. His main task, however, seems to be to define a different masculinity, a project often referred to as his 'man-making mission'.

Vivekananda's 'man-making mission' has been studied in psycho-analytical terms by Sudhir Kakar. Kakar sees in Vivekananda's life the 'struggle to free himself from his mother and the advocacy of a thoroughly masculine courage and initiative' that 'manifested itself in his historic mission to infuse Indian nationalism with a militant revival of tradition, to bring resolute manly activity and radical social transformation to that "nation of women" as he characterized the India of his time' (1981:170). Kakar reads Vivekananda's obsession with manliness in terms of an unresolved personal conflict about his own individuation as a man (pp.174-6). However insightful, this kind of psycho-analytical study of an individual is an inadequate tool for placing Vivekananda within the context of the nineteenth-century anxiety about manliness and its absence in the national life. The historical location of such allegations, and their reception by the middle-class intelligentsia who were struggling to define themselves within the colonial context, place the problem of masculinity in an arena larger than the individual mind. The British representations of the Indian as weak and effeminate were consistent and continuous. It was with reference to this undesirable self-image that the figure of the heroic ascetic was constructed. Masculinity was central to the rejoinder to charges of being emasculated, even when shrouded in metaphysical rhetoric. Opposition was articulated through this particular notion of maleness because it was the area which stood affronted. Within this discourse of heroic masculine asceticism, women were perceived as inspirational figures rather than actual participants, except for the unusual examples of Sister Nivedita and Sarala Debi before her marriage. Both these women were distinguished for having transcended their sexuality, and Sarala Debi's marriage was viewed as a loss for nationalism (see Chaudhurani 1975:186).

The nationalist self-definition of an alternative masculinity negotiated with the colonial definition of what constituted 'Indian'. However, the nationalist attitude towards the virile English rulers is often ambivalent. For even if they are admired for their strong physique, the deterioration of the indigenous Hindu population is seen to be directly linked with the spread of Western civilization. The *Sulabh Dainik* (22 May 1893) notes with reference to the Census of 1891:

> The salutary practices enjoined by the Rishis for the preservation of the health of the body and mind are now little observed. And to crown the whole, there is now a dearth of food in the country owing to an unnatural system of trade. (RNPB 1893(21):427)

If Western civilization was identified with power, there was also an awareness of its negative aspect: power that consolidated itself at the expense of the indigenous people. The oppositional masculinity was thus designed to resist this insensitive virility as exemplified by the colonizers. Vivekananda's insistence on a different manliness was therefore linked, on the one hand, with this equation of manhood and power and, on the other, with an alternative maleness that took its meaning from the worship of Shakti, embodied by a Mother Goddess. The devoted nationalist sannyasi – later elucidated by Aurobindo – was dedicated to liberating the Mother Country. Vivekananda's reconstruction of this alternative masculinity powerfully redirected the meaning of spirituality within Hindu religious norms. Vivekananda's reconstruction of the sannyasi icon in the context of its antecedents make it possible to see what aspects of this important icon fired the imagination of the youth in the Swadeshi agitation.

In 1918, the Sedition Committee, with Justice Rowlatt as President, saw both Vivekananda's mission and the exhortations of Krishna in the *Bhagavadgītā* as influencing and inspiring the beginnings of the revolutionary movement in Bengal (Sedition Committee Report, p.17). The threat contained in this 'man-making project' was personified in the Swadeshi activists of Bengal. This not only coincided with the authorization of a different masculinity in the image of the sannyasi but also set free the inherent power of youth wasted at the altar of child-marriage. In this drafting of a 'useful' masculinity through sannyas, the householder disciples (whom Ramakrishna had initiated and included in the fold) were to be excluded. 'We want,' said Vivekananda to his brother disciples at the Alam Bazar Math in 1894, 'two thousand Sannyasins, nay ten, or even twenty thousand.... Not householder disciples, mind you, we want Sannyasins' (CWSV 6:293). This redefined masculinity, in its movement towards celibacy, signalled a movement away from meaningless marriages. What was exercised in this context was the choice of a guaranteed potential achieved through celibacy as opposed to the debatable venture of marriage.

During the Swadeshi period, many activists, particularly the extremists, found the notion of sannyas both empowering and useful. The Sedition Committee Report quotes from Barindra Kumar Ghose's statement before a magistrate in May 1908. Barindra Kumar, the younger brother of Aurobindo, was a Swadeshi activist arrested because of his involvement in the Manicktola Bomb Conspiracy. In his statement, Barindra says he was convinced that 'a purely political propaganda would not do and people must be trained up spiritually to face dangers' (Sedition Committee Report, p.20). His conviction that only spiritually trained youth would be capable of sacrificing themselves is further elaborated in the autobiography of his associate Upendranath Bandyopadhyay (1954:18):

> It was decided that we shall pick some boys from the *Yugantar* office, and build a new association in the Maniktala garden. We decided that we had to take boys who had no attachment to family or material life, or even if they were so attached could easily sacrifice such ties. However, such qualities cannot be acquired without gaining religious discipline, so it was decided to impart religious education at the garden.

Geoffrey Galt Harpham's observations on the notion of self-discipline as a shield against temptation within a different ascetic culture are also applicable to this context: 'For the ascetic, self-discipline was a way of "mortifying," or making-dead the flesh. He could not seek his death as an end, but only as a means, a middle that could never end' (1987:59).

Self-discipline through spiritual education could ensure a self-sacrificing spirit which mediated between the captive present and the independent future, and made such a future possible. Aurobindo's *Bhavānī Mandir* (*Temple of Bhawani*), written around 1905, was in fact 'more Barin's idea than his'.[15] This tract, noted by the Sedition Committee, listed among the 'Three Things Needful' the specific work of building a temple to Bhawani ('the Mother of Strength, the Mother of India') which will have

> a new Order of Karma Yogins attached to the temple, men who have renounced all in order to work for the Mother. Some may, if they choose, be complete Sannyasis, most will be Brahmacharins who will return to Grihastha ashram when their allotted work is finished, but all must accept renunciation.[16]

[15] Introduction to *Bhavānī Mandir in Sri Aurobindo Birth Centenary Library* (ABCL 1972: 1.59).

[16] Introduction to *Bhavānī Mandir* (ABCL 1:69).

The appeal of sannyas lay in its self-discipline and the spiritual energy it generated. The two ideal figures – Bankim's ideal man (Krishna) and the sannyasi – were brought together and rationalized by the prevailing notion of *karma* in Aurobindo's essay 'Asceticism and Renunciation' (*Sannyās o tyāg*; ABCL 4:60-2) in 1909. Informed by the notion of *karma* – according to which action is to be pursued for its own sake – sannyas both imparted a sense of purpose to the Swadeshi activists and conferred the strength to transcend what were perceived to be the petty ties of family and community. Celibacy and non-attachment aided this transcendence. The nationalists saw themselves as devoting all their spiritual energy to the cause of the country and thus as dedicated to the greater community.

The new alternative masculinity was implicated in these formulations of a nationalist identity. It entrusted the male with the power to save his motherland by channelling the energy of procreation to the service of the country. This anticipates Gandhi's explicit sexual experiments to 'acquire the kind of moral and spiritual power he thought he needed to arrest the tidal wave of violence raging all around him' (Parekh 1989:201). In the discourse of early nationalism, it was Vivekananda who forged the link between the growing preoccupation with asceticism and sannyas in the nineteenth century and the Swadeshi sannyasi. By locating him within the parameters of this emerging Hindu discourse, it becomes possible to see the progressive construction of the sannyasi icon and its significance for early nationalism. There is in fact further scope for mapping out this complex process which is an important marker within the context of the Swadeshi Movement of 1903-8. Once its significance is established, it is possible to trace the transformation of the selfless sannyasi into the devoted nationalist son of Mother India.

Abbreviations

ABCL	*Sri Aurobindo Birth Cententary Library*. 1972. Pondicherry: Aurobindo Ashram Trust.
CWSV	*The Complete Works of Swami Vivekananda*. 1989. Calcutta: Advaita Ashrama.
RNPB	*Report of the Native Papers, Bengal.*

References

Amrita Bazar Patrika. See *Report of the Native Papers, Bengal.*
Aurobindo, Sri. *Sri Aurobindo Birth Centenary Library.* Vols. 1–10. 1972. Pondicherry: Aurobindo Ashram Trust.
Bagchi, Jasodhara. 1986. 'Positivism and Nationalism: Womanhood and Crisis in Nationalist Fiction, Bankimchandra's *Anandamath.*' In *Narrative: Forms and Transformations*, ed. Sudhakar Marathe and Meenaskhi Mukherjee. New Delhi: Chanakya Publications.
Bandyopadhyay, Upendranath. 1954. *Nirbāsiter ātmakathā* [*The Autobiogrpahy of an Exile*]. 5th edition. Calcutta: Bengal Publishers.
Bankim Chandra Chattopadyay (Chatterjee). See Chattopadhyay.
—. 1969. *Bankim Racanābalī*, vol. 2. Calcutta: Sahitya Samsad.
Chatterjee, Partha. 1989. 'The Nationalist Resolution of the Women's Question.' In *Recasting Women: Essays in Colonial History*, ed. Kumkum Sangari and Sudesh Vaid. New Delhi: Kali.
Chattopadhyay, Bankim Chandra. 1953. *Ānanda Maṭh.* In *Bankim Racanābalī* vol. 1. Calcutta: Sahitya Samsad.
Chaudhurani, Sarala Debi. 1975. *Jībaner jharā pātā* [*Life's Fallen Leaves*]. Calcutta: Rupa.
Dange, Sadashiv A. 1986. *Encyclopedia of Puranic Beliefs and Practices.* Delhi: Navrang.
Datta, Bhupendranath. 1954. *Swami Vivekananda, Patriot-Prophet: A Study.* Calcutta: Nababharat Publishers.
Dhar, S.N. 1975. *A Comprensive Biography of Swami Vivekananda.* Madras: Vivekananda Prakashan Kendra.
Ghose, Benoy, ed. 1966. *Sāmayik patre baṅlār samāj citra 1840-1905. (The Picture of Bengali Society from Journals and Newspapers)*. Calcutta: Path Bhavan.
Ghose, Hemendra Prasad. Unpublished diaries, 1893-1902. Housed at the Central Library, Jadavpur University, Calcutta.
Haich, Elisabeth. 1972. *Sexual Energy and Yoga.* Tr., D.Q. Stephenson. London: George Allen & Unwin.
Harpham, Geoffrey Galt. 1987. *The Ascetic Imperative in Culture and Criticism.* Chicago/London: The University of Chicago Press.
Hunter, W.W. 1860. *Annals of Rural Bengal.* London: Smith, Elder and Co.
Kakar, Sudhir. 1981. *The Inner World: A Psycho-Analytic Study of Childhood and Society in India.* 2nd edition. New Delhi: Oxford University Press.
Kaviraj, Sudipta. 1987. 'The Myth of Praxis: The Constructions of the Figure of Krishna in Krishnacarita.' *Occasional Papers on History and Society.* New Delhi: Nehru Memorial Museum and Library.
National Paper. 'In Memoriam of a Sannyasi Political'. 19 January 1870:32.

Obeyesekere, Gananath. 1976. 'The Impact of Ayurvedic Ideas on the Culture and Individual in Sri Lanka. In *Asian Medical Systems: A Comparative Study*, ed. Charles Leslie. Berkeley: University of California Press.

Oman, John Campbell. 1973. *The Mystics, Ascetics and Saints of India: A Study of Sadhuism, with an Account of the Yogis, Sannyasis, Bairagis, and other Strange Hindu Sectarians*. London: 1903. Reprint: Delhi, Oriental Publishers.

Parekh, Bhikhu. 1989. *Colonialism, Tradition and Reform: An Analysis of Gandhi's Political Discourse*. New Delhi: Sage.

Ray, Ajit. 1986. 'Bankim Chandra Chatterji's New Hinduism and the Bhagavad Gita.' In *Modern Indian Interpretations of the Bhagavadgita*, ed. Robert N. Minor, 34-43. Albany: State University of New York Press.

Raychaudhuri, Tapan. 1988. *Europe Reconsidered: Perceptions of the West in Nineteenth-Century Bengal*. Delhi: Oxford University Press.

Report on the Native Papers, Bengal (1875-90).

Sanjivani. See *Report on the Native Papers, Bengal*, nos. 46 and 47 of 1890.

Saraswat Patra. See *Report of the Native Papers, Bengal*.

Sarkar, Sumit. 1985a. 'The Kathamrita as a Test: Towards an Understanding of Ramakrishna Paramahamsa.' *Occasional Papers on History and Society* 22. Nehru Memorial Museum and Library, New Delhi.

—. 1985b. 'The Women's Question in Nineteenth-Century Bengal.' In *Women and Culture*, ed. Kumkum Sangari and Sudesh Vaid. Bombay: SNDT Women's University.

Sedition Committee 1918: Report. Calcutta: Superintendent of Government Printing, 1918.

Sen, Chandicharan. 1894. *Jhānsir Rāṇī [The Queen of Jhansi]*. 2nd edition. Calcutta.

Subramaniam, V. 1987. 'Karmayoga and the Rise of the Indian Middle Class.' *Journal of Arts and Ideas* 14-15 (July-December 1987): 133-42.

Vivekananda, Swami. See *The Complete Works of Swami Vivekananda*. Calcutta: Advaita Ashrama, 1989.

8

Arthur Avalon: The Creation of a Legendary Orientalist

Kathleen Taylor

Introduction

In 1916, an article appeared in the Bengali magazine *Bhārat Varṣa* entitled 'A New Way of Learning Letters' (Paṇḍulipi 1916). It was a pictorial alphabet and beside each letter was the photograph of some well-known figure of the Bengali literary world whose name began with it. When the alphabet reached *ū*, there was no name to fit, so the author had to fall back on an English writer instead: *ū* stood for 'Woodroffe' as transcribed in Bengali characters. So Sir John Woodroffe, a Judge of the High Court of Calcutta, took his place amidst a list of famous Bengalis. This was because, as the article explained, it was believed by most people that he was the real Arthur Avalon, the mysterious writer on Tantra whose books were doing so much to change the image of that previously despised cult. The article runs:

> The Tantras are obscene, the Tantras are full of indecency... the Tantras are loathsome... Such loud words of condemnation were wont to resound without pause in the mouths of the English-educated class... Having received an English initiation and education they were cutting with their own hand the branch on which they were seated. At that moment Arthur Avalon (people say he is Mr Justice Woodroffe) broke their false pride and revealed the greatness of the Tantra and the English-educated Babus commenced to rub their eyes.[1]

[1] This quotation is translated under 'Press Notices' in TT 19:iii.

The article goes on to say that this was nothing new – the English-educated were only too eager to follow after foreigners, even in the cultivation of their own nationalism – and cites Mrs Besant and the Theosophical Society, among others, as examples. The writer sounds a little sarcastic, yet he pays sincere tribute to Sir John Woodroffe's championship of Indian culture, which extended beyond his writings on Tantra. The article ends with the comment that everything Woodroffe touched turned to gold.

As well as revealing the extreme disrepute in which this esoteric strand of Hinduism was held by the English-educated middle-class in Bengal – the *bhadralok* – the article implies that it was largely because Woodroffe, or Arthur Avalon, was a Westerner that he was able to change people's attitudes. It also shows us how his use of the pseudonym for his writings on Tantra seemed to do little to conceal his identity, at least in Calcutta where he was a popular figure in its cultural life.

Sir John Woodroffe

Sir John Woodroffe (1865-1936) was a barrister at the High Court of Calcutta from 1890, and a judge from 1904 to 1922. After that, he retired from India and was All Souls Reader in Indian Law at Oxford University until 1930. His final retirement was to France, where he died at Beausoleil, a suburb of Monte Carlo.

Before his writings on religion, Woodroffe had already produced some well-known textbooks on British-Indian law.[2] But he was best known, at the time of the *Bhārat Varṣa* article in 1916, for being an Indophile and an art connoisseur. He belonged to the circle around the Tagores, especially Rabindranath's artist nephews, Abanindranath and Gaganendranath, with whom he had helped to found the Indian Society of Oriental Art in 1907. Other members of this interesting international group included E.B. Havell and Ananda Coomaraswamy, whose books on Indian art created a new idealizing and spiritualizing attitude, a sharp reaction to the denigration prevalent in the nineteenth century. An account of this change of attitude is described in detail in Partha Mitter's book *Much Maligned Monsters* (1977). The contempt towards art had sometimes been expressed in language similar to that used about Tantra, and the two of course were connected in many minds through erotic temple imagery. Woodroffe's (or Arthur Avalon's) reinterpretation of this controversial strand of Hinduism paralleled the revision of attitudes towards Indian art, as well as reflecting a much broader movement of Hindu revival and cultural nationalism.

2 The best known was a standard text book: Woodroffe and Ameer Ali 1898.

Woodroffe never expressly claimed to have been initiated in Tantra, preferring to portray himself in the role of a sympathetic outsider or disinterested scholar,[3] but there is evidence that in fact he was much more personally involved. It is believed by many in India that he was a disciple of a popular Tantric teacher, preacher and writer called Śivacandra Vidyārṇava, a brahmin from East Bengal who had a following among the Calcutta *bhadralok*. His book in Bengali, *Tantratattva*, was translated under the name of Arthur Avalon as *Principles of Tantra* (PT). Few people alive in India today could have known Woodroffe, but an account of his initiation by Śivacandra was given in the 1960s in a series of magazine articles by Vasanta Kumār Pāl, one of the guru's other disciples, who had met Woodroffe and who cites the testimony of others who had also known him (see Pal 1966). Pal was the main source for a chapter on Śivacandra in S.N. Ray's collection of biographies, *Bhārater Sādhak*, published in 1985. Several other sources describe how Woodroffe meditated regularly and even worshipped an image of Durga in his home. He was also given to wearing Indian dress, on both religious and social occasions. A photograph of him wearing a *dhoti* and carrying a water-jar at the Sun Temple of Konarak is reproduced in the latest editions of the books. Another photograph[4] taken at Konarak shows him seated on the steps of the temple with two other men, all in Indian dress. Two of the men are European: Woodroffe and his friend H.P. Moeller, a Danish businessman who was initiated into Vaiṣṇavism and was also a member of the Indian Society of Oriental Art. The third is an Indian to whom I shall return later.

It seems as if the art society had religious as well as artistic connections. Havell's and Woodroffe's involvement in Tantra is described by the artist Nandalal Bose, a pupil of Abanindranath Tagore, but he does not refer to Śivacandra.[5] Pal claims that Śivacandra lectured to Havell and Coomaraswamy on Hindu theories of art in Woodroffe's home in Calcutta, and that he was instrumental in helping Coomaraswamy to be formally accepted as a Hindu (Ray 1985:328). Whether or not he wanted to exaggerate the extent of his guru's influence over these three Englishmen, there is no reason to doubt that Woodroffe, at least, was closely associated with Śivacandra;[6] and it is interesting to see that there were other Europeans at that time in his circle who were personally involved in Hinduism, to the point of seeking initiation.

[3] For example, 'My attitude is an objective one ...' (SS 1987, preface to the second edition, pp.ix-x).

[4] I am grateful to Mr Krishna Ghosh who had a copy made for me of this photograph.

[5] See Datta 1954:309-12, where Bose's letter to the author is reproduced. Datta, however, is arguing for the influence of Vivekananda on Havells' theories of art.

[6] Woodroffe's connection with Śivacandra Vidyārṇava is recorded in newspaper reports, e.g. *The Bengali*, 28 March and 1 April 1914.

Woodroffe's relationship with Śivacandra was compared by Pal to that between Ramakrishna and Vivekananda, with Woodroffe cast in the role of the 'rationalist' modern disciple who needed winning over but who was eventually able to spread his master's fame throughout the world.

The Works of 'Arthur Avalon'

Although he did not claim in his books to be an initiate, Woodroffe seems to have made no secret of his scholarly interest in Tantra. He lectured on it in public in Calcutta; and in 1915 he did so at the Chaitanya Library to an audience which included the Governor of Bengal, Lord Carmichael (SS 1987:243, note 1). Arthur Avalon's books on Hindu Tantra started to appear two years prior to that, in 1913. No less than four books were produced in that year alone: a collection of *Hymns to the Goddess* – written in collaboration with his wife, who called herself Ellen Avalon – and a translation of the *Mahānirvāṇatantra*, published in English as *The Great Liberation* (MNT). This text was popular with the middle class in Bengal because it was regarded as a mild or 'respectable' Tantra. It is now thought to be a comparatively recent work belonging to the eighteenth century, but Avalon dated it much earlier (see Derrett 1977). He wrote a long introduction to his translation outlining the main features of Tantric ritual and philosophy. In the third edition (1952), this was published as an independent book: *An Introduction to Tantra Śāstra*. Also in 1913, the first two volumes appeared in the series *Tantrik Texts* (TT), which eventually ran to twenty-one volumes. All the texts were Hindu Sanskrit texts, apart from volume 7 which was edited and translated from Tibetan by Lama Kazi Dawa Samdup. Arthur Avalon was the general editor; many of the introductions and summaries in English which accompanied the volumes were written under this name. These made the texts accessible to those without a knowledge of Sanskrit. Most of the earlier volumes were produced by a team of Indian scholars, but many of the later ones were described as being edited by Arthur Avalon himself.

At the beginning of 1914, *Principles of Tantra* appeared in two volumes. This was the translation, from the Bengali, of Śivacandra's *Tantratattva*. In his preface and introduction to this book, Arthur Avalon did not write of the author in the manner of a disciple writing about his guru, but simply introduced him as an example of a 'modern orthodox Hindu' whose views, it was claimed, had not been modified through Western education as he did not speak English (PT 1:31). Avalon was addressing the unfavourable image of Tantra held by the Western-educated public, something which he blamed almost entirely on the prejudices of European Orientalists. He considered that Indians who condemned Tantra did so because they had imbibed Western prejudices through their English education. In this regard, he seemed to view Indians as entirely passive recipients of foreign ideas.

After *Principles of Tantra*, and throughout the second decade of the century, books and magazine articles by Arthur Avalon continued to appear rapidly. By 1922, eleven volumes of *Tantrik Texts* had been published, including two translations: *Kārpurādi Stotram* (a hymn to Kālī) and *Kāmakalāvilāsa*, a Kashmiri text describing tantric cosmogony. Two translations not included in the *Tantrik Texts* series were also published: the esoteric poem of praise to the Goddess *Ānandalahari* ('Wave of Bliss'), traditionally ascribed to Śaṅkara, and *Mahimnastava* (a hymn to Śiva).

Meanwhile, in 1918, there appeared two books which were destined to have a long life and which have been translated into several European languages. *Śakti and Śākta* (SS), was the first of the books to come out under the name of Sir John Woodroffe. It is a collection of articles and lectures; some of the articles had been published in magazines under the name of Arthur Avalon, the lectures had been delivered by Sir John Woodroffe in person during the three years prior to the book's publication. *Śakti and Śākta* reached its sixth edition in 1965 and has been reprinted many times since then. It was popular despite having some rather abstruse passages and it has introduced several generations of Westerners to Tantra, both scholars and more general readers.

At the end of 1918, a volume already edited in the *Tantrik Texts* (TT 2) series called *Ṣatcakranirūpaṇa* ('Treatise on the Six Centres') was translated into English and, with the addition of a long introduction which took up more than half the book, was published as *The Serpent Power* (SP). As the first full account in English of *kuṇḍalinī yoga*, this was to become the best known and most enduring of all the books, and undoubtedly it was Arthur Avalon who first made the concept of *kuṇḍalinī* familiar in the West. It is now well known to everyone interested in yoga, but in Woodroffe's time few Westerners knew anything of ideas about the six psychic centres in the human body and their awakening by the psycho-physical force called *kuṇḍalinī* , which is regarded as the source of supernormal powers: the *siddhi*s. Shortly after the book first appeared, it was read by C.G. Jung who claimed it had a crucial influence on his discovery of the collective unconscious.[7]

The Serpent Power was attributed to Arthur Avalon. *Garland of Letters* (GOL) was published in 1922 during Woodroffe's last year in India under his own name. It explores cosmogony and the 'science' of mantra. The letters are the Sanskrit alphabet, pronounced in monosyllabic mantras called 'seeds' (*bīja*), which are conceived of as primordial sounds denoting the first vibrations out of which the universe evolved: their garland is the necklace of skulls depicted in iconography around the neck of Kālī. This can probably be viewed as a sophisticated Tantric reinterpretation of a primitive image. As with *Śakti*

[7] Jung 1966:16, 334-5. Jung also quoted *Śakti and Śākta* on other aspects of Tantra, but he used the concept of *kuṇḍalinī* and the *cakra*s very much in his own way.

and Śākta, many of the chapters of this book had first appeared as articles by Arthur Avalon. For others, Woodroffe acknowledged the help of his friend Pramathanath Mukhopadhyay (GOL:xi). The book is of mixed quality: some chapters are very readable, explaining abstruse and – to modern Westerners – strange ideas in an attractive and fairly clear way; others are smothered under a mass of Sanskrit terminology and strained English. The book reveals two contrasting aspects of Woodroffe's style of writing.

Woodroffe's friend, Mukhopadhyay, also collaborated with him on two other books: *The World as Power* (1923) and *Mahāmāyā* (1923). These abstruse books deal with the Śiva-Śakti philosophy, and attempt to correlate concepts of Indian metaphysics with those of contemporary Western science – a project which has become increasingly popular. Pramathanath Mukhopadhyay was a teacher of mathematics at the National College of Calcutta. Much later on, he was to renounce the world and take sannyas under the name of Swami Pratyagatmanand Saraswati. His influence on Woodroffe, especially towards the end of the latter's time in India, seems to have been considerable.

The Reception of Avalon's Works and Previous Attitudes to Tantra

The books seem to have made an immediate impression and, on the whole, to have been favourably received. Both in India and abroad, most people unhesitatingly accepted the new writer as a member of the community of European Orientalists, although one or two remarked that Arthur Avalon took a surprisingly unhistorical attitude to his texts compared to what was expected of a Western scholar. Such foreign accounts as there were of Tantric scriptures were mostly concerned with Buddhist Tantra but even there little had been done. Nearly all reviewers agreed that the subject had been unjustly neglected. The French orientalist, Masson-Oursel, wrote (1921:57-8)

> A chapter of Burnouf, some remarks of A. Barth, various researches of Louis de la Vallée Poussin, constituted before 1913 all that was written on the Tantras, whose encyclopedic character, ritualistic nature and bizarre mysticism repelled the analysts. And then there appeared all of a sudden the rudiments of a Tantric library for which we thank the scholarship and courage of an Englishman concealed under the pseudonym of Arthur Avalon... he has done the work of a pioneer and explorer...

Even the contemporary missionary-Orientalist, J.N. Farquhar, welcomed the books as a valuable contribution to knowledge. Commenting on the translation of *Mahānirvāṇatantra*, he engaged in some speculation on the identity of

Arthur Avalon and (unless he was 'in the know') seems to have had an inspired guess (1915:145-6):

> The translator, who writes under a *nom de plume*, is clearly a European disciple of some pundit belonging to the Left-hand Shaktas; and he shows great sympathy for the sect. He is always ready to defend any of its doctrines and practices, even the most shameful... On the other hand, his faithful discipleship has brought him a wonderful understanding of the teaching and cult of the sect... and his introduction and commentary (is) of great exegetical value.

The 'Left-hand Shaktas' was the way in which most Orientalists described those Tantrics who practised rituals of which they disapproved. The term *vāmacāra* – the left-hand path – referred to the esoteric practices of Tantra. Orientalists were inclined to bracket Tantra with Śāktism, not only because female divinities are central to both, but sometimes also because of a tendency to associate goddess worship with degradation.[8]

The rites which gave rise to Tantra's sinister image were precisely those which also affronted Hindu orthodoxy. They involved deliberately breaking taboos and courting pollution. For example, the *pañcatattva* was a ritual practised by Tantrics of the Kaula sect (widespread in Bengal), and involved wine, meat and sexual intercourse. Other rites had to be performed in graveyards or burning grounds where the strongest kind of pollution, that connected with death, was to be encountered. The purpose of Tantric rites is two-fold: the acquiring of supernormal, or magic, powers (*siddhis*), as well as the more general Hindu soteriological goal of liberation (*mokṣa*). In the latter case, the breaking of taboos is to do with overcoming dualism: like and dislike, purity and impurity, fear and attraction, and so on (Sanderson 1992).

An association with European witchcraft was one factor which obviously influenced Western attitudes. Few Europeans before Woodroffe considered it necessary to probe any philosophical or 'spiritual' meaning behind such practices.[9] Tantra, however, had another, special place in the Orientalist discourse: it was regarded as an extreme example of the degeneration which, by general consensus of both Europeans and Western-educated Indians, was believed to have affected Hindu religion since its glorious classical past in the so-

---

[8] For example, see Payne 1933, especially the last chapter, 'The Impermanence of Shaktism'.

[9] An exception was Louis de la Vallée Poussin, who edited two short Buddhist Tantric texts, and spoke of the 'metaphysical and subtle' character of its concepts. He is cited favourably by Arthur Avalon (see, for example, PT 1:25; 2:9,11).

called Aryan civilization. It was viewed as a prime example of the 'non-Aryan culture' which was believed to have intermingled with that civilization and corrupted it (Kopf 1986:144). The 'Aryan' civilization that was believed to be associated with the orthodox Vedic texts had usually been idealized by European Orientalists; but the Tantras were texts which stood outside the Vedic tradition and hence, to more orthodox Hindus as well as to Orientalists, they were by implication 'non-Aryan' and therefore 'uncivilized'. In addition to this, for the foreign Orientalists they had the added disadvantage of being more recent than the Vedas, and therefore closer to the Indian present than to the idealized past.[10]

In his preface to the translation (PT) of Śivacandra's book, Arthur Avalon gives several telling examples of the kind of language which framed Orientalist accounts of Tantra. One of the sources he criticizes is L.D. Barnett's *Antiquities of India* which had been published the previous year, in 1913. Barnett was a respected Sanskritist who was later to lecture at the School of Oriental and African Studies in London in its earliest days, but he was a prime example of the textually-based Orientalist who had little contact with the living religions of India. He described the Aryan society in terms which have become familiar (p.3):

> Its head was a foreign race of fairer skin and Indo-Germanic speech, warriors and priests proud and jealous of their blood and traditions; its feet was a mixed populace, of which the more civilized elements had learned something of the arts of peace from the Dravidians . . . while the lower strata were wallowing in savagery.

Tantra in this view was a survival of, or a reversion to, that primitive savagery, and hence belonged to a lower order of civilization. The books of Arthur Avalon did not attempt to challenge this discourse, which was similar to the high-caste Hindu discourse;[11] rather they sought to change the place of Tantra within it. For this reason, the main thrust of their argument was to emphasize those elements of Tantra which were 'respectable' and common to all Hinduism – such as its soteriological goal of *mokṣa* – and to assert its claims to orthodoxy in relation to the Vedas. In particular, the books put forward the argument that the Tantras represent the Vedic religion in a form suitable for the *kali* age.[12]

---

[10] Indians too had the idea that time itself is corrupting and all manifestations of culture represent a degeneration from an ideal in the past. This view is to be found in Avalon's pages too (e.g. PT 1:13). But nowhere does Woodroffe himself give the impression of preferring the idealized past to the living religion around him.

[11] Barnett's analogy of the head and feet recalls the famous *puruṣasūkta* (10.90) in the *Ṛgveda*, where the brahmin emerges from the head of the primordial Man, the *śūdra* from his feet, and so on.

[12] Kopf's suggestion that Woodroffe was one of the first to put forward this idea does not seem to be correct (1986: 147). The idea appears as a standard validation of Tantra. It is found in the texts themselves: for example, the author (whoever it was) of the *Mahānirvāṇatantra* uses it (MNT:20) and so did Śivacandra Vidyārṇava (e.g. PT 1:156).

Avalon insists on a position for Tantra close to the centre, and not on the fringe, of mainstream Hinduism through its metaphysical basis in Advaita Vedānta. He ignores its role as a 'cult of the shadow' and its strand of antinomianism which set out deliberately to transgress orthodox restraints and taboos.

Although usually regarded by scholars as having an independent origin, the Tantras in fact do have many similarities with the Vedas, as has been pointed out, among others, by N.N. Bhattacharyya (1982:168 ff.). He argues that both traditions contain a primitive substratum overlaid with a more sophisticated metaphysical system. There is a similar emphasis on ritual and a belief that the rite is effective in itself, over and against the deities who are invoked in it; and both kinds of texts contain magic prescriptions – but Woodroffe's contemporaries viewed them very differently. For example, Barnett described those Vedic rituals which involved taking an intoxicating drink (*soma*), the sacrifice of animals and even sometimes of human beings – and the royal horse-sacrifice where the chief queen had to mimic copulation with the dead horse – but he could portray all these without undue expressions of horror, and they did not interfere with his highly idealized, romantic vision of Vedic society. While admitting a 'darker side' to Vedic religion, he asserted that 'it was nevertheless in its official aspect a fairly bright and respectable system' (1913:4). Of the Tantras, however, whose rituals he does not describe at all, he writes (p.17) in a choice passage also quoted by Avalon:

> Even the highly coloured Yogic imagination pales beside the doctrines of some of the innumerable sects which have pullulated on the fertile soil of India. Most famous or infamous of those are the Tantras... in which a veritable Devil's Mass is purveyed in various forms to a swarm of sects mostly of the Shaivite persuasion.

Yoga – mentioned in this quotation – was also regarded as 'non-Aryan' in origin, and hence could come in for criticism.

Similar language could be quoted extensively from other sources and Avalon himself, in many places in his writings, has amply illustrated the attitudes of Orientialist writers. Not all were so extreme; but many were, and nearly every study of Hinduism or Buddhism by Europeans at this period and earlier was extremely unsympathetic when dealing with the Tantric strand. This was especially so among early Western writers on Buddhism when they discovered the Tibetan version of that religion. In a similar vein to the idealization of Vedic/Aryan religion in relation to contemporary Hinduism, European writers also tended to idealize the 'pure' religion of Gautama Buddha and to identify it with early Buddhism: they were correspondingly pained by what they saw as the contrast with the 'degenerate' and 'superstitious' practices of the contemporary *vajrayāna* or Tantric Buddhism of Tibet and Nepal (Bishop 1989:127).

The tone and the whole atmosphere of Arthur Avalon's own writing on Tantra is therefore all the more striking by contrast with his contemporaries and those of the previous generation. Not only does he take a sympathetic attitude, but he appears to understand from within. Pañckori Bāndyopādhyay in an article in the Bengali magazine, *Sāhitya* (1913), wrote:

> We could never have dreamt that it was possible for a modern Christian Englishman to so fully understand such matters as the mode of Tantrik Sadhana... (He) has certainly learnt a great deal of the inner and secret doctrine of the Tantra... We have never heard even from any Bengali Pundit such a clear exposition of Mantra Shakti as the author has given.[13]

One or two reviewers, however, remarked that Arthur Avalon sounded rather like one of those Bengali pundits himself. It was a reviewer in an American paper who wrote: 'We suspect that Arthur Avalon is one of the learned Pundits of Bengal whose native speech has not been without influence upon his almost impeccable English' (*The Nation*, New York; TT 19:iii).

The Pseudonym: The Identity and Role of 'Arthur Avalon'

But the pseudonym carried associations far removed from Bengal. The end of the nineteenth and beginning of the twentieth century saw a revival in the West of interest in its own occultism and esotericism – and Tantra has strong affinities with this. The Theosophical Society was founded in 1875 by Colonel Olcott and Madame Blavatsky and, by the second decade of this century, it was a firmly established international organization with an influence on Indian politics. Theosophy was only one of the major nineteenth-century esoteric organizations which claimed to have inherited an older tradition. A number of other occult societies had come into existence in European countries by the turn of the century, among them that of Aleister Crowley who had borrowed superficially from Tantric philosophy and had attracted to himself through his activities something of the same kind of notoriety that a 'left-handed' Tantric held in the eyes of the middle class in India.[14]

In the context of occultism, there could hardly have been a more suggestive

[13] This translation is taken from 'Some Press Notices' in GOL 1922:i.

[14] See King 1977 and Eliade 1987: 13.189 (but the implication that Crowley was influenced by Woodroffe is chronologically impossible, and their approaches to Tantra were of course radically different).

name than 'Arthur Avalon'. The roots of the Arthurian legend lie deep in European esoteric or heretical cults, and the name seems to hint at initiations and the possession of occult secrets. The fact that Woodroffe writes familiarly of occultism from time to time, and identifies Tantra as Hinduism's version of it, enhances this impression. Woodroffe did have connections with the Theosophical Society, but according to the membership lists in its international headquarters in Madras, he did not formally join, although his wife became a member. His books are distinctively Hindu and not Theosophical as such. Nevertheless, he had other friends and contacts within the movement, including James Cousins, editor of the Theosophical newspaper, *New India*, and a close associate of Annie Besant in Madras (see below).

Avalon was the Celtic island of the dead which was transformed in Tennyson's poem *Morte d'Arthur* (1907:416) into a place of healing to which, after his last battle, the fatally wounded King Arthur was taken on a ship by three mysterious women:

> ... I am going a long way
> With these thou seest ...
> To the island valley of Avilion;
> Where falls not hail, or rain, or any snow,
> Nor ever wind blows loudly; but it lies
> Deep-meadowed, happy, fair with orchard-lawns
> And bowery hollows crown'd with summer sea,
> Where I will heal me of my grievous wound.

It seems that the legend inspired Woodroffe through a painting. An appendix in the latest editions of *Śakti and Śākta* reprints an article by James Cousins which first appeared in the Calcutta journal *Modern Review* in February 1918, where he wrote of 'the challenging phenomenon of a decried and abused Eastern scripture being championed with missionary ardour (albeit in the most judicial manner) by a writer whose name takes him outside India in race (though the suggestion of France in one magazine might be modified in front of Burne Jones' unfinished picture of *Arthur in Avalon*' (SS 1987:460). Burne Jones' masterpieces, *Arthur's Sleep in Avalon*, continues the story where the poem leaves off. The painting shows King Arthur in the island of Avalon itself, lying in an entranced sleep attended by maidens of typical pre-Raphaelite beauty. It was the artist's last painting and was unfinished at the time of his death in 1898.[15] James Cousins was probably not suggesting a direct connection between the editor of *Tantrik Texts* and the painter. From the

[15] The painting is reproduced in Harrison and Waters 1989.

context he seems to be dropping a hint about the author's nationality (British) and also perhaps hinting at Woodroffe's well-known interest in art. The words 'albeit in a most judicial manner' are another hint, this time at his profession.

The assumption behind this article by Woodroffe's friend, as well as that behind the Bengali article quoted at the beginning of this chapter, is the same assumption that has been held by nearly everyone since: that Arthur Avalon was Sir John Woodroffe's pseudonym. All recent editions of the books, whether published by Ganesh in Madras or Dover Press in the United States, come out under the name of Woodroffe, and the British Library which at first distinguished the two names now has 'see Woodroffe' against 'Arthur Avalon' in its most recent index.

But in his preface to *Śakti and Śākta*, the first of the Tantric books to come out under his own name, Woodroffe explained that it was not his own identity that was referred to by 'Arthur Avalon'. His previous books had come out under that name 'to denote that they have been written with the direct cooperation of others and in particular with the assistance of one of my friends who will not permit me to mention his name. I do not desire sole credit for what is as much their work as mine.' (second edition, p.x). We have already seen that Woodroffe was not concerned to conceal his interest in Tantra. The person who wanted to keep his involvement secret was someone else. The pseudonym did not only refer to a team of collaborators – the named editors of the individual volumes of *Tantrik Texts*, for example – but especially to one person in particular.

We have seen that only *Śakti and Śākta* and *Garland of Letters* came out under the name of Sir John Woodroffe in their first editions. Two other books were published under the name of Woodroffe in collaboration with P.N. Mukhopadhyay. All publications by 'Arthur Avalon' were directly to do with texts: either translations, editions or commentaries.[16] So it seems clear that Woodroffe was acknowledging that someone else had done the work that involved Sanskrit (which represents the greater part in terms of quantity at least, although eventually it was the essays in English which attracted most popularity). Nevertheless, with time, the sole credit Woodroffe wanted to renounce was eventually given to him, and this unknown friend has been forgotten – as indeed seems to have been his intention.

One reason for this was a certain long-established relationship between European Orientalists and their collaborators, whereby the latter received little recognition. In fact, it seems probable that Woodroffe was being rather more

[16] In *Garland of Letters*, many of the chapters take the form of simple commentaries on extracts from texts. This is especially true of those chapters which were originally published as articles by Arthur Avalon.

conscientious than was normal in using a pseudonym to indicate the work of collaborators. An example of this attitude can be seen in a review by another Orientalist, Johan Van Manen, on Volume 7 of the *Tantrik Texts* series: the translation from Tibetan by Lama Kazi Dawa Samdup. Van Manen merely congratulates Arthur Avalon for having been 'able to secure a competent collaborator to undertake the philological portion of the work, the translating and editing labour' (1919; SS 1987:142).

But another factor was that, having once made this acknowledgement of his friend in the preface to *Śakti and Śākta*, Woodroffe never referred to him again. Instead, he seemed all the more ready after that to subsume Arthur Avalon's identity under his own. In subsequent publications, he listed books that had come out under his own name along with those under the name of Arthur Avalon quite indiscriminately as 'works which I have published' (e.g. GOL 1989:xii).

In 1937, a second edition of the first volume of the *Tantrik Texts* series was published posthumously. The preface (p.viii) stated:

> Arthur Avalon... had thought of publishing a revised second edition quite a long time ago, but he was heavily engaged in editing volumes 16 and 17, and 18 and 19 of *Tantrik Texts*. He had secured some and was on the lookout for other new manuscripts. But unfortunately he passed away at the beginning of the year 1936 leaving this work unfinished.

The volume numbers mentioned refer to the *Śāradātilaka* and the *Prapañcasāratantra*, two very substantial texts in two volumes each. It is obvious that here the name Arthur Avalon referred to one person, not to a team of collaborators. But if it still referred to Woodroffe – who did indeed die at the beginning of 1936 – then we must assume that he was able not only to go on editing texts but to collect manuscripts right up to the time of his death in retirement in Monte Carlo! As this seemed most unlikely, there was one other person, a friend of Woodroffe's, whom I wanted to know more about when I visited Calcutta.

His name did not appear on the covers of the books but he was the secretary of an organization called Āgamānusandhana Samiti ('The Agamas Research Society').[17] This was a small organization which had been set up to publish the *Tantrik Texts*. Arthur Avalon's name was given as the editor and its President was the Maharaja of Darbhanga, a well-known – 'notorious' according to one account – practising Tantric.[18] There were two joint secretaries, Sir John

---

[17] The *Āgamas* are a class of scriptures to which the Tantras are considered to belong.
[18] See the Marquess of Zetland's 'My Bengal Diary', July 14th 1921, p.97.

Woodroffe and a Bengali gentleman we have hitherto heard little about: Mr Atal Behari Ghosh. He was the third man in the photograph taken at Konarak.

The Correspondence with Atal Behari Ghosh and Woodroffe's Knowledge of Sanskrit

I managed to trace the family of Mr Ghosh, who still maintain his house in Calcutta. I arrived just when his very large library and Tantric manuscript collection were about to be transferred to the library of the Sri Aurobindo Ashram in Pondicherry. There were also several letters which were retrieved from various places in the house, twenty-one of them from Woodroffe to Ghosh. All but four of these were written after Woodroffe's return to England when it seems the two friends and collaborators kept in constant touch, and so the letters represent only a small proportion of those which must have passed between them.[19]

Atal Behari Ghosh's granddaughter, Mrs Sumita Guha, said to me: 'My grandfather wrote all the books except *Śakti and Śākta*'. This strong statement needs just a little modification. I think Woodroffe also contributed most of the long introduction to *The Serpent Power* – and, as we have seen, it was these two books which carried the fame of 'Arthur Avalon' to the West – and, of course, he also wrote the books on which he collaborated with P.N. Mukhopadhyay. I think he also wrote most of *Garland of Letters* himself, but with help from others including Ghosh. On the other hand, Ghosh probably contributed something to some of the original articles which became chapters of *Śakti and Śākta*. Ghosh supervised the textual side of all the works under Avalon's name, including those in the *Tantrik Texts* series, but it seems that Woodroffe took charge of the administrative aspect, especially the financial. The correspondence between the two men gives us a glimpse of their joint role in creating 'Arthur Avalon'. The first question we need to ask is: How much Sanskrit did Sir John Woodroffe actually possess?

The answer would seem to be very little, according to one letter in the collection. It is the only one that was written by Atal Behari Ghosh to Woodroffe. It was dated 6th June 1918, the year in which *Śakti and Śākta* was published, and when Arthur Avalon's books had been before the public for five years. It was found alongside a letter addressed to Sir John Woodroffe by a

[19] I am very grateful to Mr Sobhun Ghosh, Atal Behari Ghosh's grandson, for allowing me to keep the originals of these letters and for his generous interest and support. The letters are now with the India Office Library in London. I am also grateful to Mrs Sumita Guha and her son Jayadip for their patient help and to other members of the Ghosh family, including Mr Krishna Ghosh (see note 4).

South Indian reader, which contained several quotations in Sanskrit. Ghosh's letter begins: 'Dear Sir John, I return the letter with the Sanskrit parts (except for the quotation from the Upanishad) translated. I do not translate this as you can get it from Max Muller.' The translations on the accompanying letter were scribbled above the Sanskrit passages in the same handwriting as on Ghosh's letter. Woodroffe replied to the correspondent, because two more letters from him addressed to Woodroffe were found in the collection and it seems their writer never learned that he could not read an unseen passage of Sanskrit.

Confirmation comes from another source. One member of their circle was the young Suniti Kumar Chatterji, who later became an expert on Bengali linguistics. Just after he had completed his BA, he was asked by Atal Behari Ghosh to teach Sanskrit to Woodroffe and his wife Ellen, who as 'Ellen Avalon' is named as co-author of *Hymns to the Goddess*. Some time in the 1960s, Suniti Kumar Chatterji was interviewed on West Bengal Radio. With the passage of time he felt able to express himself freely, even scathingly. He said definitively: 'Woodroffe didn't know Sanskrit' (*Woodroffe samskrit jānten nā*). Then he told a funny story about how Woodroffe had asked him the meaning of a word which did not exist because he could not even read the script accurately.[20]

This must have taken place around 1911, because that was the year in which Chatterji took his BA (Mallik 1981: preface). The first books by Arthur Avalon, including the translation of the *Mahānirvāṇatantra*, came out only two years later, but it was four years before Woodroffe lectured in public on 'Creation in the Tantras' before the Governor of Bengal and a highly literate audience at the Chaitanya Library in Calcutta. The reprint of his lecture – produced first as a pamphlet and then incorporated into *Śakti and Śākta* – is highly erudite and full of Sanskrit terms which he appears to use confidently (chapter 19, 1987 edition). This is characteristic of the style of the books in so many places that it is one reason why it is surprising to learn that Woodroffe did not know the language well. Some later lectures delivered in Europe are noticeably simpler, but that might have been because of the background of the audience.

Woodroffe seems often to have recited Sanskrit *śloka*s when he delivered a public lecture, whatever the topic, so he obviously acquired at least that much facility in the language. It seems that he managed to learn enough grammar

---

[20] I am grateful to Gautam Sengupta of All India Radio Archives, Calcutta, for obtaining for me a copy of the tape of this interview. Further testimony to Woodroffe's lack of Sanskrit comes from Agehananda Bharati in his foreword to H.V. Guenther's *Yuganaddha* where he remarks that Woodroffe knew very little Sanskrit himself but relied closely on pandits and others who did. Bharati (Leopold Fischer) lived in Benares in the 1950s and would have met people still living there at the time who had known Woodroffe.

and vocabulary to cope with philosophical concepts through Sanskrit, but that of course is a very different thing from being able to translate an unseen passage on one's own. It was an important aspect of the image of Arthur Avalon that Woodroffe should appear to be deeply versed in Sanskrit and many members of the Indian public as well as foreign scholars believed that he was.[21]

Another letter written in India suggests that Woodroffe could use Sanskrit quotations on his own initiative, but sought Atal Behari Ghosh's supervision. It was scribbled in pencil on High Court notepaper and has no date but was probably written in 1917:

> Dear Mr Ghose, Please run through this proof and make what corrections are necessary specially noting the Sanskrit quotations marked in red pencil. I shall be glad to have it back soon as it is the next article to appear in the Vedanta Kesari.

The articles in this magazine published by the Ramakrishna Mission came out under the name of Arthur Avalon, and they eventually turned into chapters of *Garland of Letters*. We have already noted the style of this book: some parts of it are so dense with Sanskrit terms as to become almost unintelligible in English, yet the letter implies that Woodroffe wrote them himself.

Most of the letters in the collection were written during Woodroffe's retirement in England and France and show that during that time, as we have already guessed, it was Atal Behari Ghosh who was still hard at work editing the *Śāradātilaka* and *Prapañcasāratantra*, which were published under the name of Arthur Avalon after Woodroffe had left India. This time it was Ghosh who submitted the English prefaces and introductions to these texts to Woodroffe for vetting.

An unusually sharp letter from Woodroffe to Ghosh towards the end of their correspondence reveals the extent to which Woodroffe attempted to control his collaborator. Their disagreement concerned the new preface to Ghosh's edition of the *Prapañcasāratantra*, which had already been edited much earlier on in the series. Woodroffe objected to what he considered an intolerant and 'polemical' tone in Ghosh's draft. He implied that in the final analysis it was he who, so to speak, owned the name 'Arthur Avalon' and that whatever went out under that name reflected on him. He wrote to Ghosh:

> I have cut out in blue pencil the bulk of the proposed

---

[21] Ray (1985:327,328), following Pal (1966), believes that Woodroffe became expert in Sanskrit. Pavitra Gangopadhyay (1956), who describes seeing Woodroffe at a party wearing Indian dress, clearly believed that he wrote all the books of Arthur Avalon.

> introduction as unsuitable and irrelevant... I am not concerned with orthodox polemics. These constant jibes at the modern Hindu become tiresome to the public. Moreover a polemic is more fittingly conducted in an article signed by the person who carries on such polemics.

The 'polemics' concerned the question of the authorship of the text. The *Prapañcasāratantra* was traditionally ascribed to Śaṅkara, an ascription which Ghosh supported but most Western scholars did not. Woodroffe sat on the fence: his tendency was to want to treat such controversial questions with great care. In the end, the original introduction to the earlier edition was preserved and the new version – the one discussed in the letter – was simply added as a 'Postscript' to it. This seems to have been a compromise. If we compare the two we see the difference clearly: the earlier introduction attempts to leave the question open; the later postscript decides firmly in Śaṅkara's favour, even if less polemically than might have been the case without Woodroffe's influence (TT 18:70 ff.).

The discussion of authorship in the earlier edition seems to have been written by Woodroffe himself for, after presenting arguments for both sides, he leaves the question like this: 'I leave however others, who may think that the contents of the work itself notwithstanding its authoritative tone and general style tell against the tradition as to its authorship, the development of their thesis' (p.2). This confusing sentence, which attempts to be 'balanced' yet also leaves us wondering just what his own position is, offers us one of the surest signatures of Woodroffe's own hand in this particular passage of Arthur Avalon. It shows us the restraints he felt about expressing an independent opinion. It also shows us that while he was in India at least he personally contributed to the English introductions to the *Tantrik Texts* series, but his influence diminished after he left India.

The letters that have come into the collection do not contain many intimacies. They are mostly to do with the business of publication, although they do include some references to their mutual health and that of their families, and they exchange advice about homeopathic medicines. Both of them suffered bad health at this time and Woodroffe was developing the Parkinson's Disease from which he eventually died and consequently could not write in his own hand. He addresses his friend and collaborator nearly always as 'My dear Ghosh', only occasionally 'My dear Atal'. They mostly deal with financial and organizational matters, where it seems that Woodroffe was always in charge. He directed all their relationships with the outside world, whether with Luzac, their publishers in England, or with 'D' by which term they designated their financial sponsor, the Maharaja of Darbhanga.

Only one letter was a little more reflective, expressing anxiety over the financial situation of the 1930s and wondering about the future. Woodroffe wrote: 'We are witnessing the birth of a new world and the final disappearance of the one which you and I have known ... We have lived to see a very eventful time, and I hope that we may live to see at least the beginnings of the new world that follows ours.'

Conclusion: The Influence of 'Arthur Avalon'

They were drawing towards the close of an eventful collaboration. One feature of that new world would be a different kind of Indologist: one more interested in the Hindu present than the Aryan past, and less inclined to keep the former at a distance. Mircea Eliade considers that Sir John Woodroffe influenced a whole new generation of Indologists, himself included: and both he and Heinrich Zimmer describe how they were inspired by him.[22] But he meant, of course, Sir John Woodroffe as Arthur Avalon, the British Judge with the profound knowledge of Sanskrit and Indian philosophy, who appeared on the world stage as a far greater figure than either Sir John Woodroffe alone or Mr Ghosh of Calcutta could ever be.

Arthur Avalon was Woodroffe and Ghosh together; he was their joint creation. Most of the English writing, whichever of them wrote the initial drafts, was the result of their mutual influence, while the Sanskrit textual work was directed by Ghosh. Sir John Woodroffe held in trust the public face of Arthur Avalon, lending him his identity and prestige, and negotiating his relationship with the outside world.

Woodroffe as Arthur Avalon seemed like another Sir William Jones, his famous predecessor at the Supreme Court of Calcutta, to whom he was compared in his obituary in *The Times* (18 January 1936:14). He was also compared by several reviewers to Max Müller, for it was said that he had done for the Tantra what Max Müller had done a generation earlier for the Veda – a prestigious comparison indeed at that time for both scholar and text.

What happened was that the image of the European Orientalist, which at that time carried enormous prestige, had been captured and utilized by two disciples of an Indian guru – for Atal Behari Ghosh was also among the group around Śivacandra Vidyārṇava. Arthur Avalon seemed like one of the Orientalists' own number, able to answer them back on equal terms. Yet he spoke with the voice of traditional Hindu wisdom and proclaimed above all what Hindus at that time most wanted to hear: the greatness and spiritual superiority of their culture; and this was said in terms that also caught the spirit of new currents of thought in the West. Atal Behari Ghosh's grandchildren told

[22] Eliade 1987, 1987:15.569 (see also Eliade 1981:1.176); and Zimmer 1984: 22-3 and 254 ff.

me that Ghosh recognized this, and that he knew what he was doing when he insisted that his own name be kept off the books.

In his introduction to the *Prapañcasāratantra*, discussed above, Woodroffe also wrote: 'It is common knowledge that in the history of all religions, works are attributed to great names to gain for them an authority which their real author could not perhaps have achieved.' One wonders if he perceived the parallel to his own relationship with the modern Tantric 'texts' he was helping to create.

Curiously, and by a strange coincidence, all three died together. I mentioned earlier my puzzlement at finding that Arthur Avalon's death coincided with that of Sir John Woodroffe. I discovered that the two friends, having worked so closely together and merged their identities in Arthur Avalon, happened to die within three weeks of each other, in January 1936.

Abbreviations

GOL	*Garland of Letters*
MNT	*Mahānirvāṇatantra*
PT	*Principles of Tantra*
SP	*Serpent Power*
SS	*Śakti and Śākta*
TT	*Tantrik Texts*

References

Primary Sources

Books published under the name of Arthur Avalon

1913. *Tantrik Texts*, ed. Vols. 1-21. London: Luzac/Calcutta: Thacker Spink & Co.

—, tr., with Ellen Avalon. 1913. *Hymns to the Goddess*. London: Luzac.

Books published originally under the name of Arthur Avalon and subsequently reprinted or revised under the name of Sir John Woodroffe

1913. *The Great Liberation* (*Mahānirvāṇatantram*), tr. London: Luzac. Sixth edition: Madras, Ganesh and Co., 1985.

1914. *Principles of Tantra*, ed. Vols 1, 2. London: Luzac. Sixth edition: Madras, Ganesh and Co., 1986.

1918. *The Serpent Power*. London: Luzac. Fourteenth edition: Madras, Ganesh and Co., 1989.

1917. *Wave of Bliss* (*Ānandalaharī*). London: Luzac.
—. *Greatness of Śiva* (*Mahimnastava* of Puṣpadanta). London: Luzac.
—. *Ishā Upanishad* (with commentary of Sadānanda), ed. London: Luzac.
Reprinted in one volume as: *Iṣopaniṣad, Wave of Bliss, Greatness of Śiva.* Madras: Ganesh and Co., 1971.
1952. *An Introduction to Tantra Śāstra.* Madras: Ganesh & Co. Eighth edition: Madras, Ganesh and Co., 1990.

Books published under the name of Sir John Woodroffe
1918. *Shakti and Shākta.* London: Luzac. Second edition: London, Luzac, 1918. Ninth edition: *Śakti and Śākta*; Madras, Ganesh and Co., 1987.
1922. *Garland of Letters.* Madras: Ganesh and Co. and London: Luzac. Ninth edition: Madras, Ganesh and Co., 1989.
With Ameer Ali, 1898. *The Law of Evidence Applicable to British India.* Calcutta: Thacker Spink & Co.
With P.N. Mukhopadhyay. 1923. *The World as Power.* Madras: Ganesh and Co. Sixth edition: Madras, Ganesh and Co., 1981.
With P.N. Mukhopadhyay. 1923. *Mahāmāya.* Madras: Ganesh and Co. Second edition: Madras, Ganesh and Co., 1929.

Secondary Sources

Barnett, L.D. 1913. *Antiquities of India.* London: Philip Lee Warner.
Bandyopadhyay, P. 1913. '*Sahayogi Sāhitya.*' *Sāhitya* 24 (*Srāvan* 1320): 363-8.
Bhārati, Agehananda. 1964. Foreword to H.V. Guenther. *Yuganaddha: The Tantric View of Life.* Varanasi: Chowkhamba Sanskrit Series.
Bhattacharyya, N.N. 1982. *History of the Tantric Religion.* New Delhi: Manohar Publications.
Bishop, P. 1989. *The Myth of Shangri-La: Tibet, Travel Writing and the Western Creation of Sacred Landscape.* London: Athlone Press.
Cousins, J.H. 1918. 'The Agamas and the Future.' *Modern Review*, reprinted in *Śakti and Śākta* (1987:458 ff.).
Datta, Bhupendranath. 1954. *Swami Vivekananda: Patriot, Prophet.* Calcutta: Nababhārat.
Derrett, J.D.M. 1977. 'A Judicial Fabrication of Early British India: The Mahānirvāṇa Tantra.' In *Essays in Classical and Modern Hindu Law*, vol 2. Leiden: Brill.
Eliade, M. 1981. *Autobiography*, vol 1. San Francisco: Harper & Row.
Eliade M., ed. 1987. *Encyclopedia of Religion.* New York: Macmillan.
Farquhar, J.N. 1915. 'Recent Advances in the History of Hinduism.' *International Review of Missions* 4/13, London.
Gangopadhyay, P. 1956. *Calaman Jiban.* Calcutta: Vidyoday Library.
Harrison, M., and B. Waters. 1989. *Burne Jones.* London: Barrie & Jenkins.

Jung, C.G. 1966. Collected Works, vol. 16. London: Routledge & Kegan Paul.

King. F. 1977. *The Magical World of Aleister Crowley*. London: Weidenfeld & Nicolson

Kopf, D. 1986. 'Sexual Ambivalence in Western Scholarship in Hindu India: A History of Historical Images of Shakto-Tantrism 1800-1970.' *Comparative Civilizations Review* 13:143-57.

Lipsey, R. 1977. *Ananda Coomaraswamy: His Life and Work*. Princeton: University Press.

Mallik, B.P., ed. 1981. *S.K. Chatterji Commemoration Volume*. Burdwan: University Press.

Masson-Oursel, P. 1921. 'Dons de Sir John Woodroffe.' *Bulletin de l'Association Française des Amis de l'Orient* 1/1:57-8.

Mitter, P. 1977. *Much Maligned Monsters: A History of European Reactions to Indian Art*. Oxford: Clarendon Press.

Pāl, Vasanta Kumār. 1966 (Agrahān 1372, Paush 1373). '*Tantrācārya Śivacandra.*' *Himādri*, Calcutta.

Pāndūlipi, A.S. 1916. *'Abhinav pranālir varnabodh.' Bhārat Varṣa* 4/1:137 ff., Calcutta.

Payne, E. 1933. *The Śāktas*. Calcutta: Oxford University Press.

Ray, S.N. 1985 (1392). *Bhārater Sādhak*. Calcutta: Karuna Prakāśni.

Sanderson, A. 1992. 'The Early History of Śaivism.' Lecture delivered at the School of Oriental and African Studies, London, 28 April.

Tennyson, A. 1907. 'Morte d'Arthur.' In *Idylls of the King*. London: Macmillan.

Van Manen, J. 1919. 'A Tibetan Tantra.' *The Theosophist*, reprinted in *Śakti and Śākta* (1987:136 ff.).

Zetland, Marquis of. 1921. 'My Bengal Diary.' MS D609/1. India Office Library, London.

Zimmer, H. 1984. *Artistic Form and Yoga in the Sacred Images of India*. Princeton: University Press.

Index